EDDI RICKENBACKER

By

Hans Christian Adamson

New York

The Macmillan Company

1946

PRINTED IN THE UNITED STATES OF AMERICA

TO

ELIZABETH RICKENBACKER

A Great American Mother

AND

ADELAIDE FROST RICKENBACKER

AND

HELEN LYON ADAMSON

Two Stanch American Wives

To the Gang That Made Eastern:

The life chart of Eddie Rickenbacker shows many peaks of accomplishment. But, as in the case of all great men, there are corresponding valleys of depression, despair, and defeat. To all of us close to the Captain, what makes his career outstanding is not so much the inspiration of his successes, but his magnificent courage in overcoming every shock of despair and defeat.

I wrote this book for many kinds of people. But, most of all, I wrote it for those who now and in the past have worked with Captain Eddie in creating the greatest monument of his life —Eastern Air Lines. You men and women who form the Eastern Air Lines' family both on the ground and in the air, should find particular interest in that part of this book which deals with the early days when Eastern was a luckless Cinderella, draped in the ticker tape of market speculation.

In my opinion, one of the towering peaks in the life of Eddie Rickenbacker was the day when he won the fight to save Eastern from being merged into another air-line company. The day when Rick jubilantly phoned his office and shouted: "I have saved Eastern for the gang that made it!"

Well, the "Gang That Made Eastern" is not a fixed and selected group. That gang is, as I said before, composed of the men and women who now and in the past, in all positions, all along the line, have done their part to keep the Great Silver Fleet flying; you whose loyalty and ability have made Eastern Air Lines one of the world's greatest transportation systems.

Hans Adamson

Contents

Illustrations

All photographs in this book are from the collection of Captain E. V.
Rickenbacker, except those of Colonel Adamson, Captain Cherry, Lieutenants
Whittaker and De Angelis, Sergeants Reynolds and Kaczmarczyk and Private
Bartek. These are through the courtesy of Twentieth Century-Fox Film Corp.

Book One

Boyhood

DEAD END KID OF THE GAS–LIGHT ERA
1890–1905

Chapter I

Turning into High Street near the old Ohio Statehouse, a gangly fifteen-year-old boy—who walked with a slight limp—came to a sudden, wide-eyed halt.

The pause lasted but a fraction of a minute. Then, his injured leg completely forgotten, the lad ran down the street as swiftly as his feet could carry him.

Why? Because at the corner of State Street a crowd was gathering near the curb, milling about like swarming bees—men and women, but mostly men. In 1905, it was not considered ladylike for women to mix in crowds.

The boy with the forgotten limp was thin and short for his age. His longish, narrow face, topped with a thick thatch of reddish hair, was liberally sprinkled with freckles. His large ears stuck out from his head like the handles of a jug. His eyes, brown and bright and alert, were deeply set under straight and heavy brows that were contracted into an almost habitual scowl. This, together with his jutting chin, gave his face an angry aggressiveness contradicted by the lively humor that warmed his eyes and the smile that flickered readily at the corners of his wide and generous mouth.

It was less than five years after the start of the twentieth century, and in cities like Columbus there were two major social divisions: the people who lived on the right side of the railroad tracks, and the people who did not.

The boy who ran down the street eager to taste the excitement of crowd contact obviously lived on the wrong side of the tracks. A blue coat and dark gray trousers hung on his scrawny frame with almost scarecrow looseness. They were, without a doubt, hand-me-downs, shiny with wear and threadbare, but spotless and neatly mended. His faded blue shirt was clean and starched in the manner of the day, and his shoes, although crudely patched where the uppers had cracked, shone with a brave new polish.

Nearing the corner, the boy saw a man tower waist-high over the swirling mob. It was a good-natured crowd, laughing, shouting, talking. And the man who seemed to rise from its center was good-natured too. His thick chest and beefy shoulders shook with laughter. On his red-meat face, under a tobacco-brown derby worn with a rakish slant on the side of his head, a broad smile sifted through the curtain of a walrus mustache. He waved a fat cigar, tipped with an inch of ash, in a pudgy hand as he shouted:

"Move back, folks! Make room! Don't shove! Don't push!"

Without heed the boy began to work his way into the throng, using a heel-and-elbow technique that made his push through the jungle of coats and pants and skirts and shoes surprisingly swift. Now he reached the inner edge of the crowd.

There it stood, smart and black and elegant: the darling of his days; the object of his dreams; the love of his life. It was a brand-new Model C Ford, gleaming with bright black paint, sparkling with burnished brass. He was not dreaming. It was there. He was actually looking at something he had feared he might never see. The angry aggressiveness left his face, and a warm happy feeling surged through him—a feeling he had never sensed before. It seemed to spread warmth, like sunshine, into every corner of his being and made him feel light—light.

In the Columbus newspapers, the boy had seen pictures of this new, wonderful automobile and read descriptions of it. He had cut out the pictures and pasted them on the wall of the room he shared with his brothers. But here was the gas buggy itself with a real steering wheel instead of the tiller bar most of the horseless carriages had; and, instead of being hidden beneath the seat, the engine was up in front under a hood and behind a radiator. The brass lamps mounted on each side of the dashboard glinted in the sun.

The car could do thirty miles an hour—well, twenty, anyway. And it cost nine hundred dollars. The boy recited these high points to himself as he looked at the queenly carriage. There it stood, right before his eyes, within reach of his hands!

Maybe he dared touch the glossy leather fenders?

No, better not.

Now, only one thing remained to fill his cup of contentment: to hear the beat of its motor, the throb of its metal heart. But the car stood still, its engine silent.

"Hey, Doc!" yelled someone in the crowd. "Did ya run out of gas? Why doncha feed it some hay? Ha-ha-ha-ha-ha."

The crowd laughed, and so did the man called Doc. And when he laughed the boy laughed too.

"Say, Doc, git a horse to take you home!" yelped another voice.

More laughter in which Doc joined.

"Don't need no horse," he bellowed. "Engine just stalled on me. That's all."

"Yeah, Doc," shouted another. "These fancy mackansy motor wagons stall on the street, but a horse only stalls in a stable—ha-ha-ha-ha-ha."

"Just you wait until I get her started," returned Doc. "Why, boys, this automobile is a real, rip-snorting, ding-tooting, mud-bucking, hill-climbing, speed-bursting road terror! Git your fastest horse, and it'll swaller my dust!"

With this sally, Doc leaned back on the high and narrow seat of the little two-passenger car, chuckled, and flicked his cigar over the small turtleback that covered the tail end of the vehicle. The ashes fell on the glossy paint.

It seemed like an act of vandalism to the boy. Without thinking, he stepped forward and reached out to sweep the ashes away.

Doc misunderstood his motion and roared: "Hey, you good-for-nothing rascal! Keep your dirty hands off my gas buggy, or I'll learn you!"

The boy returned Doc's glare as he answered in a steady, unruffled tone: "You spilled ashes on it. I was only going to wipe them off."

"Oh! Huh," sputtered the man. "You were, were you?" Then, caught by something in the boy's forthright gaze, he continued in a friendly tone: "Think you'd know how to wind her up?"

"You mean start—you mean me start the engine?"

"Nothing else but. How about it, sonny?"

"Gee, Mister, I don't know— I've never done it. But I'd sure like to try!"

"Go ahead and try then!" The man winked at the crowd. "Even a youngster can start this car. Yes, sirree." Then, louder, to the boy who by now had walked to the front of the automobile: "Just grind the crank around until the engine pops. Then drop the crank like a hot potato, for if you don't, the kick-back from this powerful engine 'll break your arm—*pst!* Like that!" He snapped his finger. "Got it, me lad?"

"Yes, Mister, I got it."

The boy braced his feet squarely before the radiator. He put one hand on its brassy rim. Ouch! It was hot. He tried not to show the great pride that engulfed him. He tried to suppress the elation that swept over him and set him trembling from tip to toe. He tried to show bored unconcern as he bent and grasped the starting crank —and then, he almost felt faint with horror. He did not know which way to swing it. To the right? Or the left? He would have to ask Doc, show his ignorance in front of this staring, laughing mob. It was too much. They would laugh at him. That was more than he could stand, and he was on the point of ducking back into the crowd.

Doc saved the situation. "Hold on a second, son, before you start. Every moment is a golden opportunity to turn an honest penny —that's what I always says. I make my living selling cars, and I never pick anything but the best. And let me tell you, folks, this new Ford automobile is a jim-dandy! Yes, indeed, gents, it is the rig you've been waiting for; the automobile that'll take you there and back in comfort and in speed; a mechanical marvel that runs faster than any horse, only"—a laugh bubbled up from his belly—"it doesn't run up the feed bill when it stops in the barn. Speed, that's what you get—thirty miles an hour, guaranteed by Henry Ford, the Speed-King himself, and one of the fastest drivers on earth.

"Come and see me sometime at the Meriam Hotel, and I'll give you a demonstration."

"What's the car cost?" yelled a voice.

"Only nine hundred dollars!"

"Do you sell it on time?" shouted another.

"Yep, brother, I sure do," replied Doc. "A dollar down and a dollar a week."

"Them ain't bad terms, Doc. How soon do you deliver the car?"

Doc smiled broadly and held his words until he had the full attention of his audience. Then: "You get the car, brother, when you've made the last payment." He laughed boisterously, and the crowd joined him.

"Come on now, boy," he shouted when the laughter subsided. "Let's get a-going. But hold your horses." He roared again at his own pun. "Hah, that's a good one—eight horses, that's what you're holding in the hollow of your hands, boy! Think of that—eight horses under that hood, and all rearin' to go. But don't be impatient," he admonished. "Wait until I push the throttle open and adjust the spark."

This was all Greek to the boy. But he grasped Doc's next words with eager understanding and happy relief: "Swing the crank slowly and steadily—like you wind a watch—when I holler, 'Now.' Understand?"

"Sure," answered the boy with a superior smile. "You needn't tell me what to do, Doc. You just yell when you're ready. I'm all set." Again he felt warm and full of sunlight. The crowd would not have a chance to laugh at him, and he would actually have started an automobile engine. Would that be something to brag about!

"Now!" snapped Doc.

The boy turned the crank. At first it was easy. Perhaps something was broken. But suddenly the crank turned hard. The resistance grew as he leaned all his weight upon it on the down stroke. Then, like lightning, the pressure disappeared, the engine caught on. It began to splutter. The splutter changed to a series of violent explosions that rocked the car and sent the crowd surging back. In those days, people had funny ideas about cars. They were afraid of all sorts of things. One widespread fear was that automobiles could explode—and they frequently did.

The scared spectators drew back, but the boy stood his ground. Tingling with excitement, he watched the man on the seat move levers up and down until the barkings and bangings within the car settled down to a fairly steady rhythm. To the boy, that even-pulsing note, which is the basic melody in the symphony of auto-mobile power, seemed to blend with the excited pounding of his heart. His heart and that engine were one and the same thing, both part of him—his heart and this engine which his hands had just brought to life. This engine! His hands!

"Hey, you, boy! Don't stand there mooning!" Doc's voice yanked him out of his thoughts. "Get out of my way. Can't stay here all day. Gotta demonstrate this car to a customer."

Metal grated. The car moved forward, and the boy jumped out of its way. He watched it as it putted up State Street, a fragrant and handsome plume of smoke pouring from its exhaust pipe.

The crowd melted away. But the boy stood rooted to the spot. He could still feel the crank in his hand. He could still feel that pregnant moment when the engine, from a lifeless mass of metal, changed into a living, throbbing thing. A thrill of fulfillment and accomplishment ran through him like an electric current. It gal-vanized him into unswerving purpose. The helter-skelter disarray of plans characteristic of a boy of fifteen suddenly fell into a pattern as definite as that of a jigsaw puzzle when all the pieces are as-sembled.

From that hour, his world would be the world of engines—the realm of power. On that April day of 1905, at the corner of High Street and State in the city of Columbus, Ohio, Eddie Rickenbacker stood at the starting line of the roaring road to world-wide renown.

Eddie was third-born of the eight children of William and Eliza-beth Rickenbacker, who had come from Switzerland in the early 1880's as bride and groom to settle in Columbus. Mary and Bill, his older sister and brother, were five and three years old when he was born on October 8, 1890, in a two-room cottage in the north-east section of Columbus, within range of the soot and noises of the roundhouse and shops of the Panhandle Railroad yards. In due time, two more sisters and three additional brothers saw the light of day—Emma, Louis, Louisa, Dewey, and Albert.

Father Rickenbacker began by working for the Panhandle; but from the very start he and his young wife had two fixed ideas. One was to own their own home, and the other was for William to go into business for himself. In the old country he had served an apprenticeship in the building business.

William knew how to handle lumber, bricks, and cement. But it took money to go into business, also to own a home. On top of that, it took money to clothe and feed the steadily growing family. But even as William worked hard and long to make the skimpy pay envelope just a little fatter, so Elizabeth, with the thrift and energy characteristic of that era, saved and toiled to make every dollar, dime, and penny go as far as possible.

After almost a decade of struggle and saving, William and Elizabeth had enough money to make a slim down payment on a lot in a new and undeveloped section far out on Livingston Avenue—in the country, almost. At any rate, the plot was about a dozen blocks beyond Sixteenth Street, where the Livingston Avenue horse car turned back.

Partly with cash, but mainly on credit, Father Rickenbacker obtained the materials for a plain but solidly built one-and-a-half-story frame house: two rooms downstairs—a bedroom and a kitchen; two attic half-rooms upstairs. Behind the house, a combination barn and storehouse for building supplies was erected.

The house itself was without the conveniences which today are taken for granted in even rural communities. There was no water in the house; it had to be drawn from a well near the barn. There was neither electricity for lighting nor gas for cooking. In the cold months, the only heat in the house came from the kitchen range. There was no stove, no heater, no furnace. After dark, the only illumination came from two kerosene lamps. One was in the front bedroom, occupied by the parents and the younger children. The other hung from the ceiling over a large table in the kitchen, which was also dining room and living room. There was no heat, and no light at night, in the two tiny upstairs rooms where the bigger boys and the girls slept.

All this construction was done by Eddie's father after his day's work and on Sundays and holidays. The day when the house and barn were finished, Father Rickenbacker quit his job and went into business for himself as a subcontractor constructing sidewalks, foundations, culverts, and so on. In moving out to the semiurban extension of Livingston Avenue, he hoped to profit by the development of that section. Like many pioneers, he did not live long enough. However, that is another story.

At the time Father Rickenbacker finished his work on the Livingston Avenue house and barn, and proudly nailed the numerals 1334 over the three steps to the short and narrow front porch, both he and his wife had high hopes and full confidence in the future. Eddie was then a three-year-old tyke and gave no evidence as yet of the pain and sorrow he was to heap upon his mother in the next ten years; nor of the tower of strength and heart-warming pride he was to become in the years after that harrowing decade.

Nowadays, it may seem impossible for a couple without much cash income to raise seven or eight children, in a city, without almost crushing hardship and near-starvation. To be sure, hardship was the Rickenbackers' constant companion; but there were also work and resourcefulness, and there were space and soil in which to grow things.

The house stood on a lot 200 feet deep and 100 feet wide. The yard was not covered by lawns, bushes, and pretty flowers. The principal reason why the family did not go hungry was that almost every foot of that ground was made to produce vegetables, including corn, potatoes, tomatoes, turnips, cabbage, parsnips, and carrots. On porch trellises and arbors grew Concord grapes that yielded not only jams and jellies but a good supply of homemade wine. In time, apple, peach, and pear trees produced abundantly. Goats provided milk. Pigs fattened themselves on the garbage. Hens clucked and cackled in a small chicken yard. Nothing was wasted or thrown away.

One of the best investments Father Rickenbacker ever made was the enormous vat which he bought secondhand from a brewery. It was at least fifteen feet across and twelve feet deep, larger than any room in the house, and was lowered into a huge hole right behind the house. Roofed over with lumber and covered with six feet of tightly packed earth, it was warm in winter and cool in summer. One entered it by lifting a tiny door on the side next to the house and clambering down a ladder.

The vat was dark as pitch, but smelled richly of the good things from the garden and the kitchen and the hen yard that were stored there—foods that carried the family through long, hard winters. On shelves there were fruits and vegetables in row on row: regiments of jars of corn and tomatoes; battalions of jars of fruits and jellies. There were big gobs of homemade goat cheese, barrels of sauerkraut, crocks of eggs preserved in water glass, also homemade wine and beer, beverages enjoyed by the whole family, just mildly alcoholic but the strongest ever used by the household. If he had ready cash Father Rickenbacker would buy a pig, fatten it up in a pen behind the barn, kill it at the onset of frost, dress it, and lay it up in the underground storeroom for the winter. On special occasions, fragrant pork would grace the table.

There was just as little money to spend on fuel for heating or cooking. By and large, most of the fuel came from the trees that still stood in that section. One of the steady jobs of the older boys was to bring wood home, cut it, and stack it up. Now and then Eddie and Brother Bill would go to the coal yards of the Toledo & Ohio Central Railway, a few blocks from Main Street and about two miles from the Rickenbacker home.

Pushing a squeaky wheelbarrow or carrying hard-to-get jute bags, the lads would head for the tracks and scout out the land. If no "coppers" or railroad "dicks" were in sight, they would gather coal that had either fallen from the loaders or been dropped along the tracks by the shovelers. The picking was sometimes good, sometimes poor. The coal supply was governed by the amount dropped from the cars and the number of children hunting it.

Now and then cars heaped high with coal stood in strings on the tracks, and Eddie, the nimbler, would climb to the top of a car and kick an avalanche of chunks cascading down to the edge of the track, while his brother stood guard, ducking back and forth under the car to watch either side of the tracks for dicks and coppers. Now and then they were almost caught redhanded by vigilant detectives, but usually they got away with it.

Where there are many mouths to food, there is work for many hands to do; and long before they reached school age chores were assigned to Eddie and his brothers and sisters around the house, in the garden, the hen yard, and the barn. They were taught, mainly by their patient mother, to share the work and help one another.

Neatness was a theme forever on her tongue.

"Clean up after yourselves, whatever you are doing," was her advice. "You can't stand in a dirty spot and do clean work."

Everything in her small domain had its place, and everything had to be where it belonged. Her favorite maxim was:

"If you put things in their proper places you won't lose them, you won't fall over them and break them, and you won't have to buy new things to replace them."

Eddie adored his mother although he usually had a poor way of showing it. Her French-Swiss ancestry gave her a gayety of mood and a gentle understanding of the turmoil and conflict that made Eddie's childhood days an almost constant anxiety. His father, of German-Swiss descent, was a heavy-handed taskmaster and a firm subscriber to the spare-the-rod-and-spoil-the-child theory; and it was a question who was the more worn out from the numberless lambastings and larrupings, father or son.

Not that relations between Eddie and his father were strained or unfriendly; or that Eddie got more lickings than he deserved. On the contrary, during the rare and short periods when he stayed out of rod's reach, Father Rickenbacker and his second oldest son were close companions.

As a boy, Eddie liked to fuss around with tools, to make things. This trait he inherited from his father—who was handier than most men even in those days when fathers were supposed to be handy around the house. From the time he was very young, Eddie had tools of his own and knew how to use them. Two of his favorite hangouts were his father's workshop in the barn and an old-fashioned blacksmith shop down near the railroad yards. He was in his element when the burly blacksmith let him pump the bellows, and he often hammered horseshoes on the anvil. Many of the tools Eddie owned, he made on the anvil with his own hands under the blacksmith's eyes.

Eddie's father, despite his strong German accent, had a broad command of English; and often at night he would try to imprint upon the minds of his children a grateful realization of their opportunities as American citizens. He would describe with anger the German wars of aggression against Austria, Denmark, and France. He hated Germany and its mania for conquest with an unflickering flame and loved America beyond expression.

Perhaps the best proof of the practical patriotism of Father Rickenbacker and his wife is that they agreed that it was his solemn duty to America to serve in the Spanish-American War. He sought to enlist but was rejected on account of his large family.

Almost every winter evening, after the supper dishes were washed and the kitchen cleaned up, the family would gather around the big table which, with the stove, took up nearly all the space in the tiny room. The oven door would be open, and the fire in the range would spread its pleasant warmth.

Chairs would be dragged up, and the children would sit at the table, the boys on one side and the girls on the other, sloping in size from Father at the head of the table to Mother at the opposite end. Father would read the paper. Mother would sew. The older children would study their lessons, and the younger would play games.

Eddie remembers those family evenings around the table as among the happiest in his life: the yellow sheen of the kerosene lamp, the heavy fragrance of his father's long-stemmed pipe, the gentle smile on his mother's roundish face that still held traces of youthful beauty . . .

As the burning wood crackled in the range, Eddie would often think of his boyhood hero—Abraham Lincoln. He would try to picture Lincoln, a boy like himself, stretched in front of a fireplace and reading by the light of the burning logs. Getting drowsy from the heat, he thought that he might like to study his lessons if he had a fireplace like Lincoln's.

Another hero in the household was President McKinley. Father Rickenbacker had made a close study of McKinley's career, and would spend hours telling the children what a fine, lovable, and clever man he was. Eddie was interested in the qualities that had enabled McKinley to rise from the rank of private to major in the Civil War.

The boy's interest in the President increased greatly when he saw McKinley in Columbus during the campaign of 1900. The

President matched the picture in Eddie's mind, and the ten-year-old was so impressed that he could not speak about anything else for days. From that time on, his interest in the campaign was avid; and he took it as a personal victory when McKinley was reelected.

In September, 1901, the world was shocked by the assassination of McKinley. Among those who were completely upset by the tragic event was Eddie Rickenbacker. The day of McKinley's death, Eddie went into hiding. He sulked for hours in the attic or in the cellar, day after day, and cried his heart out. He shunned his brothers and sisters. He would not tell his mother what was wrong. He just mourned by the hour.

One evening, when Eddie did not show up for supper, his father had had enough of it. He found his son having a good cry back of the barn.

"What's the matter with you? Out with it!" demanded the father.

"I don't want to die," lamented Eddie. "I want to live and see what's going on."

"Who says you're going to die?"

"No-nobody," sobbed Eddie. "But President McKinley died—and other people die, and I"—the tear-throttle was wide open—"I don't want to die."

A hard glint crept into Father Rickenbacker's eye, and he slowly and coldly issued the standard invitation to a larruping: "You come with me into the barn for a good lambasting. By golly, I'll teach you not to die."

Still sobbing, Eddie followed his father into the barn, got his lambasting and, miraculously, gave up all thoughts of death.

Chapter II

~~~~~~

When the Rickenbackers moved in, the Livingston Avenue section was sparsely settled. The already dilapidated Columbus Driving Track sprawled behind a rotting fence less than half a mile away.

Within a radius of three miles there were fewer than twoscore houses, nearly all small and humble like the one built by Father Rickenbacker. The land was open country that had gone to city-seed, awaiting real estate booms to sprout. Fields once fertile had become seas of tall weedy grass broken by islands of shrub oak. Here and there trees clustered in lonely-looking groups. A mile or two away, Elm Creek ran its placid course.

The thin population in those early days provided few young companions for the Rickenbacker children. In the first year or so they were virtually on their own resources; and during this period, when Eddie was almost five years old and Bill was about nine, the younger boy began to rail against big-brother authority. There is no doubt whatever but the fires of spite and deviltry that burned so steadily within him from that age until his sudden reformation at the age of eleven were lit by rebellion.

Eddie Rickenbacker was so constituted that he could not and would not knuckle down to Bill or any other lad. This was not because he was a lone wolf. On the contrary, he loved to run with the pack—but as a leader. Even as a child he knew only one real authority—himself. Anything that ran counter to it was in for a head-on collision.

Then, as now, it was impossible for him to play second fiddle. He even frowned at playing first violin because the real top dog was the leader of the band. He had an insatiable thirst for leadership; and, because he was the youngest leader of the youngest gang of boys, because he felt that he constantly had to fight to maintain his independence, he became a rash, brash, and reckless young scape-gallows who would rush in where the Devil feared to gambol. Once this burden of frustration is weighed, once this feeling of rebellion is understood, the bewildering contradictions in Eddie Rickenbacker the harum-scarum boy who often seemed headed for the Reforma-tory, and Eddie Rickenbacker who became one of America's out-standing heroes and a bright inspiration to two generations of Youth, become as clear as polished glass.

Up to the time he was twelve years old, life to Eddie was a constant challenge. When he was good—and that was often—he was better than the average boy, because he was fundamentally honest, loyal, generous, industrious, and truthful; but when he was bad he could be worse than horrid—stubborn, irresponsible, ruth-less, self-centered, ornery, and destructive. With it all, he was not a sneak, not a filcher, and not a fibber when the jig was up on some escapade or other.

Eddie's first real clash with older-brother authority, in which he came out the winner, occurred just after school began in the fall of 1895. The shortest way to school was across country through the brush, to the east of Livingston Avenue. Eddie's bright, eager eyes noticed that Brother Bill and members of his gang would dive into a thicket along the path to school. Since this was before Eddie was old enough to go to school, he had plenty of opportunity to find out what was going on. In the thicket, he found ashes, cigarette stubs, and burnt matches close to the trunk of a big tree. Young as he was, he knew what that meant: the gang had been smoking. The next morning, and the one following, he rushed out of the house right after breakfast, stole into the thicket, and climbed up among the branches of the tree. There he sat waiting for the older boys to show up. They did not come. On the third day, he had better luck.

Laughing and joking, Bill and his crowd settled under the tree. A package of tobacco and one of cigarette paper, plus matches, were produced. Each boy rolled his own, and soon they were puffing smoke in high but self-conscious contentment.

The manly, companionable silence was broken by a thin, gloat-

ing voice from the tree: "I caught you at it—I caught you smoking."

"Hey, who's that?" yelled Bill as cigarettes were hastily ex-
tinguished and hidden. "Aw, shucks! It's only my little brother,
Eddie."

"Don't you call me 'little,' " snarled Eddie as he clambered
down, "or I'll give you the old one-two from belly to beezer."

"If you tell on us," countered Bill, "I'll fix your wagon, and
plenty!"

"I'll snitch on you if you don't give me a cigarette," retorted
the miniature terror, who by this time had reached the ground
and stood truculent and firm before the older boys.

"Aw, be yourself, Dutchie," pleaded one of the boys. "You're
much too young to smoke. Skiddoo home, and leave us be."

But Eddie was not to be disposed of so easily. He declared himself in on the forbidden delights of smoking, or else . . . In the
end he won the right to use the older boys' smoking tobacco; but,
in return, he was to help pick up cigarette money.

The deal was that Eddie, being too young to go to school,
should pass some of his time collecting bones, rags, and odds and
ends of metal to be sold to Sam the Junkman for cash. That was
how Eddie got into the junk business. The boys would hoard their
pennies until they had enough money to go to the store and buy a
package of Bull Durham, "for the old man."

This working arrangement lasted only until enough boys of
Eddie's age, or slightly younger, moved into the neighborhood for
him to muster a gang of his own. With Bill at the head of the
older gang and Eddie leading the younger band, the Rickenbacker
realm was a frequent and bloody battle-ground for gang supremacy.

Most of the bad blood between the younger boys, who called
themselves the Horseheads, and the older boys was of Eddie's making. Bill was quiet, good-natured and generally respectful of the
peace and security of the neighborhood, unlike his kid brother who
was loyal and generous to his friends but "no little friend to all the
world," as Kipling put it. Eddie could hate with all the fury of a
riled-up wildcat. The heaviest cross he had to bear was that, because
the Horseheads were younger, the bigger boys would have nothing

to do with them, would not play with them or take part in their raids or other gang activities. He was called "Dutchie" in those days because, when he got into a spluttering rage, he would interlard his English with a lot of German words and phrases. Until he was about eight years old, German was the language at home.

Eddie was a boy of glaring contradictions. He was tough on the surface, but sensitive and tender beneath his bluster. He was destructive and rowdy, but not at all inclined to pull wings off flies or rob the nests of birds. An episode in his eleventh year casts a very clear light on that side of his rather complex character.

He had made a robins' house of wood which he painted an elegant blue and placed in a peach tree at the back of the house. Ignoring this, a pair of robins built a nest on a branch close to it. He began by thinking the robins did not have much sense; but day after day, with speechless fascination, he observed the building of their tiny home of grass and leaves and odds and ends—all held together with dabs of mud—watched the female shaping the nest into a deep bowl with her breast by turning around and around.

Soon after the nest was completed, Eddie began to feed the birds crumbs and bits of meat. Their friendship became so close that, when the baby robins got to be big enough for hand feeding, the mother robin would fly off the nest when he came, and would perch on his shoulder and keep up an endless chatter while he fed the ever-hungry youngsters.

Eddie liked the robins not only for their friendliness but for the kinship he felt with them. Like himself, they had to scratch for what they got. They were chased out of gardens and scared away from fruit. Like himself, they were small but tough and bold. Once he saw them drive off a battle-scarred tomcat that tried to climb their tree. The robins fought gravely against odds for what was theirs. He could understand, for that was his way of doing things too.

Eddie, loving battle and prepared to fight without the drop of a hat, was forever in one scrap or another. As the leader of his gang, he always started the fights. Many of them were rear-guard actions with gangs of bigger boys whom the Horseheads trailed or interfered with when they were swimming, playing ball, or raiding orchards.

From the first, Eddie was a good strategist. The qualities of leadership which he was to assert in automobile racing, in aerial battle during the First World War, in the pioneering days of airplane transportation, as well as over a pathetic fleet of three rafts afloat in the Pacific—those qualities were already his half a century ago.

But in his boyhood most of those qualities functioned in reverse. As a boy at home, and in a civilized, peace-loving neighborhood, he was a holy terror; and all betting favored the stand that "*that* Rickenbacker boy" would come to a very bad end indeed. Where did he get that "bad blood"? All of his brothers and sisters were nice young people. And the good Lord did not make nicer parents than William and Elizabeth Rickenbacker.

Of course, the boys in the Horsehead gang saw Eddie in an entirely different light. They admired him because he could fight and lick twice his weight in wildcats, because he could swim better, skate better, and play ball better than any other boy in his own age group in that neighborhood. He was the marbles victor over all comers. The marble season never lasted long, because Eddie, his knuckles sore from shooting on the ground, soon gathered all the "puries," the big and dandy shooters, and that was the end of competition.

Eddie received the most terrific larruping in his young life the summer he organized a baseball team within his gang with a view of entering the sand-lot league that played in a park on Lockwood Road. Lacking any baseball equipment, the Horseheads under Eddie's guidance borrowed a little here and there from older brothers or schoolmates. In this way they collected a couple of balls and a bat or two; but one item they could not seem to snag was a catcher's mitt.

It was most depressing until the Sunday afternoon Eddie went to a game in Lockwood Park. It was a good game, but the only thing Eddie could see was a catcher's mitt. It was bright yellow and had scarlet trimmings and was the biggest mitt that he had ever seen.

For a long time Eddie debated within himself whether it would be stealing or snitching to take the mitt. At first it seemed like stealing; but then he decided it would be only snitching, and therefore the mitt was fair game. He sneaked up to the end of the bench where the mitt owner sat, saw his chance to grab the mitt, and off he went with his loot.

Out on Lockwood Avenue, he hid the treasure in a culvert that ran under the street. Then he took his time, stopping for a smoke in a thicket where some tobacco had been cached. Nearing home he saw it was surrounded by a lot of people. He broke into a trot to find out what had happened. But, instead of being a spectator, he instantly found himself the center of interest. The mob was mainly made up of baseball players.

"There he is, Mr. Rickenbacker," shouted a lanky boy. "That's the boy who stole my brand-new ten-bit catching mitt. Where is my mitt, boy? Where's it at?"

"Did you steal his baseball mitt?" thundered Father Rickenbacker.

"I didn't steal it," answered Eddie. "I just snitched it, and if he wants his old mitt he can have it back."

"Ach, ach, mein lieber Gott!"

Whereupon William led his offspring down to the barn for a lambasting that had an extra Sunday punch. Eddie was used to having his posterior beaten with the frequency of a Chinese temple gong, and the licking itself did not hurt him much, although it cut him to the heart to be switched in front of a lot of laughing strangers; but his sense of justice was really outraged when he had to go away out to the culvert on Lockwood Road and give the catcher's mitt back. He felt that he had paid for it.

Once a week, usually on Fridays, a broken-down wagon would be drawn up Livingston Avenue at funeral pace by a swaybacked cadaverous refugee from a glue pot. On its backless seat was an aged man with a ragged gray beard, a greasy black derby, and a purple suit that once had been blue. The loose reins would lie in his bony left hand while his right moved a rusty cowbell listlessly up and down and he sang out in a dispirited chant:

"Any rags, any bones, any iron today—any rags, any bones, any iron today?" over and over and over like a talking machine record that had got stuck.

This was Sam the Junkman, the first person in the world with whom Eddie did business on his own account. Of course, he had collected money for goats' milk and eggs; and he would get up at two o'clock in the morning, drag his cart more than three miles down to the Columbus *Dispatch*, collect his load of morning newspapers, and deliver them to his clients; and from time to time he worked on farms and construction jobs as a water boy—but the money he earned he always turned over to his mother.

But the money Eddie made by collecting paper and iron and rags, brass and bones and bags—pennies, nickels, even dimes, that money went into his own pockets to be spent on candy, soda pop, and tobacco for the cigarettes he and his gang rolled and smoked behind the barn and in other secluded places. Wherever he went in his daily travels, through open lots, across back yards, over refuse dumps, along streets, he kept an eye roving for things that could be transformed into cash. For some peculiar reason, he specialized in bones. Cow bones, dog bones—any kind of bones. Since bones sold by the pound, he made a rather valuable discovery when he learned that dry bones would add a little extra weight if he soaked them for a few days in very watery mud.

He was rather proud of this discovery and happy over his business relationship with Sam, the Junkman until he began to suspect Sam's scales. He suspected that they were on the light side, so to speak.

Such duplicity was almost unbelievable.

To find out if it were so, Eddie took a batch of his mud-soaked bones to the grocery store and had them weighed. Sure enough, when Sam came around and started to dicker for the bones, they weighed almost five pounds less on his scales.

Eddie did not know quite what to do. He needed Sam as an outlet for his junk. He needed the money for smokes and similar small luxuries. So, instead of flying into a rage or pouting as many another boy would, he thought the matter out and stuck with his problem until he found a solution. He went to a few downtown pawnshops and shopped around until he came upon a secondhand spring scale offered for twenty-five cents. He got the money from his mother. Next time Sam came around, Eddie sprung the scales on him and won his campaign for fair weight. From that day on Sam treated the boy with the wary regard reserved for an equal, and they became firm friends.

Sam was an innocent party to a rather dangerous bit of research into applied physics undertaken by Eddie at the age of eleven after he had learned in school about Benjamin Franklin's experiments with electricity. Deeply impressed by Franklin's use of a kite to prove the identity of electricity and lightning, the boy decided to repeat the test. He made a kite, a rather large one, but instead of using string bought from Sam a spool of very thin copper thread—about one hundred yards of it.

After a patient wait of several weeks, a thunderstorm came one day toward sunset. Eddie sent his kite aloft, and while lightning flashed across the sky and thunder rumbled over the heavens he held his dipping and dancing kite aloft by means of the copper cord.

The tireless Providence that has always been on the job protecting Eddie without regard to union hours was on hand that afternoon to push the bolts of lightning away from the kite. When the storm blew over, the boy hauled the kite down with disappointment. The experiment had been a failure. Had he done something wrong? He learned in school the next day that the first man to repeat Franklin's experiment was struck dead on the spot; and he never repeated the experiment.

The Columbus Derby was another source of income. Whenever there was a meet on, Eddie and some of his Horseheads would sneak over or under the fence in order to make an honest dime or two selling soda pop for the soft-drink concessionnaires. Oddly enough, in view of his subsequent fame in the world of speed, the boy never stood frozen with suspense as the horses came thundering down the home stretch or idled away time around the stables. Definitely, his only interest at the track was in how many bottles of soda he could sell. It was all pop and no ponies with him.

To this day, Eddie Rickenbacker is more interested in the Soapbox Derby than in the Kentucky Derby. It was in his boyhood days that the pushmobile, the boy-powered forerunner of the speed wagon of the Soapbox Derby, came into vogue; and Eddie was a crackajack pushmobilist.

Nowadays the pushmobile can be a thing of beauty and mechan-

ical art. In the days of Dutchie it was a crude homemade convey-
ance, made often as not from the wheels and axles of discarded baby
carriages nailed to long boards, and the driver, ensconced in a soapbox, egg crate, or beer case, would steer the front wheels by pieces
of rope. A pushmobile team consisted of two boys—a big boy who
sat and steered and had all the fun, and a little boy who did all
the work of pushing. Eddie served a brief, a very brief, apprenticeship as pusher for his brother Bill. Then he went into racing with
his own pushmobile—and pusher.

During those early days of pushmobiles the rival gangs in the
Livingston Avenue section of Columbus buried their differences
long enough to build a half-mile oval race track on an open lot
near the Rickenbacker home. It was quite a job, for grass had to be
cut, bushes had to be dug up, stones had to be carried off; but
eventually they had a fine smooth track for pushmobile speed
maniacs.

There were only two rules on that speedway. The first was that
every team entering the race had to post a penny entrance fee:
this money, plus pennies wrung out of spectators who could be in-
timidated, made up the three purses for winners of first, second,
and third prizes. The second rule was that all other rules were
written with flailing fists. Dirty driving, such as bumping into
pushers, sideswiping, tearing off wheels, throwing dust into the eyes
of rival drivers, was permitted if you could get away with it. The
outcome was that races were frequently broken up by fights. These
usually began between clashing teams but, often as not, ended in a
battle royal—drivers and pushers fighting like wildcats and everybody having fun.

In these races Eddie showed flashes of the inborn skill and
ability to plan for which he was to become known on land and in
the air. He was forever figuring out some scheme that would give
him an edge on his rivals. At that time, baby carriages with wheels
mounted on roller bearings were coming on the market. By sheer
accident, Eddie discovered that a new carriage with ball bearings
that belonged to a neighbor was much easier to push than the old-
type baby carriage in which he sometimes had to push his younger
brothers.

This discovery set Eddie thinking. Would the new kind of wheels improve the speed of a pushmobile? There was no time like the present, and he made up his mind to find out then and there. The fact that there was a nearly brand-new baby in the carriage did not stay the experiment.

Grasping the handles firmly, Eddie swung the baby carriage out on the pavement, headed it up the street, and took off on the double-quick. As it steadily gained momentum, he felt that he had never raced that fast before. The smooth turning of the ball-bearing wheels seemed to put wings on the baby cart. He was oblivious of the frightened baby's yowls and deaf to the screams of its mother, who was running hard behind him. When at last he came to a stop, he left the baby and its carriage at the curb, hurried home, and made a road test with the old-fashioned chariot occupied by his brother Albert. The test showed that the ball-bearing wheels had it all over the other kind. The only difficulty was to get a set of four wheels. Scouting around in junkyards and among secondhand dealers, the boy discovered that this type of baby carriage was still too new to turn up secondhand.

Finally Eddie thought of Sam the Junkman. When Sam showed up on his regular rounds, he presented his problem. Sam said he would see what he could do. And, lo and behold, when his cart rattled up Livingston Avenue seven days later, he had two sets of ball-bearing wheels mounted on axles for his friend. Price? Nothing! On the house!

If Eddie had known about the seventh heaven, that would have been his address for the next two days. With care and pride, he mounted the wheels on a board which he painted bright red. On it, he fastened a soapbox which he painted a golden yellow. He plaited a stout steering rope of clean white cord. And when everything was ready he hid his secret entry for the pushmobile sweepstakes under a paint-stained canvas in the darkest corner of the barn. Then he took the boy who was the fastest pusher on the track into his confidence, made a deal with him to split the prize money they would win the next day.

Eddie and his pal made a clean sweep in every race. The roller-bearing wagon and its team were almost ruled off the track. But both boys were first-rate scrappers, and rewrote the rules.

Incidentally, Eddie called his speed wagon "Mile-a-Minute Murphy." At the tail end of the nineteenth century that name stood for speed and skill and stamina—plus. Charles Murphy was a bicycle racer who in 1899 set the globe agog when he pedaled a mile a minute on Long Island and established a world record which made him the first man to travel on land or in the air at that terrific pace. As the new century began, there were 10,000,000 bicycles in the United States, and they made America speed-conscious and good-roads-conscious. The pushmobile was the invention of speed-crazy youngsters who could not afford bicycles. The automobile industry was still in its swaddling clothes, and there were fewer than 10,000 horseless carriages in the entire United States, many of them of European manufacture.

Eddie was six years old in 1896, when he first saw an automobile. It was the now famous Duryea that won the first auto race in America, staged in Chicago over a fifty-four-mile course which it covered with the dazzling speed of seven miles per hour. This "racing car" was for several years the star-feature of the street parade of the Barnum and Bailey Circus, and that was how Eddie saw it. It made no impression upon him whatever. During his early teens he saw some motor trials and many bicycle races on the old Driving Park track, but they did not rouse his interest. During that same period, two young bicycle merchants in Dayton, only sixty miles away, were working on plans for a power-driven flying machine, but it was not yet time for Eddie Rickenbacker to turn his eyes either toward the roaring road of auto racing or toward the invisible path of the skies, where he eventually was to match his daring and skill against danger and death.

This seems to be the proper place to mention that, even as a boy, Eddie had his share of miraculous escapes from disaster. As a child of three, he ran in front of a trolley car, was bumped into the gutter and not even bruised. Two or three years later, he tumbled twelve feet to the bottom of a well. He did not even get wet—because the well was dry. No bones broken, either.

Once, the Man with the Scythe almost caught up with Eddie. The near-meeting was in an abandoned sand pit near his home. There was a rusty track from the rim of the pit to the bottom, and fitting this track was a small four-wheeled truck with high sides. When the pit was in operation, the car would be hauled up loaded with sand, unloaded and sent down again by means of a cable.

Eddie and his Horseheads would slide to the bottom of the pit and then, blocking the car as they shoved it up foot by foot, would finally push it to the top of the track. The gang would pile aboard while Eddie, the self-appointed control man, sat on the forward edge of the car. As he kicked the blocks away, down the car would hurtle to the bottom of the pit. This informal way of courting death went on for quite a spell, until one afternoon Eddie fell out of the car just as he kicked away the blocks. He sprawled on the track in front of the truck, which hit him, turned over, and spilled its human cargo. Young Rickenbacker almost, but not quite, broke a leg, and had to be helped home. He could not walk for nearly a week, but that was all. It was also the end of the sand pit as a playground.

This did not mean that Eddie neglected his chores. On the contrary, he always had a flock of goats to tend. At one time he had as many as twenty-one milch goats. It was his job to stake them out where there would be grass enough to feed on; he had to milk them daily and deliver the milk not used at home to neighbors who paid Mother Rickenbacker five cents per quart. The nanny goats were tied to stakes in the open country near the house, while their offspring, the young kids, ran free; but these seldom drifted far from their mothers.

Eddie had a strong feeling of responsibility toward his flock, and this sense of loyalty made him, on one occasion, expose himself to serious danger. A mongrel dog, as big as a collie, ran amuck in the herd one summer evening when Eddie sat on the porch with his father. A terrific commotion broke out among the goats, and above their bleating and jumping and braying could be heard the deep barking of an angry dog followed by a long-drawn throaty growl. Eddie dashed off and found that the dog had attacked one of the goats and, with its teeth in its throat, was trying to drag it down.

Without thinking twice, Eddie, then only about nine, hurled himself upon the dog, grabbed it by the neck, and started to try to choke it. The wild dog released its hold and was just about to turn upon Eddie when the boy's father came up with a stick of wood and sent the animal running with a few clouts on the head. On the way home, Eddie noticed that his father was so upset that he was shaking. Thinking it was with anger, he made up his mind that another lambasting was on its way. Instead, Father Rickenbacker took his son by the hand and, in a voice that was unusually gentle, warned him that a dog that was large enough and bold enough to tackle a full-grown goat would not hesitate to spring upon a boy.

"But what should I do, Pop?" asked Eddie. "Let the dog kill one of my goats?"

While he had fun watching the kids buck one another, Eddie did not make pets of them. His relationship with the goats was strictly business.

Chapter III

~~~~~~

When Eddie reached the proper age, he was packed off to school. With the first strokes of the bell, he developed a terrific crush on his teacher, Miss Alexander. He adored the ground she walked on, and nothing was too good or too beautiful for her. This feeling deepened as the school year went on.

Other youngsters brought apples for teacher. But no apples for Eddie! Not enough class. So in the spring our gallant leader of the Horseheads brought Miss Alexander fresh and lovely flowers—tulips, lilacs, daffodils, and jonquils. At first he brought her merely two or three flowers. But when he saw how these little offerings pleased her and brightened the rather bare classroom, he increased his offering from small bouquets to big bunches.

As Eddie's floral contributions grew larger and more frequent, Miss Alexander became alarmed. She wanted to know where he got the flowers. He was vague about their source : he brought them from home, or somebody had given them to him—he was not sure which.

That very week, Eddie's flower boom came to a cataclysmic end. People along his route to school had noticed a sharp thinning out in their flower beds. They discovered that a little boy who attended the East Main Street Public School nearly always carried flowers into the building. They put two and two together and—Eddie was caught redhanded.

Miss Alexander forthwith gave him a spanking to remember. But that was not all. Bad news travels fast, and when he got home the news of his flower piracy had arrived before him; and for the second time that day Eddie got a whaling.

For such a lover of competition as Eddie, who insisted on being the front-seat driver in all activities, it was rather odd that he should be a back-seat student in dumbbell row. But that is exactly what Eddie was.

It is quite possible that Miss Álexander's swift and thorough use of the hickory stick cooled Eddie's ardor for learning.

However, it is more likely that an unfortunate situation which made Eddie a laughingstock of other children, the recipient of ridicule, jeers, and gibes throughout his second year in school, had more to do with making the boy develop a resentful attitude toward school and a chip-on-the-shoulder mood toward his schoolmates. It all began with a pair of shoes. No, that is not correct either, for "pair" implies two shoes exactly alike in shape, color, design, and size, except that one fits the right foot and the other the left.

Now, the year Dutchie entered second grade had been one of disappointments in the Rickenbacker family. Every time William made a bid for a job, he was either too high and did not get it or too low and lost money on the transaction. The result was that when winter set in, the parents had no money to spend on clothing. Everything had to be bought secondhand for the bigger boys and girls, and one of Father Rickenbacker's bargains was brand-new, thick-soled, stoutly made shoes for Eddie. They were the same size, but that was all they had in common. The left was a reddish brown with a blunt nose. The right was a butter yellow with a long nose that ended in a point. Eddie remembers that beyond doubt, because he used the pointed right shoe to kick the stuffings out of his tormentors.

With the cruelty of children Eddie's schoolmates held him up to ridicule, day after day, week after week, month after month throughout that winter. They laughed at him and his funny shoes. They laughed at him as he tried to catch them. They called him names when he hit them and kicked them. In the classroom, in the school yard, and on the way to and from school—two long and torturous miles—boys and girls would make him squirm and whiten with fury as they twittered:

"Look at Dutchie's funny shoes—"

"Hay foot, straw foot, get a shoe from Lilliput—"

"Eddie's old woman don't live in no shoe—"

It was torment. Never since that terrible winter has Eddie Rickenbacker known such goading fury or bitter resentment. He weathered the winter of derision, and the agony ended in the spring when his father had the price of a new pair of shoes. Meanwhile, something had happened to Eddie inside. The scowl had become a permanent fixture on his face. He always carried a chip on his shoulder, ready for some youngster to knock it off. He never courted trouble but, on the other hand, never allowed anything to pass by with a shrug. Even a smile could be a challenge to a fight. He did not like school, and yet he had the stamina to stick it out to the seventh grade. His teacher, Miss Gifford, felt a deep pity toward the truculent little bantam who always sat in the last seat of her class. Time and again she would talk to him after school in the hope of wiping the scowl off his face. At times she succeeded, but only for a little while.

His mother, too, tried to give him strength and consolation. A sensitive soul, she understood the boy's torment; but, on the other hand, she knew the value of an education.

"Aw, Mom, I want to quit school—what does it get me?" Eddie would plead.

Often as not, his mother would reply:

"Don't get the idea that the world owes you a living, my boy. To get anywhere you've got to meet the world at least halfway!"

Even rebellious Eddie knew that this was sound advice. He remained in school as long as he could.

The pity of it was that, but for the mismatched shoes, Eddie would probably have liked school and become an excellent student. He was keen on spelling and arithmetic, even if geography and English were a chore. But his favorite period was the one devoted to art and painting. He loved to work with crayons and water colors and made some rather fair pictures of flowers, landscapes, and animals. A landscape he painted in school still hangs in Mother Rickenbacker's room. He made the frame himself and gave it to her. The secret ambition of this strange little ruffian who carried a chip on his shoulder and a thirst for beauty in his heart, was to be a great artist. Miss Gifford sensed this gentle quality, as did his mother, and tried to help him, but Eddie could not be helped. He remained at the foot of the class because of a deportment rating that always was somewhere between zero and double zero. He was always getting into fights or, like a Chinaman in a bull pen, heading into trouble even when he did not try to do it.

Strangely enough, Eddie's dislike for public school did not extend to Sunday school. He liked it. Rain or shine, when he was eight to nine years old, Dutchie marched off every Sabbath to Sunday school in St. John's Lutheran Church in the South End of Columbus. Kindly old Pastor Pfister had baptized all the Rickenbacker children and knew them and loved them as his own.

Remember Eddie's crush on Miss Alexander? Well, in Sunday school, Dutchie "went sweet" on a little schoolmate named Blanche Calhoun. Some say the main reason tough little Dutchie was a constant and model Sunday-school pupil was Blanche, a child of almost his own age. The South End was quite a distance from Livingston Avenue, and so Blanche did not go to Eddie's public school.

Having learned that flowers pack an unexpected kickback, he did not bring Blanche floral offerings. Instead he gave her specimens of his early paintings, mostly landscapes. Some of these were surprisingly good copies of the art work on the calendars which building companies and insurance firms sent his father at the start of each year.

As a boy, Eddie was not deeply religious, although he said his prayers dutifully every night—a practice that has remained unchanged with him throughout the years. Grace was not said at meals in the Rickenbacker home. However, in the front bedroom, on a table, there was a book which all the children looked upon with awe. It was large and heavy; it was bound in black hand-tooled leather, and on the cover were the words "Holy Bible," emblazoned in gold. Its pages were big, the print was large, and there were many pictures.

Many nights, when she did not have to sew or mend, Elizabeth, the mother, would sit at the kitchen table and read in her Bible, and there was great rivalry among the children for the honor of bringing her the Sacred Book from the front bedroom. The picture of his mother reading the Bible made a tremendous impression upon Eddie. She was too reserved to reveal the weight of her burdens; but he knew, without her ever having told him, that the Bible was her sword and buckler.

The armor that protects the poor is an alloy of Hope, Patience, and Faith, and Mother Rickenbacker was amply supplied with these. Above all, her faith protected her from disappointment that otherwise could easily have brought her down.

"God will look after us!" was her firm and living belief, and no one who knows the story of this remarkable woman could ever doubt that He did. Otherwise, her many burdens would have been unbearable.

Time has the faculty of cutting down the sharp edges of things we remember.

In the passing of twoscore years, the tapestry of Eddie's boyhood takes on a soft patina which did not exist during the hectic years when his harried parents tried vainly to change him from a reckless little ruffian into a well behaved boy.

His mother would plead with him, and pray for him to mend his ways. His father would reason with him and try to lick the old Nick out of him. But nothing could change Eddie.

"They'll send you to a reformatory," his mother would prophesy.

"You'll grow up to be a jailbird unless you learn to behave," his father would predict.

Eddie did not regard his way of life as radically different from that of other boys. Being used to poverty, he regarded plain fare, hand-me-down clothing, and the utter lack of luxury as matters of course.

He knew that his parents had to labor long and hard, providing for the younger children. He knew that his older sister and brother, Mary and Bill, had gone to work on completing grade school. He knew that his own meager earnings were badly needed.

There were many nights when Father and Mother, sitting at the kitchen table under the kerosene lamp, would try to figure out ways of spreading their scant savings to meet interest demands, mortgage payments, and other costs. Young as he was, Eddie could understand the crushing burden of debts that had to be met. One evening in the early spring of 1902, the parents sat in the kitchen discussing that kind of problem. His sisters and brothers had gone to bed, but Eddie was working at a crayon landscape on a grubby bit of cardboard.

"If business only would pick up so I could collect some of the money, people owe," complained the father, "we could pay the interest on the house up to date. But forty-eight dollars! Where will we get forty-eight dollars?"

Forty-eight dollars, thought Eddie idly. A lot of money. Even forty-eight cents was hard to get.

"Don't take it too hard, Will," Elizabeth replied. "God will look after us!"

"But what will we do, Liebchen?" asked William Rickenbacker impatiently. "The payment on the mortgage is due—two payments, remember?—and I still owe for the last load of cement and lumber."

He leaned across the table and stroked his wife's straight black hair, drawn flat against her head. She smiled at him, a little sadly, but the smile grew brighter and warmer.

"Don't worry, Will." She patted the back of his hand and repeated: "God will look after us—he always has!"

"I know. Say, that sidewalk contract I have been bidding on looks good. I'll go and see if I can draw some money on my way home from the job tomorrow morning."

"I'm sure you can." Elizabeth got up and put her sewing aside for the night. "Don't you worry, Will."

"Hey, Pop!" shouted Eddie as his father was about ready to leave. "Got time to come out in the shop? Wanna show you something I made."

The boy was of an experimental type of mind, always tinkering, always trying to make some kind of gadget or other in his father's tiny workshop. In this the father encouraged him, with surprising insight into the machine age that was to come. A few days earlier, Eddie had "found" some billiard balls and, using them as weights, he had built a wheel that revolved as the billiard balls dropped into cups fastened on the rim of the wheel.

With great pride, Eddie showed him the engine. To his chagrin his father did not show the slightest enthusiasm.

"What good is it?" he asked. "What does it produce? Machinery must have a purpose—that's why it is made."

This cut Eddie to the quick. Suddenly realizing the fact, Father Rickenbacker put his arm around the lad's shoulder and continued in a softer voice:

"You know that little bridge I'm building down at the Elm Creek crossing? and how I had to rig up a pile driver to sink the bridge pilings solidly in the creek bottom?"

The boy nodded. He had been a fascinated spectator when the weight-dropping gear was set up.

"Well, that pile driver is so simple that almost any fool can build one and run it—but it does useful work. It helps to build a bridge, and bridges help to keep all sorts of traffic going—wagons, automobiles, and railroads. It's all right to build a wheel that goes 'round, as you're doing here. But unless it does something useful— unless it goes some place for some real purpose, it is nothing but a lot of wasted time and motion. Stick to machinery, Eddie. Tie your wagon to an engine, but always be sure of two things: first, that you know how to control it, and, secondly, that it serves a useful purpose. Today, people laugh at automobiles and scoff at flying machines; but I'm telling you, son, that they are only the forerunners of greater things to come. You're a lucky boy, Eddie, to be born when you were. There's a lot of new things in the making, and you want to be ready to have a hand in them. Tools, Eddie—hands and heads and tools, Eddie, will make a new world."

Father Rickenbacker stopped abruptly with a short laugh that was half cough. He spun the free-wheeling gadget with a horny forefinger and walked toward the door. Just before he reached it, he said:

"I'd give most anything to have my life to live over again, Eddie, if I could only start at your age. Well, so long, son. Time to get on the night shift."

He bent to pass through the low and narrow door. The boy listened to his departing steps. He heard the front gate creak on its hinges and slam shut. Throughout his entire life, Eddie Rickenbacker has remembered every word his father spoke to him in the shop that night, because it was the last time his father ever spoke to him. William Rickenbacker did not come home the next day. In fact, he did not come home at all. A workman with whom he had an argument flew into a rage, hit him on the head with a heavy three-foot level made of hardwood and tipped with brass, and broke his skull. He was taken to a hospital, where he remained between life and death for more than a month—and then died.

They brought him home on a sunlit April day in a plain coffin with nickel-plated handles and placed him in the front room with the window shades drawn down and the kerosene lamp standing lit on the table. The lid of the casket was open so that friends and neighbors and relatives who had moved to Columbus from the old country could say their last farewell. Elizabeth Rickenbacker sat in silent vigil near the head of the coffin. Her seven children, self-conscious and tongue-tied, sat on camp chairs the undertaker had brought in and placed along the wall. The house, usually so full of the light voices and many sounds of lively children, was silent. Only the shuffling footsteps of people coming in—pausing briefly— and going out again. Now and then low voices. A stifled sob or two.

Eddie was conscious of this change around him, but he was more conscious of an even greater change within himself. Death had come before, to take his sister Louisa away, when he was too young to understand. Now, going on twelve, he understood. He knew that his father had gone, never to return. He looked at the coffin, soberly, then at his mother. In the dim light, he could see her bowed head, her rounded back, and the work-worn hands resting in her lap.

"God will look after us!"

The boy recalled the often heard phrase, spoken by his mother on the last night his father was home alive: "God will look after us!"

He looked at his sisters and brothers, ranged on each side of him according to age. Mary, the oldest, almost sixteen, sat at one end of the pathetic line; Albert, the youngest, only four, at the other on the lap of a neighbor. Eddie's eyes drifted to the tips of his new black shoes, to his new black stockings, and up his new black suit. He had gone with his mother when she bought the clothes of mourning for herself and her children. The man in the store had been kind. He took a small down payment. The rest, she could pay on time. But where would she get the money?

"God will look after us!" Yes! But still that debt worried Eddie.

Now Pastor Pfister entered the house to conduct the final rites.

He spoke gently to Elizabeth, who rose to greet him. They talked briefly in whispers. Going over to the neighbors who stood by the foot of the coffin, he spoke softly and waved a hand toward the kitchen door. They nodded and preceded him slowly from the room, Elizabeth accepting Albert without a word from the woman who had held him on her lap. The door was closed.

For a few seconds there was complete silence in the little room. Then the mother called upon the children to step close to the coffin. As the little group looked at William Rickenbacker for the last time, she spoke clearly and slowly—without a tremor.

"You will never see your father again. He has gone, but he continues to live in all of you. His spirit goes on in you. Try to be as brave as he was. Try to be as good as he was." Elizabeth Rickenbacker paused and looked each child in the eyes. "Promise me that you will help me take care of all of you. I will not always be with you, so promise me that you will always aid each other. Some of you may be stronger, brighter, more lucky than the others, and it is your duty to help your less fortunate brothers and sisters wherever and whenever you can."

Again she looked at each child, asking each in turn, "Promise?" When she had finished she once more looked at the still features of her husband and whispered, "God will look after us!" And the strength of an iron faith was in her voice.

Late in the night after the funeral, Eddie tossed on his bed. His thoughts boiled, keeping sleep from his eyes. The room was dark. There was no moon. He knew that the door to the hall and the stairs was open. Everything was dark. To the boy it seemed as if the thick black night were closing in on him, making his world smaller, darker, and more uncertain.

Eddie kept on thinking, and began to reconstruct scenes of yesterday. Acts of which he suddenly felt bitterly ashamed came back to mind. All the sorrow and fear and agony he had heaped upon his parents suddenly took pattern, and it was not a pretty picture.

"God will look after us!" he repeated the oft-heard phrase. "O dear God," he prayed tearfully, "help me to help!" Words welled to his lips and took wings of faith. And suddenly it seemed as if he heard an answer. A strength and confidence he had never felt before swept through him.

Human beings, like plants, mature differently: some early, some late; some slowly, and some suddenly. Maturity came early and swiftly to Eddie Rickenbacker. The balance wheel of responsibility that had remained at dead center until that moment took up its functions suddenly. He was no longer a foolish, reckless, irresponsible boy. He felt that, in the span of a night, he had become a man.

A faint light stole through the darkness. Eddie listened and looked. Someone had lighted the lamp in the kitchen: his mother. But not a sound came up the stairs. After a brief wait the boy slipped out of bed and stole down to the kitchen, where he found his mother at her usual place at the kitchen table, with her chin cupped in her hands. Eddie walked over and clumsily put his arms around her.

"Mother," he whispered, "I'll never make you cry again."

She stroked his head and smiled.

"Don't worry about anything any more, Mother. Everything will be all right. I'll take care of all of you," he promised as he went to the other end of the table.

Mother Rickenbacker laughed, but her laugh was choked by tears.

"Why, Eddie," she said as the boy sat down in a chair—a boy with fiery eyes and a set chin. "Do you know what you're doing?"

"N-no," he replied, shaking with fear that he had done something wrong. "What am I doing?"

"You are sitting in your father's chair! You're sitting at the head of the table!"

"Well, Mother, that's where I belong, for I am going to be the head of the family in Father's place."

Chapter IV

The next morning, Eddie dawdled around the house so that he would not be saddled with any of his gang on their way to school. He carried a lunch when he left, which was unusual. He had no intention whatever of going to school that day—or any other day. Instead, he was on his way to get a job. He took his self-assumed role of head of the household in deadly earnest. In his own eyes, he was no longer a child but a man in the place of his dead father with the responsibility of providing for his mother and his younger sister and brothers.

Eddie did not consult his mother because he knew that she would have packed him off to school. Nor did he mention his plans to Mary, his eldest sister, or to his brother Bill—both of whom were working in a clothing factory out on East Main Street. He was afraid that they might tell on him.

The boy had hardly slept a wink the night before. After his mother had sent him off to bed, he had lain wide awake trying to think things out and plan his immediate future. His main problem was where to look for a job. After a while he remembered that one of the very first jobs Bill had had was in the Federal Glass Works in the South End of Columbus.

"They have kids working there all the time," said Eddie to himself, "and there's your chance."

Yes, but there was a law that a boy had to be fourteen years old, or through eighth grade in school, before he could get a job—Eddie was not sure which. He was only eleven and had not finished the seventh grade. He mulled that over and eventually decided that the safest bet would be to claim that he was not only fourteen years old but had gone through the eighth grade.

The Federal Glass Works was quite a distance off, and he would

not be able to get down to the plant, talk himself into a job, and
get home again in time for lunch. Besides, he might get a job right
off the bat. Hence the sandwich and pickle in a paper bag. Oh, yes,
Eddie the Strategist had it all figured out.

As he had figured, it was a long trek to the glass plant. It took
him the better part of two hours to get there. At the gate there was
a big sign reading, "No Help Wanted"; but that did not stop
Eddie. He found the employment office and asked for a job. The
man looked at him quizzically, shifted the cud of chewing tobacco
in his mouth and spat judiciously and accurately into the bowels of
a huge brass cuspidor.

"Kinda young, ain't you?"

"Fourteen. And I'm all through school."

"Kinda puny, ain't you?"

"I'm as strong as a horse," answered Eddie, "and I can lick
every kid in my gang."

"What's your name, boy?"

"Eddie—Eddie Rickenbacker. My brother Bill, he used to
work here."

"Bill? Rickenbacker? Yeah, I remember him. Good worker, he
was. Good scrapper, too! Well, if you're that breed of cats, mebbe
I can find you a job—mebbe so, mebbe no."

"Gee! Thanks, Mister!" exclaimed Eddie.

"You say you're fourteen and all through school," said the man.

"Yep."

"I think you're lying by the clock—but I can't prove it. Why do
you want a job, youngster?"

Eddie told him what had happened at home.

The man rubbed his heavy chin, shifted the cud once more, and
spat. The cuspidor went *bong* as the liquid bullet hit it. "Helps me
think," he explained. After a pause he said: "We're all filled up—
ain't hired nobody for nigh on a month—been layin' off instead.
But if you want a job carrying tumblers mebbe I can fix you up.
It will be hard work, though."

"I don't mind, Mister," broke in Eddie, trembling with happy
excitement. "I can work hard."

"Mebbe so, mebbe no," said the man. "Ain't no harm trying

though. You'll start on the night shift at six o'clock this evening. Your quitting time is six o'clock tomorrow morning. Twelve hours! You think you can stand it, heh?"

"You just bet I can!" was Eddie's triumphant answer.

The distance home was at least six miles, but he made most of it at a half-run. He told his mother what he had done.

"But, Eddie," she remonstrated, "you're too young to leave school."

"We need the money, don't we, Mother?"

"Yes, yes, my boy—but an education is worth more than the money you can make. You must not quit school. And working nights, besides!"

Thinking fast, Eddie the Strategist came up with a quick answer: "Look, Mother. Suppose then that I don't quit school. I'll go to work for a while to make a little money—and then I can always go back to school. And about working nights, maybe they'll soon put me on the day shift. But a feller has to start some place."

By the uncertainty on his mother's face, he knew that he was winning.

She laughed and shook him gently as she tried to hide her perplexity. This was such a different Eddie, and she did not quite know what to make of him or what to do with him. If it had been Bill or Mary or Emma at the age of eleven, she would have known. "Back to school, and stay there," would have been the verdict. They were good and easy to handle, but Eddie—always in trouble, always fighting; unhappy in school but smart as a whip and full of energy. Oh, if William were only alive!

The boy saw her brush away a tear.

"Oh, Mother! Don't, Mother—I promised that I would never make you cry again."

That decided her. Eddie needed her help, even as she needed his. Perhaps work was what his tireless, driving energy needed. Getting away from school, for a while at least, might knock the chip off his shoulder.

"All right," she said, "let us see how it works out. But remember, if you go back to being the way you were, you'll be the one who is sorry."

Both were silent. Then, to break the tension, she asked: "How much will they be paying you?"

Eddie's face fell a mile and turned beet-red. That was a question he could not answer.

"I don't know, Ma. The man didn't tell me—and I didn't dare to ask."

That afternoon Eddie felt more important than ever when he told his brothers and sisters and the Horseheads that he was through with school and going to work. "Like a man," he said with cocky pride. "Like a self-made man!"

And to a great extent he was right, for, as a man at the age of eleven, he was a self-made man indeed.

On that first working day he had dinner about three o'clock and then, with his father's lunch pail as a proud token of his new status, set off on the long hike to the factory.

"Be careful, Eddie," warned his mother as she kissed him goodbye. "Be careful what you say and do. You'll find out pretty soon, my boy, that to get on in the world you've got to know how to get along with people."

The boy nodded.

"You are going to a different kind of school now, son—the bitter school of life; and you've got to study the people you rub elbows with. Remember, they'll be studying you. To make them respect you, you must have respect for yourself. There's an old French saying, 'We awaken in others the attitude we hold toward ourselves.'"

She broke off with a laugh, and gave him a light push. "Run along now. Good luck."

When Eddie reached the factory shortly before six o'clock he reported to the night foreman, John Crawford, a rough and burly man who proved to have a heart of gold and took a liking to the boy. He was assigned to the job of carrying thick glass tumblers from the blowers and the presses to the tempering ovens.

The tumblers alone were heavy, and they had to be carried on a large steel tray with a long handle not unlike a baker's paddle. In addition, Eddie had to line the molds with a mixture of molasses and flour, to prevent the glass from sticking; and the molds were cumbersome and hard to handle.

That first night seemed endless, but at last the six o'clock whistle let out its shrill blast. Again Eddie walked the full distance home, because it saved a nickel carfare and he was determined not to spend a penny unnecessarily. At the end of the first week he received his first pay. It was in a small and light brown envelope, carefully sealed, that bore his name. He looked at the envelope, turned it over—looked at it again and wondered how much it contained in return for six nights' work of twelve hours each. He tore the envelope open and spilled its contents into his left hand. There were three dollar bills and a fifty-cent piece.

He whistled. Three dollars and fifty cents to bring home to Mother this week and every week! He counted the money again, fingered each dollar bill almost lovingly, and turned the fifty-cent piece over and over in his hand. It was more money than he had ever owned at any one time.

"Boy, oh, boy!" he chortled to himself. "What a bang it will be when I hand all that to Ma!"

For a moment he thought he might spend a nickel on a trolley ride home, just to celebrate. But no! The real celebration would be to turn over his pay intact to his mother. So he walked. On the way home he figured out that he had to work over an hour to earn five cents. And from that time on, whenever he felt inclined to spend money foolishly, he remembered how hard he had to work to make a nickel.

On the job, as the weeks went on, Eddie made friends with his fellow workmen. During the midnight lunch hour, he visited with the glassblowers. And they taught him how to make flowers, especially lilies, out of colored glass. The artistic aptitude he had shown in school cropped up, and many of the boy's glass flowers were surprisingly lifelike. Some of these he gave to his mother. Others he gave to Blanche, whom he still saw in Sunday school.

As a rule, he left for work about four-thirty in the afternoon and returned around seven-thirty in the morning. Before breakfast each morning, he would milk his goats. After breakfast, he would deliver the milk, which he sold at five cents a quart. He also sold eggs as a side line for six or seven cents a dozen. Then he would go to bed and sleep until about three o'clock in the afternoon, when his younger brothers and sister came home from school. Then he would help them lug water from the well, gather wood, and chop it up.

Life was rather stern for Eddie, much work and little play; but he seemed to thrive on it. He did not have time to lead his old pack or even run with it. From a rambunctious black sheep, he transformed himself into a patient and reliable man-of-all-work. He was never tired, he never complained; but, on the other hand, he seldom whistled or sang. He had only one purpose: Work! Only one creed: Responsibility!

Surprisingly enough, the authorities permitted him to play permanent hookey from school. Or maybe it was not so surprising. Chances are they shared Mother Rickenbacker's attitude toward Eddie and his problems. At any rate, nothing was done.

One afternoon after Eddie had been working about a month, the truant officer came to the house and wanted to know where the boy was. The mother took him upstairs to the room where Eddie was sleeping, dead to the world. Downstairs again, the truant officer was told the whole story. He left and never came back.

Among the things Eddie wanted in those days was a bicycle; but his puny earnings and those of Mary and Bill all went to keep the wolves called Liens and Foreclosure away from the door. Not a penny could be spent on such an unessential as transportation when time was cheap.

Shoe leather was of comparatively minor importance. For many years, Father Rickenbacker had done all the repairs in the family, buying sheets of sole leather at factory price from the tannery. From him Eddie had learned not only how to sole and half-sole shoes and put on new heels, but also how to patch cracks in the uppers. Therefore, shoe leather, too, was cheaper than transportation.

Naturally enough, Eddie the Strategist figured out a way to beat part of the transportation problem by stealing free rides on the trolley. It could not be worked too often, or the conductor would get wise; but those rides were wonderful because they gave him a chance to get forty winks.

After three months of working in the glass plant, Eddie suddenly decided one night that he had had enough. He went up to the foreman and, without preliminaries, asked for his time.

"What's the matter, boy? Hang on, and you'll learn a trade and get a raise."

"Don't want to learn this trade. I don't like this job. I'm all tired out working nights, and I've got to make more money than I am getting here."

"Well, Eddie, if you look at it that way, I won't try to hold you. Got another job in mind?"

"Some of the boys told me," replied Eddie, "that they are using kids at the foundry up the street."

"So they do—and what does it get you?"

"A whole dollar every day, Mr. Crawford, and a ten-hour day, in the daytime—"

"If you get it," cut in the work boss. "Well, Eddie, I'll give you your time, and I'm sorry to see you go. If you don't get the job, come back."

When the night shift left the glass plant at six o'clock, Eddie walked the mile farther out on Parsons Avenue to the foundry. On his way he offered a wordless prayer for a job. But the thought that he might not get the job never entered his mind. His one besetting ambition now was to bring as much money home every week as Bill and Mary did.

"Six bucks," he muttered. "That will do it." He recalled his mother's prayer: "God will take care of us!"

Eddie walked into the hiring office soon after it opened, made the employment agent realize that he knew something about molds and castings, which took a little explaining. He also swore up and down that he was fourteen years old. In brief, he talked himself into a job on the day shift.

"When can you start, boy?"

"Right now!" he answered.

"All right, you start making cores for castings at seven o'clock—half an hour from now."

Eddie rushed out to a lunch wagon. Had some breakfast, reported for work at seven, and remained on the job until five o'clock in the afternoon. He had been on his feet, walking or working, for twenty-four hours when he stopped work that day. Also home was a mile farther away than it had been before—seven miles.

That afternoon, he spent a nickel to ride home. He felt the trolley was a luxury he could afford.

What with a ten-hour day, and working in the daytime, Eddie had more time for sleep but less opportunity for work around the house. While a dollar a day was not to be scoffed at, there must be ways to make some money at night. The boy looked around and found a job in a bowling alley just a few blocks away.

After working all day, Eddie would come home, have supper, and then work in the bowling alley until midnight, making as much as a quarter a night. This he would do three or four nights a week, particularly on Saturday and Sunday evenings.

By rigid economy with the earnings of Eddie and Bill and Mary and the pin money from the sale of eggs and milk—for the younger children had now taken over the chickens and the goats—Mother Rickenbacker was able to relieve the financial pressure that had threatened her home and family. On Sunday, after Sunday school, she would give Eddie an allowance of a quarter. Ten cents of this would be spent, in the summer, on a round trip to Olentangy Park on the Scioto River, which was then the Coney Island of Columbus. That left fifteen cents for a ride on the Ferris wheel or a fling on the roller coaster and a five-cent box of Cracker Jack.

By this time, too, the future seemed sufficiently safe to risk an investment of eighteen dollars on a secondhand bicycle for Eddie bought on a basis of a few dollars down and fifty cents per week. On his wheel, Eddie covered the distance between home and foundry in almost nothing flat.

Late on a blustery December afternoon, a few days before Christmas in the year 1903, Eddie came speeding up Livingston Avenue as fast as he could pedal his bicycle, which was of the speed-bug type, with low handlebars, a high saddle, fancy toe clips, and no fenders. With his backsides high in the air and his chin resting on the handlebars, he looked, someone said, like a bumblebee bound for combat. As a bike rider, he was definitely a "speed merchant."

On reaching home, the boy braked the bicycle by sticking his right toe between the front forks and pressing the sole of his shoe

against the tire. That was the "hot-potato" way of doing it, and he
was a stickler for form. However, instead of parking his bike in the
barn, he let it drop to the walk in front of the kitchen door and
slammed through pop-eyed. The whole family was there waiting
supper and stared at him with unrestrained amazement as he yowled
like a demented Indian. Finally, he shouted at the top of his lungs:

"They've done it! They've done it! Golly, if they ain't flew!"

Shaking with excitement, he showed the front page of the newspaper. It revealed that two Dayton brothers named Wright had
traveled a distance of forty yards in twelve seconds in a flying
machine from Kill Devil Hill at Kitty Hawk, North Carolina. From
that day millions of American boys, including Eddie, had a deep
interest in the Wright brothers, built miniature planes out of canvas
and wood, declared that some day they would drive through the air
in their flying machines. But the slow progress of aviation, and the
discouragement that greeted the Wrights, in time dulled the edge of
Eddie's interest in flight.

Before that happened, he put the theory of human flight to the
acid test—the one of proving that the pudding is deadly by eating
it. He and two of his closest companions, Karl Yerglier and Sam
Wareham, rigged up a device consisting of a rather weather-beaten
wagon umbrella attached to the handlebar of Eddie's bicycle. The
idea was to take off on a flight with this power-driven "glider" from
the roof of a barn.

The Yerglier barn was selected because it had a corrugated iron
roof and was rather close to the old sand pit where Eddie had been
almost killed by the runaway truck. The advantage of the iron
roof, the lads figured, was that the bike would get more speed over
an iron surface than a wooden one, especially if they took the tires
off the bike. As for the sand pit, its nearness made it possible for the
boys to haul up a load of sand and heap it by the barn for the
daring young flier to land in. This intrepid young man was, of
course, the indomitable, incomparable, indestructible Eddie Rickenbacker.

Came the day of the experiment. After much trouble, the boys
brought the bike and the umbrella up to the ridge of the barn roof,
and Eddie got into the saddle. Pedaling with all his might, he shot

down the sloping roof and hurtled out into the open air; but the ancient umbrella, instead of arresting his fall, turned inside out, and down he plunged some thirty feet into the sand heap below. He was not hurt, but his precious bicycle was somewhat damaged.

This experiment was staged shortly after the Wrights had made their epoch-marking hop. Early in 1904, Eddie was getting tired of his job in the foundry. His hands and face and hair and clothes were always grubby with sand and grime from dirty work. Almost feline neatness was one of Eddie's outstanding traits, and so the foundry got into his hair in more ways than one.

Spring was on its way when Eddie quit the foundry and got a job with the same wages and hours at the Hoster Brewery, putting caps on beer bottles. But he soon decided that beer capping held no future. Again he quit, and he landed on both feet in Goodman's shoe factory on West Broad Street, where his job was to turn out heels on a piece-payment basis and he made more money than ever. He soon earned as high as ten dollars in a week, which was not bad then for a boy of thirteen.

Thus far, everything had been fine and dandy. From his first day in the glassworks, through the foundry and brewery to the shoe factory, Eddie had been delighted and happy with his ability to work and bring cash home to his mother. He had the satisfaction that he, as a thirteen-year-old boy, was doing the work and earning the wages and having the home responsibilities of a real man. But suddenly all this paled. Dissatisfaction set in, and his days turned drab and dreary. He was tired of factory drudgery. The boy wanted to be an artist—a great artist.

At first, he tried to feed his inner hunger for artistic expression by taking lessons at night in a small art school. The fee was twenty-five cents per lesson, and the teacher was barely equipped to teach the A B C of drawing. Night after night, when he was not at art school, the boy would bend over his drawing board on the kitchen table while his mother would try to encourage him.

For the first time in his working career, Eddie was not interested in money. He did not give a hoot how much or how little money an artist made. He was driven by a desire to be an artist with paintings hung in the great museums and admired. During this period, he frequently called on his old friend, Miss Sarah Gifford, who still taught the seventh graders in the East Main Street school. Her interest in the boy had never waned, and she was the first to introduce him to the delights of museums and art galleries. During this phase, Eddie spent virtually all his leisure hours either in an art collection or taking art lessons at twenty-five cents an hour.

Miss Gifford, who hated to see the boy waste his money on lessons that could never help him realize his dream, called him into her classroom one afternoon during this, for Eddie, very grueling period.

"Why don't you forget this art business, Dutchie?" she asked. "You know, a lot of people, young and old, get fixed ideas about some dream existence they want to live—things they want to be, but never can be, because they haven't the skill. Now painting—"

"But I am studying," cut in Eddie.

"Certainly, my boy. But one of the things you'll learn in life is that the things we do best are those we are best equipped to do. No one can teach you to be a painter or a writer or a singer or musician or even a good mechanic unless you have equipment for it to begin with. All that a teacher can do is to hone whatever talent you have and put an edge on it."

But Eddie clung to his ambition. As time went on, he made himself more and more miserable. He was racked by the destructive frustration of yearning to be a great painter crowded by fear that he would never realize his dream. And yet, even at thirteen, he was able to control his emotion. One day he sat down with pencil and paper, but instead of drawing began to figure out how much it would cost and how long it would require for him to take a full-fledged art course. The cool black-on-white of these figures convinced him that he had neither the income nor the time to take such a course if he were to continue to help his mother and family. He threw the slips of paper into the kitchen stove and consigned to oblivion his dreams of being a great painter. It is an indication of his great native caution that, all through this rather long-drawn emotional upheaval, he stuck to his job at the shoe factory, of stamping out heels.

At this time something happened that was to give Eddie's artistic

urge a different form and expression. Mother Rickenbacker desired
to place a headstone upon William's grave. Thanks to the money
earned by the children, the cost of the plot in Greenlawn Cemetery
had almost been paid; and now she felt that the time had come
to honor the memory of her husband by placing a headstone and
four cornerstones on the plot. The matter was taken up in family
council one night at the kitchen table, and everyone was in favor
of it.

The upshot was that Mother Rickenbacker went to the Zenker
Monument Works on the west side of town near the Greenlawn
Cemetery. Then Mr. Zenker began to come to the house to talk to
her about the type of stone she wanted, and show her many pictures
and different designs and types of marble and granite.

This gave Eddie the idea that, if he could not win world-wide
fame as a painter, he might become a great sculptor through the
back door of the monument trade; and he finally persuaded Zenker
to give him a job.

Eddie's first task was to polish stones. He used water and
gradually got down to honing the surface to a polish. Having an
aptitude for art and a great gift for tools and the use of his hands,
he took to the work, and within a few months he was hacking
monuments out of rough marble. In time, he began work on the
chunk of granite out of which he was to hew the headstone for his
father's grave. This simple memorial, when completed, was about
five feet wide, six inches thick, and five feet tall. It was rounded at
the top and bore the word "Father" in big block letters with dates
below in sunken letters.

Zenker had a showroom in front. The workshop was outside in
summer but in a shed with a coal stove in winter. In the year
Eddie worked here, one thing that worried him was tuberculosis.
His feet were always wet because of the necessary use of water; and
monument workers, like all stonecutters, in those days, were constantly inhaling stone dust (dust masks had not yet come into use).
It was a well known fact that the dust had an effect on their lungs
and they seldom lived very long, usually dying of tuberculosis.

Eddie figured he was subject to the disease anyway, because
he had been told there was tuberculosis in his mother's family; and

it worried him a lot at night. One day he heard his mother, on a visit to the monument works, say to old man Zenker that she was afraid Eddie would not live to be a man because of his tendency to tuberculosis, although it had not shown up yet. He was paralyzed by surprise, but not for long. The moment she left, he walked in on his employer and declared:

"I've had enough! I'll never die a stonecutter! I quit!"

One peculiar thing about Eddie's flitting from job to job was that he never suffered from unemployment. He did not plan; he would just quit, trusting to luck; and always luck rode with him. Eddie has never been out of a job. He has had one specific formula and it is very simple:

Work hard, apply all your know-how and learn all you can!

If that did not work out, if Eddie did not like a job or found he could not adjust himself to it—he quit it. If he did not like his boss, he got a new one.

When Eddie left Zenker he had no definite idea except that he would like to get into mechanics. His job at the monument works had deepened his interest in fine tools. He had begun to understand the relationship between art and tools on one hand and tools and mechanics on the other. And he made one firm decision: The job he took now would not be unskilled labor! Moreover, it would be in some sort of mechanical trade. The reason for this was the number of cars he had seen on the highway along the cemetery. This stretch of road was favored by automobile salesmen for driving lessons to buyers.

Although Eddie had seen trials for automobile races at the Columbus Driving Park, they had not particularly stirred his imagination. Most people still regarded the automobile as very foolish and impracticable. Cars were known as crazy fire wagons, and foolish horseless carriages. On top of that, they made horses run away, so that horse owners, particularly farmers, looked upon the automobile as a public menace.

Cars were still held captive, more or less, on city pavements in 1904. They were no match for quagmire roads. They were fair-weather vehicles, open to all kinds of weather, and the usual thing was to store them for the winter like straw hats and summer coats.

Doleful prophets held little hope for automobiles because there were no roads for them to run on and the fifty thousand or more in use were most of the time stalled on streets or stuck in the mud on highways.

But all these factors were far beyond Eddie's horizon as he saw the fire wagons drive over the road near Zenker's. They stirred his interest, but he did not visualize himself as being associated with them. He quit Zenker's with one specific aim: to be a mechanic. After thinking things over, he decided that the way might be through the machine shops of the Pennsylvania Railroad on the northeast side of town.

Again the boy landed a job without the slightest difficulty. His first assignment was to clean out passenger cars when they came in for renovation. That paid a dollar a day, less than he had earned at Goodman's and Zenker's; but Eddie was less interested in his wages than in the kind of training received. One profitable discovery he made was that passengers in trains lost a lot of money from their pockets: it just slipped behind the cushions and would be waiting when the crews started to clean the cars. The boy found as much as three dollars some days, cleaning those cars. That would be the accumulation of three months.

After a while Eddie succeeded in being transferred to the machine shop as an apprentice. He might have remained in the railroad shops indefinitely if an accident had not sent him home on the sick list for a week or ten days. This took place when one of his fellow employees pushed a load of lumber on a hand truck past his lathe. One of the wheels came off, he was scuffed badly about the legs and had to go home.

One day, just before he was ready to return to work, Eddie decided to go downtown, and there, within the shadow of the old Statehouse, he saw the Model C auto which, through its seeming mechanical perfection, had caught his fancy. When that spindly little horseless buggy, one of the first Henry Ford ever made for commercial consumption, puttered up the street, Eddie Rickenbacker's decision was made. As soon as possible, regardless of sacrifice in pay, he would get a job in one of those newfangled garages. The limping boy started aimlessly down the street deep in a motor-driven dream. He did not know where he was going, but he knew he was on his way. His sense of strategy told him so.

He drifted along until he reached Chestnut Street and a run-down little building that bore a sign reading, "Evans' Garage—Bicycle and Automobile Repairs." Through a grimy window he saw the outlines of two or three cars. Sticking out from under one of the cars, he noticed the legs and feet of a man. They flailed around almost constantly as their invisible owner squirmed and wriggled under the car.

"Boy," said Eddie to himself, "that's the kind of a job I wish I had! Well," he added, "why don't you go and get it?"

Without further ado, he walked into the garage and, in doing that, he left the starting point and began his journey over the roaring road that was to take him far and fast to world-wide renown.

Book Two

Youth

EDDIE THE STRATEGIST
1905–1909

EARLY PORTRAIT OF EDDIE RICKENBACKER

WORKMEN AT COLUMBUS BUGGY WORKS. EDDIE IS STANDING FOURTH FROM THE LEFT, WITH ARMS FOLDED.

Chapter V

~~~~~~

"Where's the boss?" boomed Eddie loudly to the legs and feet sticking out from under what the boy now recognized as a Locomobile steam car.

"What's that?" queried a voice from under the car.

"I want to see the head man!" answered Eddie.

Slowly and laboriously, the feet and legs stretched into hips and torso and head as the man squeezed out from under the car. He was youngish and square-built: strong, square shoulders; strong, square hands; strong, square jaw.

"Well, what do you want, young one?" The man puffed as he got up from the dirty cement floor and rubbed his hands on the seat of his overalls.

"Are you the boss?" Eddie asked.

"Yes, I'm Mr. Evans. Why?"

"Well, I was just wondering if you need any help. I am looking for a job."

"Why? Did you lose the one you had?" Evans asked sharply.

"Nope. I have a job working in the machine shops on the Penn Railroad."

"Then why aren't you working this time of day?"

"Because I've been laid up with a bum leg. Listen, Mister, I'm all burned up about automobiles. I want to work on them, learn something about them."

"You do, do you?" Evans looked the boy over and evidently liked the cut of his jib. "Well, I'll tell you. I'm not making much money, for I haven't as much work to handle as I'd like to; but I could use a bright, hard-working lad who is willing to learn."

"That's me all over!" injected Eddie.

"How much are you making now, kid?"

"A buck and two bits a day."

"Too steep for me!" said Evans with a grin.

"I don't expect to get that much," countered Eddie, "to start with. I'm not interested in money. I want a job fixing automobiles. I want to learn something!"

"How about seventy-five cents a day?"

"That's O.K. by me," answered Eddie, quick as a flash. "When do I start? Anything I can fix today? Now, Mister?"

"No," laughed Evans. "Give me your name and address and some references, and show up at seven tomorrow morning."

The weight of good news Eddie carried that afternoon was much too heavy to be borne by foot. He boarded a trolley and got home just as Bill was washing up in the kitchen after his day's work. Mother Rickenbacker was bending over the range.

"Guess what?" shouted Eddie. "I've got a new job!"

"Again!" replied Bill with heavy sarcasm. "Doing what?"

"In Evans' Garage. Fixing automobiles."

"Phooey!" Bill, with some justification, regarded Eddie as a black sheep that had been transformed into a rolling stone. "Why don't you stick with the railroad and learn a trade? Gosh, will you ever stop gallivanting around?"

"Hush, Billy. Don't talk to Eddie like that!" cut in the mother. Then to Eddie: "Tell me all about it, son. What has happened?"

As well as he could, the boy reconstructed the day's events, starting with the new Ford and ending with his new job. His mother smilingly said that, if he were happy, that was all that mattered.

"Gee whillikins!" shouted Bill. "You mean to say that instead of coming home with seven and a half bucks a week, Eddie, you'll bring in only four-fifty?"

"That does not matter," said the mother. "We'll make out."

"Gosh, I never thought of that!" said Eddie, crestfallen. "All I thought about was a chance to get into the automobile game— everybody says it's a good one."

"Bah!" sneered Billy. "There ain't a baker's dozen cars in all Columbus—and there never will be. Those motor buggies are no good and never will be!"

"That's because you, and people like you," stormed Eddie, "have your minds hitched to a horse and buggy. Pretty soon there won't be any horses left—nothing but automobiles; and when that happens I'll be in on the ground floor!" He was almost in tears. "Yes, sirree, I'll be on the ground floor!"

The ground floor in the automobile game, at the start, consisted of Evans' dinky little garage, which housed one each of the three leading types of cars of the day. These were the battery-driven, the steam-propelled and the gas-engine-powered vehicles.

In Evans' Garage there were a Waverly electric, a Locomobile steam car, and a two-cylinder Oldsmobile. But the cars were mainly there for storage and did not provide much revenue. The real support of Evans' Garage was unromantic but profitable bicycle repair work. In addition, Evans made and charged batteries for electric cars and wagons. In those days the electric car was more popular than the gasoline-driven car. It was fairly reliable, noiseless, and speedy. Its main drawback was the frequency with which the batteries had to be recharged, which gave it hardly any cruising range. The steamer model was also popular, but its many advantages over the hit-and-miss gas engine were offset by the propensity of the steam to "go boom" when something went wrong with the water pressure. Steam cars did not just stop—they exploded.

For the first time in three years of job-holding, Eddie found contentment in what he was doing. He took to the work with great application, started early and quit late. He lived, thought, and talked nothing but automobiles. Fortunately, Evans gave him full scope to satisfy his constructive curiosity and to learn through trial and error. Some of Eddie's lessons were not on his employer's agenda, but definitely sub rosa. For instance, when Evans was out, the boy would climb into one of the cars and teach himself how to handle it by driving it forward and back in the narrow space between the walls of the little garage. He did not ask permission to do this because the answer would have been a most emphatic "No!"

To his brothers and sisters, the neighbors and "the Gang," he bragged about his job, painting vivid word pictures of the world of engines he worked in. By his own representation, there was nothing that he did not know about motor wagons of any kind. As for handling them, well, modesty forbade him to place himself above

Winton, Ford, Vanderbilt, and other leading drivers of the day; but, confidentially, he admitted that he was a "demon driver of mechanical monsters."

One day, Evans was called to Toledo. He caught a noon train and would not be back until evening. His absence gave Eddie a grand opportunity for a little indoor driving practice on the Oldsmobile, which had a two-cylinder engine. If he had known as much about motors as he thought he did, he would have seen to it that the small engine was properly oiled. Instead, he ran the car with a motor that was out of oil. The outcome was that the pistons froze to the cylinder walls. Streaming with sweat, Eddie did all he could to break the pistons loose. No luck. At last, in desperation, he removed the crankcase coverings and stuck a crowbar in behind a connecting rod and pulled. It was kill-or-cure medicine and, luckily, it cured. The frozen pistons broke free. Eddie administered a heavy dose of oil and replaced the crankcase lid, let the oil seep into the scored cylinders and, after a while, started the engine. Jiggers! It ran.

This successful coup was advertised by Eddie far and wide among his cronies. One of them sneered:

"If you're so good at driving gas buggies and electrics, why don't you drive one out here?"

"Betcha can't," added one of the veteran Horseheads.

"Betcha a million that I can!"

All the gang laughed their disbelief. This annoyed Eddie, and he made up his mind that he would show them. He knew that Evans was going to Cleveland on Wednesday and would not return until Thursday morning.

"I wasn't going to tell you," he said in a lordly manner. "But stick around Wednesday afternoon. If it's a nice day I'm going to take Mother for a spin in a Waverly electric before supper."

With mouths agape, the boys digested this announcement. Eddie gave them a lifted-eyebrows look and stalked off. But on Monday he was shaky. On Tuesday he had cold feet. On Wednesday he felt as a condemned man must feel on the day of his execution. He had prayed for rain, so that he would have an excuse to call the drive off; but the sun shone brightly. He ate a heavy breakfast—the con-

demned always do. Down in the shop he did his work until closing
time, and then the hour struck.

His legs wobbled as he got into the electric; his hands shook
as he guided it out of the garage. He locked up the shop, boarded
the Waverly again, rolled over Chestnut Street, and headed toward
home.

The shaky feeling left him as he piloted the silent vehicle
through the thin traffic. Nervousness was replaced by a feeling of
authority and power. Pity the doleful pedestrian, the slowpoke
drivers of horse-drawn vehicles. In due course, he swung into
Livingston Avenue. Kids came running out to meet him. Neighbors
opened their windows or stood on their porches to watch him. It was
a triumphant procession. Laughing, yelling children kept pace with
the Waverly. Neighbors shouted from house to house. Eddie honked
his horn—a wonderfully hoarse and loud contraption—and, as if in
answer to this call, Mother Rickenbacker appeared on her own
porch, came down the steps, and stood at the curb as Eddie drove
up in front of her and stopped the car. She stepped in briskly, and
off he drove on a jaunt that took them all over the neighborhood.
It was almost dark when the trip was over.

No one will ever know, from Eddie or his mother, how much
that ride meant to them. She did not know, for many years, that
she was enjoying a slice of stolen fruit; but she must have known
that this drive was to her boy what his coronation ride must be to a
king. To Eddie, the mother whom he adored, sitting by his side in
a car that he was driving, must have been a symbol of success and
accomplishment.

The neighbors who had pitied Mother Rickenbacker because
her Eddie was a scapegallows, who had whispered that he would
come to no good end, would have something else to talk about
from that day—for was not he the only one in that whole neighborhood, man or boy, who had ever driven an automobile and taken
his mother out for a ride? Yes, indeed, that was a "cream day" in
the lives of the Rickenbackers.

But great days do not always have happy endings. Certainly
this one did not. In parading his mother up street and down avenue,
Eddie used up so much juice that the small battery ran out of power

on the way back to the garage. Luckily, it had rolled out of the Livingston Avenue section before it came to an ignoble stop. At first Eddie did not know what had happened. But it did not take him long to figure it out.

What to do now?

He did not have money to hire a horse to haul the electric back to Chestnut Street, and there were no spare batteries in the garage.

He was in a fix that was a *fix*, and no doubt about it. His job hung in the balance. If Evans ever found out, if the owner of the Waverly ever found out—goodbye, job! Farewell, automobile game! So long, Eddie, demon driver of mechanical monsters!

But Eddie the Strategist came to the rescue. He recalled that all batteries, no matter how far they were run down, would recharge themselves just a little if they were allowed to stand. If he let the car stand for a while, then, the battery might build up enough energy to push the car a block or two. Then, another rest. Another run. Another stop. And so on, until he reached the garage. So it worked out. However, it was a long, long way of working. He had left the house before supper, and it was a hungry, thirsty, and tired boy who opened the garage door at almost four o'clock in the morning and jockeyed the Waverly into its allotted space.

Eddie drew a long breath, but his work was far from over. The dead battery had to be recharged before Evans came in. Hastily connecting it with the charging plug, he switched on the life-giving electric current. Then he locked up and hopped an owl trolley that took him home. He raided the larder, wolfed down some food, washed up, caught the next trolley, and returned to the garage.

Everything was as he had left it. No one had seen him. Now, if only the battery would charge up! He stood near the window and watched for Evans. Just as the boss came up the street, he pulled the charging plug out of the battery. His fate was now in the hands of the gods—and the gods were good. No one knew about the incident until several years later, when he told Evans about it.

In the Chestnut Street garage, Eddie had a chance to learn what makes a gasoline engine go. He learned about gears and timing, carburetors and compression. He also realized that there were many things he did not understand about autos, because he lacked the basic scientific knowledge. This discovery came slowly, and it took much of the cockiness out of him.

For the first time in his life, the boy realized the handicap of ignorance, but instead of being discouraged he decided to overcome it.

Again he sought the advice of his mother and Miss Gifford. It was agreed that it was too late for Eddie, now going on sixteen, to return to school. Anyway, he didn't want to. But he had a "good head for figures," his mother said—wasn't there some way he could study at home and learn about engines? Miss Gifford approved the idea and proposed a mail-order course in automobile engineering. She had heard that there was such a course, but she did not know who offered it.

Falling in line, Eddie wrote to a number of colleges and similar institutions for information. None of them could help him. This was before home study courses were created in great numbers to help increase the brain-power of the land.

He was on the point of giving up when he heard about a mail-order college in Scranton, Pennsylvania, called the International Correspondence School. Again he wrote, hoping against hope that he might find his long-sought automotive course. A letter came. The answer was, "Yes!" The International Correspondence School had what he wanted, and he enrolled immediately for the only printed and prepared home study course in automotive engineering available at that time. It cost some sixty dollars, but students could pay it on time. The length of the course was a year.

Eddie worked on his lessons without let-up. At night, under the kitchen lamp, he studied automotive principles. In the daytime, when he could, he checked his slowly growing book knowledge against his steadily increasing practical knowledge of automobile engines and their ways. Two others who took the same course had names that were to shine brightly in the headlights of motordom—Walter Chrysler and Jesse Vincent.

Eddie's interest in automotive engineering was not confined to automobiles. It ranged aloft to the flimsy airplanes that then were making the first faint trails across the sky. The Wrights were experimenting on Hoffman Prairie, outside Dayton. In France,

Santos-Dumont was making pioneer flights, and all over America balloonists were risking their necks in exhibition flights under feebly inflated gas bags.

Evans did much to increase Eddie's interest in the magic of motors. Like so many others, he had gone into the perilous "automobile game," as it was then called, by way of the bicycle business. On looking back, one must realize that the world of wheels and wings owes much to the pioneers who left the solid security of the bicycle or carriage making to take risks in the automobile business. These daring pioneers were the real fathers of motor-driven transportation on land and in the air, and they include such outstanding motor makers and plane designers as Charles Duryea, R. E. Olds, William Durant, the Wright brothers, Glenn Curtiss, and Glenn Martin. They pitched themselves against popular disfavor and economic skepticism. Early automobile and airplane designers had one major handicap in common: all were stalled by the lack of faith of the big-money men in their ventures.

No one will ever know the sum total of the dreamers who, at the turn of the century, pursued fabulous riches through the belief that they had the plan from which foolproof automobiles could be made. In cities and in hamlets, in factories and in barns, all over the country amateur auto builders were trying to make golden pots for the end of their rainbows out of crude contraptions of metal and wood.

While there were a few well established manufacturers, home automobile making was engaged in by thousands of men who had little if any knowledge of what they were doing. There were, of course, exceptions. Some amateur automobile builders became famous, and among them was Lee Frayer, organizer and mainspring of the Frayer-Miller Automobile Company which occupied a square and unadorned three-story brick building at the corner of Fourth and Chestnut streets, some four blocks from Evans' Garage.

Here was built the Frayer-Miller car, an air-cooled "job" that subsequently sank into oblivion.

Almost from the very day he went to work in Evans' Garage, Eddie Rickenbacker had his eyes on the Frayer-Miller plant. In time, he would work there, and Eddie the Strategist knew how to bide his time. The boy knew exactly what he wanted and where he was going; and, starting with his home studies in automotive engineering, he made his moves with the firm, deliberate precision of a general planning a campaign, the strategy of which was not to be disrupted, nor its tactical procedure speeded up or slowed down. This is a rather formidable way of describing the program of a sixteen-year-old boy. But it fits. For, at sixteen, his plans for the invasion of the automobile industry were complete to the last detail.

Eddie, whose outstanding trait was an almost painful candidness, told his employer what he was after. Evans showed a friendly interest and refused to stand in the way. He told the boy to learn as much about automobiles as he could in the garage and, meanwhile, to keep his eye on the main chance—a job with Frayer-Miller in any capacity, no matter how poorly paid or humble. It was about this time, the fall of 1905, that Eddie began his quest for a home study course. During the early part of 1906, when he felt that his studies had given him a knowledge of engines above the average garage mechanic's, he began going to the Frayer-Miller plant every Sunday morning. To do that, he had to give up Sunday school. He did that reluctantly, for several reasons; one of them was Blanche Calhoun. Sunday after Sunday, he hung around the Frayer-Miller plant all morning, biding his time. He would stick his head into the employment office first thing.

"Anything doing?" he would say.

"Nothing doing!" he would hear.

Then Eddie would amble around the plant, where skeleton crews of machinists, cabinetmakers, painters, and electricians were whittling away at their respective tasks.

To Eddie Rickenbacker, this plant where human hands made almost every single item in a car was a wonder-world. He saw men make axles and steering gears, transmissions and crankshafts, carburetors and wire wheels. He marveled at them and knew that each of these jobs required expert skill which he lacked. This made him unhappy, but also acted as a barb to prod him on.

In the course of these Sunday visits, Eddie learned to know Lee Frayer by sight—a hard-working, hard-bitten man of few words, but long working hours. Frayer showed no signs of noticing the boy, and Eddie, since he had no definite job in mind, did not bother him. He just made his weekly routine check with the employment office:

"Anything doing?"

"Nothing doing!"

Shortly before Easter of 1906, Eddie kicked his heels one Sunday morning in the machine shop on the first floor of the Frayer-Miller plant. His eyes roamed about the room as they had done many times before. They took in lathes, drill presses, steel saws, and other tools, small and large.

Suddenly they took in something else—something that had been there all the time, that would land him a job in the Frayer-Miller plant if anything would.

He jumped up from the bench he had been lolling on and dashed up to the second floor, where he found Frayer putting an ignition system together. Frayer looked up to find the boy staring at him, and frowned.

"Well, what do you want?"

"Oh, I just thought I'd tell you that I'm coming to work here tomorrow morning!" answered Eddie.

"Oh, you are, are you?" Frayer's brows arched. "And who hired you?"

"Nobody yet," retorted Eddie, "but I'll be on the job here in the morning. If I'm worth anything, you can keep me; if not, you can fire me!"

With that, he turned and headed toward the stairs. Frayer scratched his head and muttered: "Well, I never!"

The next morning about six o'clock, Eddie left a note in Evans' Garage, short and to the point:

DEAR MR. EVANS:

      I quit.

          Resignedly yours,

             EDDIE RICKENBACKER

Then he ran up to the Frayer-Miller plant as fast as his feet could carry him. He entered the machine shop and found, after some trouble, the tools he wanted: a broom and a shovel. He now set to work on the job he had seen that needed to be done—ridding the floor of the machine shop of the thick accumulation of dirt and shavings that covered every inch like a carpet and rose in heaps under and around the tools and machines. He fell to work with a will. With broom and shovel, he hacked away at the unsightly litter. An hour later, he had cleaned up half of the machine shop. When Frayer arrived to start the day's work, he was rooted to the spot by what he saw.

Halfway down the shop ran a ridge of dirt and shavings and trimmings. In some spots, it was a foot high. On one side of that ridge was the dirt that had always been there, but on the other side the floor was so neat and clean and spotless that anyone, as the saying goes, "could have eaten off it."

Eddie saw him out of the corner of his eye, but kept on hacking away at the crust of dirt.

"You sure meant it, eh?" Frayer observed at last.

"Yep," replied the boy.

"Know the difference between a gimmick and a gimper?"

"No, sir."

"Well, a gimmick is a large hole made up of little holes. See? And a gimper is the same thing, only more powerful. Keep it up, Rick! You're a good gimper!"

Eddie wondered what a gimper might be good for. He did not know, but he decided that it must be something pretty potent and useful.

Anyway, in this manner, he breached the ramparts of the Frayer-Miller plant. His invasion tactics had succeeded. He was *in*. But the only way to stay *in* was to work, and work came his way in large doses. There were no assembly lines, no body builders, no manufacturers of parts in those days. Virtually every item of the Frayer-Miller car, except the tires, was made and fitted in the three-story plant. That was why production was slow and expensive.

From the very start, Lee Frayer watched Eddie with a sharp eye. Once he realized that the boy wanted a job in his plant as a means to a career and not for just what the weekly pay envelope might hold—once he understood that, Frayer took him in tow and showed his interest by being a hard-driving and exacting taskmaster and teacher.

First he put the boy through a course of sprouts in the machine shop, from grinders to lathes, from shapers to drill presses. It was while Eddie was working on the drill that he invented his first labor-saving device.

His main job on the drill was to make four small holes in the casing for the blower assembly. This was slow, tedious work. Eddie got terribly bored drilling hole after hole all day long. So he rigged up a simple jig by means of which he could make four holes grow in one operation where only one hole grew before.

Frayer saw the device, nodded brusque approval. "What do you call that gadget?"

"That's no gadget," laughed Eddie. "That's a gimper, Mr. Frayer."

It is worthy of more than passing comment that by this time, the summer of 1906, Eddie had undergone considerable expansion. For one thing, his disposition had changed a great deal. Where before he had been grim and aggressive, he was now cheerful and easy-going—not soft, mind you. He no longer had a chip on his shoulder, but he kept some handy in his pockets, just in case. He had learned to laugh and joke, josh and be joshed. The dimples in his cheeks and the crinkles near his eyes had become part of the frequent and infectious Rickenbacker smile—a broad grin that went from ear to ear, full of teeth and warming friendliness.

During lunch one day, Frayer found Eddie so deeply absorbed in a little book that he did not get back on the job on time.

"What you got there?" he demanded.

Eddie handed over the booklet, an I.C.S. lesson on carburetors. Frayer looked through it carefully and wanted to know all about the course, then handed it back without comment; but he transferred the boy the following week to the carburetor department, where he learned how to make a carburetor and what the functions of it were. He went on to the steering-gear department and from that by way of axle, and transmission and clutch, to the motor department, where he learned how to build engines. Frayer kept shifting the boy from place to place until he knew how almost every single item that goes into the building of a car was made and assembled.

"Come down tomorrow morning about nine, Rick," said Frayer one Saturday, just before quitting time.

The next morning Eddie found him in the office and stood before his desk.

"Do you know how to drive a car?" asked Frayer.

"Well, yes! No!" stuttered Eddie. "I can drive, but I haven't driven much."

"Doesn't matter, anyway. You know we've been building a car for the Vanderbilt Cup Race?"

"Yes!"

"And that I plan to drive it in the race next month?"

"Yes!"

"O.K. Eddie, how would you like to go into the Vanderbilt Cup Race as my riding mechanic? Well?"

Eddie was too amazed to speak. He went limp all over and had to sit down. There was no chair, so he sat himself on the floor— *plunk!* Like that. He looked up and saw Lee Frayer glowering at him over the desk.

"Well? Do you want to be my riding mechanic?"

"Mister, it's the cream dish of all I ever want to do!"

The racing car was what was known as a "special job." It consisted of a frame, a four-cylinder engine and other vital parts, four wheels, and two bucket seats. The engine, with pistons big as regalsize grapefruits, was enormous and developed all of eighty horse power. When it ran without a cut-out to muffle its explosions, it roared like an artillery barrage.

The car was finished almost a month before the race and shipped to New York for extensive elimination trials demanded by the Vanderbilt Cup rules. Along with Lee Frayer and a few handpicked mechanics, Eddie went to New York by train. This was the first time he had ever been away from his native town, but all he thought of on the train and in New York was the race. He was blind to the thrills of travel and the wonders of Manhattan.

Garden City on Long Island was the center of activity in connection with the Vanderbilt Cup Race. The stately Garden City

Hotel, standing aloof in its own exclusive park, was the headquarters of the officials as well as the favorite hangout of the millionaire racing enthusiasts whose free-flowing dollars did much toward transferring automobile supremacy from France, Italy, and Germany to the United States. Many factors entered into making America the leading producer and user of automobiles in the world, but chief among them was the money spent by rich men to encourage mechanics with inventive minds to experiment with auto construction or the encouragement given through road and track races to test and develop new automotive ideas. The Vanderbilt Cup Race was one of the earliest and most important spark plugs in firing American inventive genius into automotive production power and in building up public interest and faith in the automobile as a useful and dependable means of transportation. Father of the Vanderbilt Cup Race was George Vanderbilt, one of America's early amateur racing drivers. In February, 1904, Mr. Vanderbilt set a world record by driving a mile in thirty-nine seconds over the Florida sands of Daytona. In the fall of that year, he sponsored the first Vanderbilt Cup Race on Long Island, in order to give American cars and drivers an opportunity to show their speed and skill as against European cars and drivers.

The early cup races were staged on a thirty-mile course blocked out from public highways, and the length of the run was almost three hundred miles. The 1904 race was a huge success from all standpoints but two: first, it was won by George Heath, born in America, but a resident of France; second, the car he drove to victory, at a speed of 52.2 miles per hour, was a French Panhard. The 1905 Vanderbilt was also a rousing show but, alas, this time Victor Hemery, a Frenchman driving a French Darracq, made the American drivers swallow his dust. These two victories by European cars and drivers drew more attention to the 1906 Vanderbilt than any other sports event in the United States up to that time had received. American car makers, knowing that winning the cup would put their product to the fore, planned and slaved to put out an auto with the winning punch. Lee Frayer was one of these. Should he win the cup, his car would be a national success and orders would pour in.

On arriving at Garden City, the Frayer team pitched its tents and set up shop at Krug's Corner, where drivers, mechanics, and managers of all the competing teams were testing and checking their various speed wagons. Here, Eddie saw the great drivers of the roaring roads of two continents. He also met a man who was to become an important figure in his life: Fred Wagner, long, lean, and saturnine starter for a quarter of a century or more of the motor meets sponsored by the American Automobile Association—Fred Wagner, the man with the checkered flag, who in time was to become one of Eddie's closest friends.

On that first meeting, Wagner caught the eye of the obscure little mechanic with his sartorial elegance. He wore polished, knee-high boots, swanky riding breeches of checkered material, and a wide-crowned cap of the same gay design. He faced a group of European drivers and mechanics who smiled and snickered as "Wag," embarrassed and unhappy, recited:

"Un, deux, trois, quatre, cinq—" He paused—stuck. Turning, for a laugh, to the undersized grease monkey who stood off to one side, Wagner shouted: "What comes after five, in French?"

"Six, sept, huit, neuf, dix," rattled Eddie. "In German, it goes eins, zwei, drei—" He was cut off by a roar of laughter. "What do you want to know for?"

"Have to start these foreigners off in French on the count of ten," answered Wagner, smiling broadly. "I'm just rehearsing for the race. Who taught you French and German?"

"My dad and my mother!" replied Eddie proudly.

Getting ready for the race meant hard work and long hours, but the fever of anticipation fired his blood so that it all seemed a gigantic, untiring game. To begin with, this was his first taste of speed, and it was a dish suited to his taste. Every morning at daybreak, he and Frayer would pull out of the camp and roar down the road on mile-a-minute test runs—high speed even in racing those days. The speed Frayer and his fellow Americans had to beat was a potential sixty-one miles an hour, for Louis Wagner was driving the 1905 cup-winning Darracq on these runs. Frayer would push his argonaut up to sixty-five—seventy—miles an hour for long stretches without straining the engine, but there were other things than engines to reckon with, such as brakes and tires. Toward the close of one test run on Jericho Turnpike, the brakes failed on a curve. The car plunged off the road, into a ditch, and came to a stop, upside down on a sand dune. Both Frayer and Eddie were flung free and landed in soft spots without injuries.

"That was a sudden stop, Mister," said Eddie, as he dug himself out of the sand.

"Yeah, Rick," answered Frayer, "but you'll learn in racing that any stop is a good one—if you can walk away from it!"

In grim jest, veteran drivers called the night before the Vanderbilt Race "The Last Night on Earth"; and, for some of them, it was to be just that. Of all the major races in motordom, the number of accidents and deaths in the Vanderbilt was by far the largest. Not only drivers were smashed up or killed, but onlookers as well. The reason for this was that the races attracted anywhere from 150,000 to 200,000 spectators, many of whom had a reckless disregard for their own safety. Since it was impossible to police a line of spectators that stretched some thirty miles along both sides of the speedway, they would lash themselves into wild, harum-scarum mobs. They surged out upon the road as the cars came roaring down upon them, leaving only a narrow lane between walls of humanity for the racers to travel through at breakneck speed. That had been the experience in the past two Vanderbilt Races, and now, on the eve of the third—the "Last Night on Earth"—it looked as if history were about to repeat itself.

In the racing camp, drivers and their riding mechanics tried to rest while worn-out, sweating mechanics kept reaching for perfection with wrenches and screw drivers.

The high voltage of excitement with which he was charged kept Eddie from sleeping much that night. When dawn came, he was up and ready. He was gulping a sketchy breakfast as Frayer came in and sat down beside him.

"Well, Rick!" he exclaimed. "This is the big day!"

Eddie just nodded.

"Don't forget to do your stuff, now! I'm betting on you! Keep the oil pressure up. Keep the gas pressure up."

"Betcha," affirmed Eddie, "I'll keep pumping! Don't you worry,

Mr. Frayer, I know my stuff. I'll watch the rear and let you know when another car is coming up fast enough to pass us—I'll keep watch on the wear and tear on the tires and listen to the beat of the engine."

"Good enough," answered Frayer as he emptied his mug of coffee. "Keep pumping, keep looking, keep listening, and you'll be an A-1 riding gimper. Come on, Rick! Time to get going."

Unfortunately, Eddie's first venture down the roaring road did not take him to the finish line. Shortly after the start, a burned-out bearing sent the car limping to the side of the road. Lee Frayer did not win the coveted Vanderbilt Cup in 1906, nor did any other American driver or car win it. For the sake of the record, let it be noted that the 1906 cup was won by Louis Wagner, who covered the 297 miles at an average speed of about sixty-one miles per hour in his French Darracq.

Eddie did not finish his first race, but even so he gained a lot by this experience. For the first time in his life, he caught a glimpse of the world outside his narrow orbit in Columbus. He also found time to visit with other mechanics, and in this way increased his knowledge about cars. When Frayer and he returned to Columbus both of them had broadened their automotive horizons; and during the spring and summer of 1907 the bond between them grew both wider and stronger.

Chapter VI

On a blustery November day in 1907, about a year after their unsuccessful quest for the Vanderbilt Cup, Lee Frayer called Eddie into his office. Without preliminaries he said: "Rick, I think you've been around here long enough."

"I'm fired?"

"No, but I think you'll want to make a change. How old are you, Rick?"

"Seventeen last month."

"Seventeen, eh? And you already know what makes a car tick from timer to transmission. You can make almost everything that goes into a car."

"You bet I can," replied the boy with conviction.

"In that case, Rick, how would you like to quit here and come along with me over to the Columbus Buggy Company and help design and build a new type of touring car for them?"

The boy looked at Frayer in open-mouthed wonder.

"You're only seventeen, Eddie, but I'm offering you the job of experimental engineer."

"Who! Me?" blurted the lad. "Me, an experimental engineer?"

"That's right. I'm going over as chief engineer to build the new C.B.C. car, with a free hand to do as I want. And you are my number one man. The job pays twenty dollars a week. How about it, Rick? Is it a deal?"

"You bet your boots it is," shouted Eddie. "Boy, oh, boy— twenty smackers a week. Wait until Mother hears this. Twenty dollars I can give her every Saturday." Then, with quick concern: "Say, is this a steady job?"

"I think it is, Rick. Something tells me that the horseless carriage is here to stay."

Eddie was burning with enthusiasm that evening when he brought home the fine news about the new job, the thrilling news about the big money he would be making.

Mother Rickenbacker smiled and patted him on the head. "I knew it, Eddie, I knew it all along. God will take care of us." She smiled and shook a warning finger. "But don't ever forget that God is most likely to help those who help themselves. You have worked hard, and you have studied hard, and you have given God an opportunity to help you. And you have made friends, Eddie. Remember what I told you some years ago, that we arouse in others the attitude we have toward ourselves. Always remember that!"

The Columbus Buggy Company was a firm of long standing. It occupied a sprawling plant on the west side of town. Its slogan, "Standard the World Over," was known wherever horses were hitched to buggies and wagons. The head of the firm was Charles E. Firestone, a keen businessman with a wide streak of imagination and daring in his make-up. Toward the turn of the century, when he saw the threat of self-propelled vehicles to the wagon and buggy trade, he decided to join the changes in transportation trends rather than to fight them.

He began with the building of electric cars and established a thriving business. Then, in 1906, the company began making its famous High Wheel Buggy. This vehicle was nothing more than a buggy with a small, asthmatic, two-lung engine under the seat, but it sold. The high wheels had solid tires. It was driven with a steering bar and its speed was about fifteen miles an hour under the most favorable downhill conditions. But Firestone, seeing gas buggies yield to automobiles, wanted to get aboard the bandwagon.

He decided to build and market a five-passenger touring car. Knowing Frayer as a clever engineer, he induced him to leave Frayer-Miller and join him in making the C.B.C. car.

"Write your own ticket," Firestone told him, "and don't bother me again until you've got a real automobile to show me."

It was natural that Frayer should select seventeen-year-old Eddie Rickenbacker for the job of experimental engineer, despite his youth. He knew him as a skillful worker, with endless energy and constant initiative, who had the same sensitive touch with tools and

machinery that a violin virtuoso has with his instrument. The boy
had completed his home-study course in automotive engineering.
In some respects, he knew more about combustion engines than even
Frayer did. Hence, he was put in charge of the C.B.C. experimental
shop from the very start. His specific job was to assemble the parts
of the new car as they were made, and test them out.

But making by hand, and one by one, the hundreds of parts
that form a five-passenger touring car is a slow and exacting job.
So, while the design of the new car was going forward, Eddie decided to study the Columbus high-wheeler. He soon learned that
it had one outstanding foible—stopping because of the weakness of
small locks that held springs on the intake valves in place. Ever
anticipating that one of these valve-spring locks would pop out,
Eddie always carried an extra supply in his pocket. His preparedness against this source of trouble was to be of great help to him.

One day an extraordinarily deep rut on the Storage Dam Road
brought Eddie into the ken of Charles Firestone, who was exactly
the sort of man one would expect to find the president of the big,
solid Columbus Buggy Company to be. He was big and solid
throughout—a big, solid stomach, and big, solid jowls, but a small
warbling voice. Being a progressive man, Firestone had discarded
the team and buggy that for many years had taken him back and
forth between his handsome home on Broad Street and the plant—a
ten-mile journey that crossed the Scioto River by way of the Storage
Dam Road. Now, early in 1908, Firestone used a spick-and-span
high-wheeler, the single-cylindered asthmatic engine of which grew
a little breathless under his almost pachydermal weight.

One morning Frayer rushed into the experimental shop and
shouted to Eddie: "The Old Man is stuck up at the Storage Dam.
Go out and fix him up!"

The boy started a handy high-wheeler, jumped in and headed
for the dam, where he found a big solid scowl on the big solid face
of big solid Mr. Firestone. The Old Man looked with a sour eye on
the pale and scrawny youngster who had come to help him.

"What do you think you're going to do?"

"I understand you're in trouble, Mr. Firestone, and I was sent
out here to fix you up."

"Heaven help me," moaned C. F. "I am in trouble; I am a busy person, wasting time sitting here. I ask for a man to get me going, and they send me a sprig from the bloom of youth."

"Well, maybe I can help you," said the sprig cheerfully. He swung the crank and turned the engine over. Aha! No compression. With wrench and screw driver, Eddie quickly reached the spring of the intake valve. Sure enough! The locks had jarred out. From his pocket, he fished two little V-shaped pieces of metal which he slipped into place. He put back the parts he had removed, placed spark and throttle where they should be, turned the crank, and, *pop*, went the engine.

"There you are, Mr. Firestone," shouted Eddie. "I think that'll take you in."

Mr. Firestone smiled a small, sheepish grin and drove on.

Later that afternoon, Frayer came into Eddie's shop. "Say, Rick, the Old Man told me about this morning. He wanted to know your name and all about you—he thinks you're the Seventh Wonder of the World."

"Don't tell him too much about me and change his mind. I may need him some day."

Although Eddie had ended his I.C.S. course, he still spent a great deal of time with the books, making up new sets of lessons. In addition, he began a systematic course of reading, but in strictly limited fields. He read, with avid interest, all he could get on modern inventions and patents. When he tired of this he would turn to biographies of great Americans. His "cream dish" among these was the lives of men who had started poor and obscure and ended rich and famous. Oddly enough, Horatio Alger had no fascination for him at any time. He cared only for the real-life success story; it gave him the feeling of support and inspiration he needed. Let the truth be known: even when he was going on eighteen and other boys of his age went "sparking" on Wednesday night, Eddie's life was all work and no play.

To begin with, every dollar Eddie made had a definite place to go: His younger sister and brothers must complete school and get a better start in life than he had had. Also, with the extension of gas and electric utilities and the city water system, his mother must benefit from them. All these and other improvements to the house cost money and left Eddie's string short at both ends, in spite of the fact that he was earning good pay.

Another reason for staying at home was that it took a lot of scrubbing to get ready to call on a girl. While work in the experimental shop may have been creative, it was also very productive of grit and grime.

Thus, Eddie's social activities were very limited. These were mainly parties held in the basement of Pastor Pfister's church. Blanche Calhoun was very active in them, and her friendship with Eddie had continued over the years. When he ventured forth to the Vanderbilt Cup races she gave him a rabbit's foot mounted on a small silver stem. He came to place great faith in this charm and was never without it. In fact, his co-workers at the Columbus plant used to chide him mercilessly.

One of Eddie's greatest tormentors was Harry Dienst, a daredevil test pilot on the high-wheeler. Harry took particular pains to chide him about the folly of charms and tried to make him throw the rabbit's foot away; but the boy, with his characteristic grim stubbornness, held onto it.

While he had no money or time to spend on girls or fancy clothes, Eddie saved enough out of his slim allowance to make one of his boyhood dreams come true: a small machine shop of his own. He bought lumber from a house that was being torn down and built a shop some twelve feet long and ten feet wide. He made tool cabinets and a workbench. His plan was to make an automobile out of defective parts that he could either buy cheaply or get for nothing at the C.B.C. plant. He started on a small single-cylinder car; but it was never completed, for this reason: Soon after he began making the car, a long-time mystery was made plain to him by a lightning flash of inspiration. One night he went to bed obscure and poor; before he closed his eyes, hours later, he was famous and rich. Eddie had found what others had failed to discover, the elusive key to perpetual motion.

Lying in the dark, the former leader of the Horseheads figured out, step by step, a machine that would keep in self-sustained motion until long after the last echo of Gabriel's horn had died out. He

pictured every detail of the apparatus. But how could he build it
without arousing suspicion? How to test it without someone stealing
it? The mere thought of losing this great invention gave Eddie grave
concern.

He could not make all the wheels and gears and rods and struts
himself. So, in order that no one might know what he was doing, he
had various shops make different parts. When, after weeks of anxious
waiting, he collected all the pieces, he locked himself in his tiny shop
and sat in the dark until midnight. He wanted to be sure that none
of his friends would make a late call.

When all the houses in the neighborhood were dark, when distant chimes struck twelve, Eddie lit a kerosene lantern and hung it
on a hook near the blacked-out window. From their hiding places—
boxes, cabinets, drawers, chests, and pockets—the young inventor
brought out the parts of his world-shaking machine. Briefly, it consisted of a series of springs, weights, and counterweights. As he
worked at it, Eddie was struck by another flash of mental lightning:
the machine would never work. He did not even bother to put it
together; in fact, he did not even bother to tear down the part he
had completed. Being an intense realist who never cried over spilt
milk, Eddie just put out the light and went to bed, as obscure and
poor as he had been before the vision of perpetual motion came to
him in the night.

There was one perpetual motion machine in which big and solid
Mr. Firestone was deeply interested, and that was the C.B.C. high-
wheeler. Unfortunately, the venerable vehicle—with the nerve-
racking stubbornness of inanimate things—would stop all semblance
of motion on inauspicious occasions.

For instance: In 1908, when the Million Dollar Pier was a new
attraction at Atlantic City, one of the early automobile shows was
held on the pier. The C.B.C. sent an exhibit of electric cars and high-
wheeled gas buggies to the show. One of the routines of the agents
was to take their cars on exhibition drives and demonstration runs—
just to show the wonders their mechanical monsters could perform.

The trouble was that nearly all the highways in and around
Atlantic City were ribbons of deep, soft, yielding sand, and the

narrow wheels of the old-time cars would sink into it; the harder the driver tried to get out, the deeper the wheels spun into the sand, for the reason that the 1908 type of clutch did not have the grip required to pull the car out.

Since potential car owners would not buy unless they had two or three or more demonstration rides, and since the cars made such a poor showing on the sandy roads, agents and salesmen saw their sales go a-glimmering.

Among car makers who received frantic calls of distress was Mr. Firestone. What to do? Ah, he decided, there was but one thing to do, send that Eddie Rickenbacker to Atlantic City to soothe the agent and fix his wagon.

Eddie went. Soon after his arrival, he braved the sandy road to motor doom with a brand-new high-wheeler. He left the pavement, hit the sand, stuck. He tried both forward speeds. The car still stuck. He went into reverse. No motion. He killed his engine and put on his thinking cap. The clutch just did not have what it took to battle sandy roads. After considerable pushing and hauling, Rick got the car onto the pavement and took it back to the shop. For two days and as many nights, the young experimental engineer battled his problem. Finally, on the third day, Eddie the Strategist pulled his rabbit's foot out of his pocket and put it to his lips. He had a plan to stop the slipping clutch. Like all great plans, it was very simple. The clutch band would not hold because it could not get a grip on the metal surface of the clutch. But brakes took hold because the rough, heavy brake bands gave them gripping power.

"Why not, then," reasoned Eddie, "put brake bands into the clutch and set their grip to work?"

It was worth trying, and after a day or two of patient work a new clutch lined with brake bands was installed. On the morning the job was finished, Eddie and the exhibitor took the car out and tested it. It ran like a scared rabbit through sand ruts and sand heaps that had defied all other cars. Eddie had won!

Later that day, there was a public demonstration before hundreds of spectators, several reporters, and the photographer of an Atlantic City newspaper. Eddie put the high-wheeler through its paces and won wide acclaim. The photographer took his picture and put it in the paper. The next day, the name and face of Eddie Rickenbacker appeared in a newspaper for the first time. It showed a very self-conscious young man who scowled at the camera to hide his embarrassment. Inside, of course, he was proud as punch. The "cream" of his trip was not knocking the bug out of the clutch, but that he could come home and show his mother that her son had his picture in the paper.

Eddie got more out of this mission than mere satisfaction. Old Man Firestone not only praised him loudly but raised his wages; and above this recognition of his worth Eddie had the heart-warming satisfaction of seeing his clutch improvement become a standard part of all the C.B.C. high-wheelers. It ended the flow of clutch complaints.

Eddie's days with the high-wheelers were almost over, for the experimental model of the C.B.C. touring car was nearing completion.

Lee Frayer and Eddie ran most of the tests on the new automobile on the track in the old Columbus Driving Park or on the highway between Columbus and near-by Newark, including the belt-line run around Buckeye Lake. On one of these occasions, two cars were being tested. Harry Dienst, who did not believe in lucky charms, drove one, and behind him, Eddie drove another.

As he drove along the lake at a fairly rapid clip, Dienst blew a tire. His car swerved off the road and crashed into the lake. The car's momentum took it several feet from shore and it sank, with Dienst held behind the steering-wheel in ten feet of water. Eddie pulled his car to a screaming stop, hauled off his coat, threw off his shoes, went in after Dienst, and almost drowned pulling him out more dead than alive.

"Now what do you think of my rabbit's foot?" asked Eddie, when Dienst came to.

"It's the berries," gulped Dienst. "Don't ever let it go!"

The many tests showed the C.B.C. car satisfactory beyond expectation. Being a brilliant but careful designer, Frayer had turned out an automobile that had all the comfort and reliability that could be packed into the machine of that period. One of its great selling points was that it was cooled by a thermo-siphon cooling system, which sent water through the engine without the need of a pump.

Frayer decided to exhibit the new car at the Chicago Automobile Show in January, 1909. Instead of shipping it by rail, he believed that the publicity the car would get if it ran all the way from Columbus to Chicago, a matter of a little more than three hundred miles, would be helpful. So Frayer and Eddie drove to Chicago.

It took them three days to reach the Windy City because the roads were highways in name only. Even then, an average of one hundred miles a day was considered almost sensational. When Frayer and Rick arrived in Chicago, with the record-making run of Columbus to Chicago behind them, they were celebrities and, therefore, news.

An important part of Eddie's job during the Chicago show was to demonstrate the car to potential buyers. One day he was driving down Michigan Avenue at a fair rate of speed after ending a demonstration run. A policeman ran out into the street a few yards in front of him, held up a hand, and ordered him to stop.

"You're under arrest for speeding!"

Eddie tried to explain that he was barely moving.

"Come along, stranger, and tell it to the judge," ordered the minion of the law. With that, he hoisted himself into the seat next to Rick and said, "Turn to the right when I tell you!"

After a few blocks Eddie obeyed orders and turned into a dinky alley.

"Stop here. Now you know what this would cost you if I took you in—twenty-five bucks."

"Yes, officer," observed Eddie meekly.

"Tell you what," the Law continued. "You give me a five-spot and I'll let you go."

Taking the easiest way out, Rick dug into his pocket, fished out some crumpled bills, and gave five to the officer. Eddie hated to lose that five dollars—it was a lot of money. But how could he get it back? Then Eddie the Strategist went to work. He knew that it was illegal for policemen to take money. That was the target to aim at.

"Now, take me back to Michigan and Twelfth Street and let me off," ordered the cop.

Eddie complied. He drove very slowly and made many stops, all the time keeping his eyes glued on the policeman's badge which also bore his number. Under this constant scrutiny, the man began to squirm. When he got out of the car, Eddie said casually, "Well, Officer Number Blank, Blank, Blank, I'll be seeing you!"

"No," answered the cop, "I guess not. Here, you're a pretty good sort of a kid. Take your money and get going."

Whereupon, he handed Eddie the five dollars and the score was even.

Eddie always maintains that this Chicago officer should not be judged too harshly. For many years, before the A.A.A. won its fight for state rather than local motor-law enforcement, fine-splitting constables and justices of the peace preyed on motorists. With a financial stake in dealing out convictions, these fee-hungry local enforcement officials had little or no regard for the rights of the motorist. They cracked down for the purpose of lining their own pockets rather than for safety and law enforcement.

During the period of the Chicago Automobile Show, Eddie made numerous demonstration runs up and down Michigan Avenue and when Officer Number Blank, Blank, Blank was patrolling his beat, Rick would honk his horn in greeting, while the policeman would wave a beefy hand in return. On the last day of the show, Eddie gave the officer a box of fifty genuine six-for-a-quarter Havana cigars. He could well afford to. Between them, he and Frayer had sold eleven cars.

Chapter VII

~~~~~~

After its highly successful debut at the Chicago show, the new C.B.C. car went into production. Carloads were shipped to dealers all over the country. Three of the autos were sent to Dallas, Texas, and that is where trouble began.

It seems that the thermo-siphon cooling of the engine worked wonders in climates adjacent to the arctic fringe, but that in warmer zones the water in the car boiled away almost as fast as frantic drivers could pour it in.

At first the complaints were mild as the spring weather that caused them; but with unseasonably warm weather in June came a telegram from Dallas that lifted big solid Mr. Firestone straight out of his office chair and sent him rushing into the plant in search of Lee Frayer.

"Listen to this telegram from Fife and Miller in Dallas," he piped. " 'Unless you send expert immediately to stop radiators from boiling out after cars have run only ten miles, all further orders are hereby canceled.' "

"That's a fine mess, Lee!" complained Firestone. "What are we going to do? Send an expert! Bah! We haven't any expert."

"Nope, Mr. Firestone," answered Frayer. "None of us knows enough about that car as yet to cure that trouble."

"But we must do something! We can't lose that contract. Fife and Miller are among our oldest and best buggy agents. We've gotta do—" Suddenly a light broke through the clouds of despair on Mr. Firestone's brow. "I got it! We'll send that Eddie of yours. You pack him off to Dallas, and I'll wire Fife and Miller that our expert is on his way."

As Firestone thundered off, Frayer laughed until his sides ached.

"Eddie, the Texas two-gun trouble shooter," he chortled to himself. "Gangway, Texas, here comes Eddie Rickenbacker!" With that, he went in search of his protégé.

A few hours later, Rick was on a train bound for Texas, on a journey that was to change the entire course of his life.

No one knows what he would have grown into—what kind of man, what kind of life—if he had not been sent on this particular mission to Texas. The ticket in his pocket read "Dallas"; but his destination was far beyond that thriving city. To reach it, he was forever (though he did not know it then) crowbarred out of his Columbus home to become a rolling stone that gathered plenty of greenback moss as it gained speed.

Those June days of 1909 were hot, even for Dallas. When Eddie got off the train, the heat that surrounded him rose like a solid wall. He got into a hack and was driven to the Southern Hotel, then the leading hostelry. After washing up he went to Fife and Miller, and introduced himself to the two partners.

Fife looked at Miller. Miller looked at Fife. Then both glared at Eddie and swore—swore long, fulsome, cowman oaths that would frizzle the ears off an onery longhorn.

They stopped, glared again at the pale, gangling youth, and finally Fife drawled:

"Don't take this too personal, young feller. It ain't your fault that you're too young even to be branded, but those blasted Yankees up in Columbus have a blankety-blank-blank nerve to send a green shoot like you down here to fix cars."

"You said it, pard," broke in Miller. "We've been swindled. We'll go to law, that's what we'll do."

More two-fisted cussing.

Eddie stood in quiet admiration as he drank in the Niagara of expletives. Even as a drop of water never repeats its plunge over the brink of the falls, so the words that poured from the oral caverns of Fife and Miller for a solid half-hour never had a double-take.

Suddenly, as men will, they stopped the torrent of cussing, slapped Rick on the shoulder, and told him that, so long as he was there, they would give him a chance. He would have one week, and no more. Rick accepted the challenge.

The next morning he took one of the cars out and headed toward Fort Worth, some thirty miles to the west. It was piping-hot, and as the sun rose higher the heat battalions launched their attack in waves. The touring car did not have a top, and soon the leather upholstery was hot enough to fry an egg. One-third of the way to Fort Worth, the engine steamed up and pounded in bitter complaint for lack of cooling water. Then it stopped. He let it cool off as he sat in the scorching sun. He knew that if he poured cold water into the red-hot engine the water jackets would crack. So he sweated. And waited. And swore. Having a good memory, he repeated some of the more pungent phrases spewed forth by Fife and Miller.

After a wait, Eddie poured water into the radiator, started the engine and headed for Fort Worth, twenty miles away. Things went well for another ten miles or so, when, again, the water boiled out, the engine stopped, and he resumed cussing.

The same thing happened on the way back. It happened every day. Like Lewis Carroll's famous characters in "The Hunting of the Snark," he tried every trick he knew, and many he did not know, to stop the car from boiling over. But nothing worked. A dozen miles was the limit. Eddie ran out of ideas—and out of words.

One of the strange things that happened to him on this trip was that he actually got acquainted with a girl. She worked in the office of Fife and Miller. Perhaps she felt rather sorry for the trouble-laden trouble shooter, young and far from home. At any rate, she invited him to her house one night to meet her folks and have a bite to eat. His lone and unsuccessful fight against the red-hot devil that had taken possession of the car had left him rather low, and he was glad to accept some human companionship. Besides, the girl was nice and friendly.

Rick had promised to be at her house at six o'clock. As usual, he was out that afternoon trying to learn why the engine could not be cooled. He had had more stops than usual and had used up all the water he had brought along in cans. There were no service stations along the roads in Texas then, which were barely more than cow trails. There were no ranch homes, no houses of any kind along this road, and when the car stopped once more he was in a bad spot. It was after five o'clock and, unless he got going, he would be late for his supper date.

Eddie took a chance. Although the engine was as dry and hot as a bake oven, he started it and crept toward Dallas at the slowest possible speed, the engine banging and pounding like a boom-time boiler factory. At last, he came to a gentle decline in the road, slipped the clutch and coasted down to the bottom of the slope where, lo and behold, there was a pool of muddy, dirty water, a ·drinking hole for cattle.

He filled one of his buckets with the brown and smelly stuff and lugged it up to the car.

Now he would have to wait for the darn thing to cool. That engine was hot enough to press his pants on.

But if he waited he would be late!

Still, if he did not wait, but poured the water into the red-hot engine, the water jackets would be sure to crack!

Eddie debated briefly and reached a firm decision. He would not wait. The car was no good anyway.

Off came the radiator cap, down went the water, up rose a geyser of live steam. Inside the long-suffering engine, demons banged and clanged, cracked and whacked so that the motor rang like the tintinnabulating anvils of Abaddon on Beelzebub's birthday.

After an eternity, the geyser shot itself out. The torment within the engine subsided. The countryside resumed its normal quiet, while Rick waited—waited to hear those fatal ripping, tearing cracks that meant ruined water jackets. But the silence was unbroken. He started the motor. It ran. He drove the car the twenty miles into Dallas without a stop. The water did not boil out.

That evening, Eddie was an absent-minded guest, sometimes failing to answer questions, and missing much of what was said. His mind was with that car in the garage, wondering what made that auto run without boiling over. Perhaps it was just the cool of the evening? Perhaps it was just a grim mechanical jest.

The next morning, Eddie loaded the car with cans of water and headed for the country. He drove, hour after hour, and nothing happened. The engine did not boil out. The motor ran smoothly mile after mile. The day was just as hot as the days that had gone before, but there was no boiling. He could not understand it at all. First, he thought that there must be something in the water, some chemical, that caused it. In fact, he drove back to that same water hole, collected a bottle of the water, and took it to a chemist in Dallas. His analysis, a day later, showed it was nothing but muddy rain water.

Well, as Eddie kept on thinking, he came to the conclusion that, by accident, he had caught the metal while it was expanded and, by pouring the cold water on the red-hot metal, had frozen the parts while they were mated and thereby kept the clearances. The answer was, he now knew, that back at the factory they had been fitting the engines too tightly. By freezing the metal, he had fixed the clearances, and that was all there was to it.

Having found the key to the mystery, Eddie the Strategist decided to keep it in his own pocket until he was sure it was the right one, and could decide what to do with it. That afternoon, he turned the first car over to Fife and Miller with the brief comment, "It'll run now!"

Then he took the second car out, put it through the same treatment of heat, cold water, and steam—and it ran. The third car was also cured of its low boiling point in the same manner.

Naturally, Fife and Miller were filled with curiosity. Eddie just sat tight, saying that the cars would run—and they did.

On the strength of this success, the agents bought four carloads of C.B.C. autos. They came three in a car, but with the understanding that Eddie would remain to give them his mysterious but effective treatment.

Back at the factory, both Firestone and Frayer were agog with curiosity. What had Eddie done? To letters and telegrams, he replied that they would have to wait until he returned to the plant. Firestone and Frayer were not the kind to look a gift horse in the crankcase, so they waited; but Frayer sent the boy a wire that warmed his rather lonely young heart. It repeated a phrase that had given Eddie the green go-ahead light in the old Frayer-Miller plant in 1905.

"Keep it up, Rick," the telegram said. "You're a good gimper!"

The situation was just about under control in Dallas when Rick received a wire from Frayer ordering him to proceed to

EDDIE RICKENBACKER IN FIRESTONE-COLUMBUS CAR IN TEXAS AS A ROVING SALESMAN IN NEW TERRITORY FOR THE COLUMBUS BUGGY COMPANY. NOTE THE STRAW SKIMMER ON HIS HEAD. IMMEDIATELY BEHIND HIM IS WILLIAM JENNINGS BRYAN, WHO WAS DRIVEN UP THE MAIN STREET OF A TOWN WHEN HE WAS TO GIVE A LECTURE.

EDDIE RICKENBACKER AT THE WHEEL OF HIS ONCE-FAMOUS FIRESTONE-COLUMBUS RACING CAR.

Tucson, Arizona, and see Dr. Fletcher, who had a brand-new
C.B.C. touring car that boiled like a steam laundry. That would
be a quick and easy job: he had the magic key in his pocket. But
this time the formula did not work. He poured cold water on the
piping-hot engine time and again, but the car kept boiling.

One day Eddie went up in the mountains on a camping trip with
Dr. Fletcher. It was the first time he had been on such an expedi-
tion, and while he was impressed with the beauty of the desert scene,
he was also intrigued by the quick way the water boiled off in the
pot when they were making coffee. Suddenly, he recalled what he
had read about the effect of altitude on boiling water—that the
higher up you are when water boils, the quicker it vaporizes. In the
twinkling of an eye, the thought came to him: "That is why the
cooler boils dry! Dallas is close to sea level, but Tucson, in a valley,
is more than half a mile up."

Well, maybe that was the reason for the cooling trouble? But it
did not provide him with a solution. However, it gave Eddie the
Strategist a starting point. If he could increase the circulation of
the water in the water jackets and radiator with a pump and thus
take the circulation load off the thermo-siphon system, the boiling
problem might be solved.

After vainly nosing around in various stores, he finally stumbled
on what he wanted in a back-alley repair shop: a secondhand Fair-
banks-Morse engine with a small double-geared water pump. Eddie
bought the pump. After several days of experimenting with the
pump, chains, fan belt, and crankshaft, he finally created a force
system for the circulation of water. And it worked. The water
stayed on its cooling job instead of steaming into space as vapor.

While in Arizona, Eddie sent in a full report on what he had
done to make the cooling systems function, both in Texas and in
Arizona. He got a letter full of glowing praise and orders to go to
Abilene, Texas, where John Hall, a long-time Columbus Buggy
Company agent, had gone into the automobile business and now
was having cooling headaches. He had just received his first three
cars, and Mr. Firestone wanted Old Man Hall to get a good start.
By now, he regarded Eddie as a first-rate starter.

The folks of Abilene were less automobile-minded than the

people of Dallas—at any rate, would-be buyers did not crowd up
for demonstrations. Eddie felt that it was up to him to start the
ball rolling for Hall, and went into executive session with his board
of strategy. The idea for his course of action came from a billboard.
It announced that William Jennings Bryan was coming to town to
lecture. It would be big-time stuff, Eddie decided, to get Mr. Bryan
to use a C.B.C. auto, with him at the wheel, as his official car. He
recalled the helpful publicity the Atlantic City agent had got out
of his conquest of the Jersey sands. Taking Bryan around in a
C.B.C. was bound to get into the papers.

Hall gave reluctant consent to the plan, for he was not a great
admirer of Mr. Bryan. When the famous orator arrived Eddie went
to his hotel, introduced himself, and offered the use of his car, which
Mr. Bryan accepted with pleasure. The outcome was that where
Mr. Bryan went in Abilene, Eddie drove him. And did Rick and
the C.B.C. get into the newspapers? He could not have avoided the
front page had he tried. There was Bryan sitting big as life in the
rear seat of the C.B.C., and right in front of him sat the driver.
Remember him? Dutchie, the scapegallows leader of the Horsehead
Gang, driving a near-President of the United States. If Mother
could only see him now!

Eddie had found vast satisfaction in beating the bugs out of the
new C.B.C. car, but in recent months a new idea had come to him:
there would be more profit, more fun, and more prestige in selling
cars. In the months since June, he had tasted the spice of trading
and he found the flavor to his liking. On top of that, he liked people,
and liked the great Southwest. He found meeting people easy,
chiefly because people liked him, found him real, a shrewd trader,
yet warm and kindly like themselves.

The change Eddie had undergone, physically, mentally, and
temperamentally, since he left home was truly amazing. The out-
door life had made him grow. He now reached a height of six
feet two inches and filled out in proportion, becoming a broad-
shouldered, slim-waisted man who radiated cheer, energy, and health.
His boyhood habit of writing all the rules with clenched fists vanished completely. The reason for this might be that he was in such
perfect mental and physical balance that, like the Man Who Car-

ries a Big Stick, he felt he could afford to walk slowly and speak softly.

Another factor that contributed to Eddie's inner serenity was that, with the help of his earnings, his mother had paid all the debts that had hung over her home since the death of William Ricken-backer. The little house was free and clear. All other debts were discharged. This happy news came to him while he was in Abilene, and made him feel solid and worth while all the way through. He was now making about a hundred dollars a month and expenses, and he sent most of his wages home to Columbus.

After completing his mission with John Hall, Eddie was assigned to Mr. McClaren, who was district sales representative of C.B.C. for Texas, Louisiana, New Mexico, and Arizona.

McClaren was going on seventy—tall, thin, and with a hacking cough. He had sold Columbus buggies for many, many years, and he still looked with greater favor on horses and mules as transportation providers than on automobiles. He compromised by using an early-vintage high-wheeler, but always had a whip socket on the dashboard with a whip in it, just in case it should be needed.

At that, he was not far off the track. All too often, the jeer "Why don't you get a horse?" really meant that the friend in need was a horse indeed. Like everybody else, Rick was hauled home by horses time and again; often, too, when stuck in deep ooze up to the hubs, it took horse or mule power to get the car unstuck.

The rural good Samaritans who came to the rescue of automobilists usually "soaked the city slickers" who needed their teams. There were times when help could not be had for love nor money because of the intense hostility of many horse owners toward machines that often sent their horses into tantrums of fright. Some owners, in fact, were more afraid of cars than their horses were. In the pioneering days the rules demanded that an automobile driver, when a horse approached, should pull to the side of the road, stop, kill his engine, wait until the horse had passed, get out, crank up, and drive on.

Being a salesman out to make friends, Eddie always obeyed this rule to the letter.

Among his experiences was one with a farmer who point-blank

refused to unhitch his horses from his wagon to pull Eddie out of hub-deep mire.

"It's agin my religion," he· explained.

"Why?"

"Because the Good Book says that 'a righteous man regardeth the life of his beast.' "

"Then why don't you buy a car and save your horses?"

"Eh!" ejaculated the man. "Spend my hard-earned savings on one of those contraptions!"

Eddie had not attended Sunday school for nothing. "Well," he answered, "remember what Solomon said: 'We can't tell who will be after us, wise men or fools.' "

It would be wonderful if the record showed that he made a convert and a sale. But the man drove off and left him in the mud until some one of greater heart came along.

From time to time, Eddie got many suggestions for improvements on the C.B.C., some of which he passed along to Lee Frayer at the plant in Columbus. The one complaint he heard most frequently came from ranchmen and farmers. "Why," they would ask, "do we have to drive from the wrong side of the seat? We sit on the left side on a wagon to drive a horse, but on the right to drive an automobile. Why?"

He did not know the answer, and asked Frayer to give him some sort of argument. To his surprise, Frayer wrote that the farmers were perfectly right, and that he was happy to learn they felt the way they did. American cars, he said, had right-hand drives because they were copied after European cars. Frayer added: "I am thinking about a left-hand drive on the next C.B.C. model. But keep this under your hat. I haven't told the Old Man as yet. I know he'll raise the roof, but I believe it will make driving easier and safer."

"Also a good sales point," observed Eddie the Strategist to himself, as he tore the letter into shreds.

Eddie's sales talk did not follow a regular pattern. People then did not know or care about mechanical niceties on automobiles. After an often dubious, "Can it run?" their questions usually concerned the car's speed, its power to climb hills, and its riding comfort, questions the car answered best itself through demonstration rides.

Of course, there were tricks in the trade. For instance, if Eddie was giving a prospect a hill-climbing demonstration and the engine began to buck, he would kick out the clutch, slide in the brakes, and show with great pride how well the brakes held on a steep hill. Then he would quietly shift into low gear and end the climb before going back into high.

Eddie was a good salesman because he not only knew cars, but had been experimental engineer in the designing and building of this particular make. He radiated the confidence he felt in it, and, as they used to say, he could do everything with a C.B.C. except make it "beller like a longhorn steer."

Just before Christmas, 1909, while he was in Dallas, Eddie was ordered back to Columbus. He had been wishing that he could get home, and even worked his rabbit's foot overtime in the hope his wish might come true. When the order arrived, he went Christmas shopping. Among the trinkets he bought in a Dallas pawnshop was a gift for Blanche. The gift was a slim little gold ring with a pin-point diamond which, if you held it right, would sparkle like *anything*.

That first evening in Columbus, he spent at home with his mother and brothers and sisters around the big table in the warm and cozy kitchen as in the old days—not *the good old days*, for things were much better now than they had been that night only seven years back when a little boy made the solemn promise: "Mother, I'll never make you cry again."

He had kept that promise. "God will take care of us," his mother had predicted. And He surely had done so.

The second evening, Eddie went over to the Calhouns' and presented Blanche with the ring. He did not slip it on her finger, he did not kiss her—he just handed her the ring and thought no more of it; but a few days later the fellows at the plant started to congratulate him.

"On what?" he wanted to know.

Why, on his engagement to Blanche Calhoun!

"Engagement?"

"The ring!"

Why, that ring was not an engagement token—just a gift! Marriage was as far from his mind as Dr. Cook was from the North Pole. It was a terrible shock to Eddie.

"But when you give a girl a diamond ring," people said, "you're engaged."

"Not me!" affirmed Eddie.

When he called on Blanche again, he was so wooden and self-conscious that it was a very dull evening. His conversation was dull. She was plainly bored. He went home early. His calls after that were shorter and shorter, and might have stopped altogether even if he had not been sent out of town again.

A day or two after Christmas, word came that Mr. McClaren had died. Frayer told Eddie to go see the Old Man about getting a chance to fill the vacancy.

"You're too young," said Firestone. "How old are you, anyway?"

"I was nineteen in October!"

"Holy Moses!" shrilled Firestone to the walls of his office, as he thumped his desk. "He's only nineteen, and he wants to be a district agent! He's crazy!"

Eddie realized that he had to sell himself, and went to it with all the persuasive power at his command. What did Mr. Firestone want—a Civil War veteran? Sure he was young. But that had not stopped him from fixing slipping clutches in Atlantic City.

Had it?

No-o-o!

Nor had it prevented him from fixing Mr. Firestone's own car in a jiffy.

Had it?

No-o-o!

Or stopped him from putting an end to cooling troubles in Texas and Arizona.

Had it?

No-o!

Or prevented him from selling autos by the carload and getting good publicity for C.B.C.

Had it?

No!

"Well, then," argued Eddie, "why don't I get the job?"

"You do," answered Mr. Firestone with firmness. "Get out of here before you talk me out of my own. Get back to Texas and sell some cars."

When Eddie gushed the great news, Frayer smiled and whanged his protégé on the back. "So you're now a district agent, eh! Well, since you had that pleasant surprise for me, I'll give you one. We're bringing out a new car in the spring, Eddie, with left-hand drive. The car will have one of the new American-British engines, a small, high-speed four-cylinder with a lot of power for its size and weight. Come on, I'll show you the model!"

"Oh, boy!" sang Eddie. "That car ought to sell like hot cakes! A left-hand drive!!"

So anxious was he to get on the job that he left for Dallas before the holidays ended. He had barely established himself in Texas when a telegram instructed him to get to Omaha as soon as he could—the C.B.C. agents there were having sales troubles. They had heard about Rick the trouble shooter and wanted him at once.

"When can you leave Dallas?" was the closing sentence of Firestone's telegram.

"I have left," wired Eddie from the station as he caught the train.

Chapter VIII

Eddie reached Omaha in January, 1910, to do a brief job of trouble shooting, but he remained almost three years. In that time he was transformed from a somewhat methodical expert on auto engines into an energetic sales executive and suddenly blossomed forth as a leading contender for the speed crowns of the wheat region of Nebraska and the corn belt of Iowa. While this transformation was rapid, it resulted from a swiftly conceived plan.

It was early on a bitter cold morning that Eddie reported at the Omaha office of the Racine-Satterly Company over the railroad viaduct.

The only person on hand was a young man who introduced himself as Charles F. Dunkle. Yes, he worked for Racine, but not in the automobile end, thank Heaven! He sold good, substantial farm machinery.

Over a cup of coffee in the railroad lunchroom, Eddie learned from Charley that the Racine people had been having a peck and a half of trouble with C.B.C. cars throughout their territory.

The main grief, Eddie soon discovered, was that most of the salesmen and agents who handled the car knew little or nothing about it, and were ill fitted to advise their customers. The results were overheating, underlubrication, and other abuses which not even a cannon caisson could have survived. He instituted an educational campaign among dealers and owners which soon left everybody happy.

He was about to return to Dallas when, out of a blue sky, he was offered the job of branch manager at $150 per month with a staff of six district salesmen covering Nebraska, Iowa, and the Dakotas. This was in March, 1910, on the very day when the newspapers announced that Barney Oldfield had broken the automobile speed record by making a mile in 27:33 seconds at Daytona Beach.

94

"That's the cream of speed," said Eddie when he discussed this feat with Charley Dunkle at lunch.

"No one will ever beat it!" asserted Charley.

"Oh, I don't know. Give me the right kind of car, and perhaps I will."

"Wouldn't surprise me, at that. You've grown into quite a speed merchant lately."

"Well, what do you expect?" laughed Eddie. "That's what people want to buy—speed. That's what they spend their greenbacks on—fast cars. Give them gooseflesh at a mile-a-minute clip and, Charley, you sell cars. You hit sixty, and they think you're chain lightning."

Cars sold on their speed performance, and to sell them you had to have a heavy foot on the throttle and a firm hand on the wheel. Beyond that, you had to be a tireless entertainer. When Mr. Corn or Mr. Wheat came to town to buy a car, he demanded not only all-day speed demonstrations but all-night parties—a rip-snorting time with all the trimmings and, in the end, maybe you would make a sale; or, again, maybe you would not. At any rate, Eddie worked like a dog at it and sold carload upon carload of C.B.C. autos, with a heavy foot, a steady hand, and a gay heart.

His closest competitors were George Rheim, the Cadillac dealer, and "Swede" Frederickson, who sold the Chalmers. These long-time friends and business rivals tried to skin Eddie alive in automobile deals and gave him warm companionship between deals. The favorite talk of the hard-fighting trio was how they had failed or succeeded in nailing their mutual hides on the proverbial barn door in auto sales.

That spring came the new four-passenger C.B.C. with the first left-hand drive ever produced on an American-made car. It was a sensation—and a center of controversy. But it sold. How it sold!

There was something about the quick get-away of the car and the smooth energy of the small high-speed, thirty-horsepower engine that reminded Eddie of his Vanderbilt Cup dreams. The C.B.C. seemed to have some of the qualities of the small cup-winning European cars he had admired at Krug's Corner on Long Island. The racing bug was planting its egg in him, to hatch later.

The fashion of the time was to stage speed events with stock cars to promote sales. So it was natural that Eddie should take one of the new C.B.C.'s, strip it down to little more than a framework and an engine on wheels. Then he rebuilt some of the weaker points of the car and redesigned others, put a bucket seat on the chassis, and gave the car a coat of white paint. He selected that above a brash color because a white car *had* to be kept clean. He also had white linen overalls made for himself. And for the same reason—neatness.

Just about this time it was announced that Aksarben Week in October, which is to Omaha what Mardi Gras is to New Orleans, would feature two days of auto racing that fall. The races would take place on the oval mile-long track on the fringe of Omaha. But the speed bug, now making test runs in Eddie's bloodstream, was not to be curbed so long—not when there were races to be run on half-mile tracks all over his territory. By fall, he had an almost unbroken string of victories, collected a lot of insignificant prizes and sold a lot of cars. Selling cars—that was the big pay-off.

Toward the end of July, he received a long night letter from Frayer in Columbus. "How would you like to swap dust with Barney Oldfield?" it began.

Eddie caught his breath and held it as he read the rest of the telegram. Its substance was: Would he come to Columbus and race with Frayer against Oldfield in a hundred-mile event on the Columbus Driving Park track in August?

Shades of soda pop and push mobiles, frogs' legs and bike races! Would he? Eddie Rickenbacker home on the old track but on the big time. Racing against King Barney himself! Would he? His answer was: Yes!

Arriving in Columbus, he handed over his racing car for a thorough factory overhaul while Frayer gave him all the details. During his absence, Frayer had built his Red Wing, a special racing job with a fifty-horsepower engine as against the thirty developed by Rick's.

The famous Barney was driving his speed-making Knox, a giant that had a hundred horsepower under its mammoth hood.

"This is how we'll have it in the bag, Rick!" explained Frayer.

"You have the lighter car, so you can make the most speed on the inside fence without skidding or slowing down. The Knox and my Red Wing are both heavier and have to take wider turns."

"Sure," replied Eddie, "I get that. But while I can beat Barney on the curves he can run rings around me on the straightaway."

"All right, let him," answered Frayer, "you push as hard as you can. That will make Oldfield start pressing. My guess is that his tires won't be able to stand the gaff like yours will."

"And he'll burn up time changing tires, eh?"

Frayer grinned. "Yeah, that's the system. We'll call it the Rickenbacker Razzmatazz!"

"But what'll you be doing while I break Barney into little pieces?"

"I'll just keep an even pace that'll save my tires and engine and leave me with a haymaker speed punch at the finish in case you break up in giving Barney the works. See?"

When the day of the race came, with the largest crowd that had. ever lined the track, the strategy was all worked out. But what actually happened was that on the thirtieth or fortieth mile of the race Oldfield blew a tire. He was about a lap and a half ahead, but by the time he had changed the tire Eddie had caught up with him. Oldfield roared out on the track and drove like the devil. In doing that, he blew another tire.

Around the ninetieth mile Rick was leading when Oldfield, about to overtake Frayer, blew a third tire. At the same instant Eddie broke a connecting rod, which put him out entirely; but by the time Oldfield got the tire changed, Frayer was too far ahead to be caught. Frayer's and Eddie's teamwork had won the race for them.

Frayer watched his protégé with deep interest during the days of testing and in the race and found in him the right mixture for automobile racing. He did not flinch from speed, but made the car give all it had every inch of the way, which was what this particular race demanded. But, at the same time, he was not rash. He was daring, but cautious too. His ability to think rapidly was innate.

"He showed himself as a clean, square racing man," Barney Oldfield was quoted as saying afterward. "There was no dirty work.

He took his share of track and no more. The sole of his right shoe is heavy as lead, and it keeps the accelerator pressed into the floor-board."

The wear-them-out, break-them-down, blow-them-up "razzma-tazz" technique developed in that race by Frayer and Rickenbacker soon became a successful formula for teams of professional racing drivers.

When Rick returned to Omaha in September he was no mere automobile salesman with a side reputation as a speed merchant. He was a full-blown racing celebrity, and people stood with checks in hand hoping to buy his cars. He was definitely "in," but he still carried his rabbit's foot and wore the same size hat. Although he was a happy-go-lucky young fellow, he already had the fixed habit in the race of life of driving to win. And so it was in the Aksarben races. There were five races on the first day of the meet. Rick won them all. There were five races on the second day. He won the first four. It was easy, like shooting iron deer on Bill Jeffers' lawn. Among those who fought like bear cats to beat him were Frederick-son and Rheim. Neither succeeded.

Just before the fifth and last race, the two dealers asked Rick to stay out so that there would be a chance for one of the two to beat the other without outside competition.

"We don't care about the prize money," said one.

"No—win, lose, or draw, you can have the money, Rick. Just give us a break!"

Rick laughed. "Sure, I'll stay out," he answered. "And I don't want anything but the fun of seeing you two sweat it out."

Being a fresh-air fiend, Eddie had formed the year-round habit of leaving the window open mornings in his office over the railroad tracks. One day early in 1911, he was at the window talking with Charley Dunkle when an engine puffed a cloud of smoke and steam past it.

"Ouch!" yelled Eddie.

"What's the matter?" asked Charley.

"Got a red-hot cinder in my eye." Eddie danced up and down with agony.

"Stand still, and I'll try to get it out for you."

But it was not as easy as that. An eye surgeon had to dig the cinder out—a delicate operation that left a permanent defect. From that time on, a black spot obscured a small sector of his vision; but, with some experience, Eddie learned to make allowances.

This impairment might have put an end to the racing activities of some men; not to those of Eddie Rickenbacker. The spot that danced before his eye did not interfere with his inner vision as he looked down the roaring road and glimpsed the gate to fame. The fact that the Grim Reaper also stood there with the blue flag of warning and the checkered flag that marks the final lap after the Last Night on Earth did not deter him one whit. Eddie would just as soon stop living as he would stop racing.

Throughout that winter, Eddie was in correspondence with Lee Frayer who, elated by the victory over Barney Oldfield, had set his sights for bigger game. This was the first 500-mile automobile race ever staged—the 1911 Memorial Day spectacle on the Indianapolis Motor Speedway, the great American automobile classic that was to become the Mecca of global motordom.

Book Three

Racing

RICK OF THE ROARING ROAD
1909–1917

Chapter IX

~~~~~~

The Time: Memorial Day, 1911, about an hour after sunrise.

The Place: The grounds of the Motor Speedway outside Indianapolis.

The road to the race track is jammed with traffic as far as the eye can see—automobiles, wagons, and carryalls, buggies, bikes, and pedestrians—human lava flowing toward the main entrance of the Speedway, where tens of thousands of men and women already wait for the gates to swing open.

They look at watches.

"5:57," say the timepieces. "5:58—5:59—6:00!"

On the dot of the hour, a bomb bursts inside the grounds: the signal to open the gates for the spectators, more than 75,000 from all parts of the country, from all walks of life, drawn by the contest in daring. Today the greatest drivers in America will tilt against one another for gold and glory. Some of these racing men are millionaires to whom gold means nothing, but who love Queen Speed for her own sake. Others are professional drivers who, caring little for the glory, are perfectly willing to risk their necks for gold. And the stakes today are Twenty-five Grand.

Famous among the drivers of the twoscore cars entered are clever Ralph De Palma, dashing Roy Harroun, reckless David Bruce-Brown, smiling Ralph Mulford, wild Bob Burman, lead-foot Arthur Greiner, jovial Louis Disbrow, chance-taking Harry Knight, and silent Joe Jaegersberger—just to mention a few whose names in those days figured in bold and screaming headline type. All men with lead in their shoes and a flippant regard toward fate.

Eddie and Frayer had reached Indianapolis several days before the race and set up shop in Gasoline Alley. They took the Red Wing

down, part for part, and assembled it again. Like other drivers and
mechanics, they tinkered eternally with their speed wagon. Nothing
was left to chance. No detail was too small for close attention, no
labor too tedious to be done over and over. To them the Red Wing
was a real, living personality. They spoke to it with tender gratitude
or exasperated emphasis, as occasion demanded.

On the morning of the race, last-minute tinkering until the hour
for the cars to be pushed into starting formation before the crowded
grandstand. The blare of bands is drowned out as thirty snarling
engines are tuned to start their blood-stirring symphony. Ragged
lengths of flame burst from the stacks of stubby exhaust pipes, and
the fumes in blue and lazy clouds spread over the scene and drive
off the fragrance of the May morning.

Ten o'clock? Almost ten o'clock! Four solid hours since the
crowds began pouring through the gates. Now it is time for the race
to start. Thirty drivers in thirty cars open wide the throttles, throttles
that release thundering thousands of horsepower. Slowly, almost
sedately, the cavalcade rolls after Carl Fisher's pace-making car on
the first lap around the track, a two-and-a-half-mile oval paved with
bricks. Once around—and the race leaps into high as the drivers set
themselves for the heavy grind of two hundred times around the
track, six to seven hours of endless strain for man and machine, if
they last.

Eddie knew that, however well he and Frayer drove, they would
never have a chance at the big stakes. The best they could hope was
to finish somewhere in the money. Their plan was to keep the car
at a speed that would save engine and tires and time in the supply
pit.

Eddie, as relief driver, was at the wheel in the early part of the
race. He was rolling along with plenty of daylight between the foot
throttle and the floorboard when the huge Amplex, driven by Art
Greiner, passed him on the back turn of the thirtieth mile. Throwing
up a cloud of brick dust and exhaust gas scented with pungent
burning-hot castor oil, Greiner swept past the Red Wing while
Dickson, his mechanic, was pumping up the gas pressure as one
beset.

Keeping his gaze fixed straight ahead, Eddie suddenly noticed that the big spot that always sailed before his eye had grown larger. Not only that, it was sweeping wildly across the track just ahead. In a flash, he realized that the spot was not the defect in his sight but the body of a man hurtling head over heels across the track. A split second later he swerved past a wildly gyrating Amplex. Both driver and mechanic had been flung out of the car, and the rim and tire of one of the front wheels were gone.

This was the first serious accident Eddie had ever seen on the roaring road. In that cloud of red brick dust and blue gas smoke, Death had come with his checkered flag. Dickson was killed instantly; Greiner got by with a broken arm.

In that cyclonic moment, Eddie reached deep down inside himself and found the stuff it takes to see men die without stopping to help, and without letting the urgent whispers of Fear compel his foot to ease up on the accelerator and slow down the pace.

This wreck was Eddie's baptism to Disaster, aside from the small preview he had had of it when his car somersaulted into the ditch on the Jericho Turnpike in 1906. Wrenching his wheel with all his strength, he swung his heavy car around the Amplex with tires that screamed in protest.

About a hundred laps later, he narrowly missed a head on collision with disaster again when Harry Knight's big gray Westcott swung off the track in front of him. There was a sickening smash as Knight's car crashed into Burt Lytle's Apperson, which was refueling at its pit opposite the grandstand.

Next, Rick's heart stood still.

Straight ahead the blood-red Case, driven by Joe Jaegersberger, with Gil Anderson as mechanic, stood dead on the track. Badly hurt, Gil was crawling from it, right in the path of Eddie's Red Wing. For the third time, he swung away from doom. Inside he was soft and jelly-wobbly. His hands held steady on the wheel, but his feet were so heavy that the car spurted forward as he fed it more gas than he intended.

From the grandstand came the ugliest animal sound in all nature: the frenzied screaming, yelling, howling of men and women who in their lust for thrills and blood had torn their garments of human dignity to shreds.

Gooseflesh rose on Eddie's skin as the ear-piercing babel came to him over the snare-drum beat of his engine. For a brief moment he felt that, if this were the pay-off for victory, it would be too putrid to collect. But a second later, as his spinning wheels carried him past the grandstand into a realm of hurtling cars, roaring engines, red dust, and blue smoke scented with burnt castor oil, he grinned with deep satisfaction and set himself for the sweeping curve into the back stretch.

In the grandstand, spectators settled down for the next buckets of blood.

"Peanuts, soda pop, ceegars," shrilled the strident voices of the candy butchers. "Get your program for the big race."

In this, the first of Eddie's many entries in the spectacular five-hundred-mile Indianapolis event, Red Wing finished in eleventh position. Being among the first twelve cars to complete the long and grueling run was not bad. But as Eddie, black with grime and whittled down by fatigue, slumped in the pit, he made up his mind that next year—or the year after—*some* year—his name would head the list of winners.

That first of the five-hundred-mile grinds was won by Ray Harroun in a Marmon; close on his heels, in second place, came Ralph Mulford, in a Lozier. Third man was hard-driving but luckless David Bruce-Brown in a Fiat.

After the Memorial Day race, Eddie went back to Omaha with a fever for racing. His thirst for speed and danger—and still more speed and danger—was so strong that he spent less time at his desk than ever and almost became a professional racer then and there. He took part in dirt-track and road races in various parts of Nebraska, Iowa, and South Dakota.

In one of these, at Red Oak, Iowa, he had his first real racing accident. His chief opponent was Walter Smith, Chalmers agent at Red Oak, who drove a Chalmers Blue Bird with lots of power and speed. In order to beat Smith, he had to push his C.B.C. for all it could deliver, and on one lap it went into the flat turn of the dirt track too fast. The rear wheel was torn off, the car nosed into the rough and turned over. Through some miracle, he was completely unhurt. He paid no attention to the incident until the next morning, when the newspapers carried a story about his smash-up. On seeing this, he sent his mother the first of many telegrams like this:

Wreck not what it is cracked up to be. Don't believe what you read in the papers. Love and kisses.   EDDIE.

When Aksarben Week arrived, Eddie drove again. Once more he garnered his full share of the prizes. At these races he met a quiet, studious young engineer from Waterloo, Iowa, named Fred Duesenberg who, like Frayer, was interested in designing racing cars because he believed that the reliability of the passenger or commercial automobile could be developed only through the car-breaking grind of the race track. Rick had long ago concluded that one two-hundred-fifty-mile race took more out of a car than twenty-five thousand miles of normal operation. That winter and spring, whenever his trips took him near Des Moines, he made it a point to visit Duesenberg who was chief engineer for the Mason Automobile Company.

Among the events that claimed Rick's attention in the fall of 1911 were the almost daily progress reports carried by the newspapers of the airplane flight by Calbraith Rogers across the United States from New York to Los Angeles. This first coast-to-coast aerial hop really became an endless series of minor leaps. The flight began in New York on September 17 and ended in Los Angeles forty-nine days later. This was during the period when stunting exhibition fliers flew, like moths, into the flame of destruction, and the airplane was getting a bad reputation.

Rick frequently discussed Rogers' flight with Charley Dunkle, who could not see much future for flying machines.

"What good are they?" he would argue. "It took Rogers forty-nine days to fly to the coast!"

"Sure, but he made it, didn't he?"

"And what does it prove?"

"Not much, maybe," Rick agreed. "We had to learn how to build cars before they got to be any good. And now we have to learn to build roads for them to run on. Perhaps flying has to grow the same way."

"Yeah, maybe."

"Anyway, I don't know and I don't care, Charley. A buzz-buggy under the seat of my pants is worth ten planes in the bush to me!" Rick concluded with a laugh.

Winter ran its slow and chilly course. With the coming of spring in 1912, young Rickenbacker's thoughts turned to Queen Speed and the Memorial Day race at Indianapolis. Again he drove the Red Wing, with greater determination to win than in the 1911 race. But his luck did not hold. At the ninety-five-mile mark, he was running fourth and crowding Joe Dawson, who won that year. But after passing the hundred-mile turn Red Wing's center crankshaft bearing burned out, and Rick had to watch the rest of the race, low with disappointment. Still, he reaffirmed his pledge of the previous year, that he would come back and that, some day, he would win. Perhaps it was just as well that Eddie could not look into the future and learn that to him the Indianapolis race would always be Heartbreak Hill on whose winning peak his wheels would never leave their imprint.

Eddie returned to Omaha bored with his selling job. The racing bug had hatched in him with epidemic results. Why waste time kowtowing to prospects whose foolish questions almost drove him into discourtesy, would-be clients who demanded dinners and suppers and late shindigs as part of the business of buying a car? He was fed up! He was disgusted. He was through—done with selling. Racing was his meat from now on.

He selected the racing end of the automobile business in 1912 for three major reasons. The first and second of these were material and in plain sight: Racing was profitable. And he loved competition and lapped up speed. To drive a fast car and make money doing it—hey, that was cream!

The third reason for his going into racing was deep beneath the surface—so deep, indeed, that he was barely conscious of it. It was the ambition some day to build the Great American Car. The race track was a school that gave both technical and practical training; and the classrooms of motordom were the brick, board, and cement speedways, the dirt tracks of gumbo and gravel, and the rutty highways of dust, rocks, and mud that challenged the endurance of racing cars and drivers all over the country.

Pulling the trigger of action the moment the time came to shoot, Eddie quit his job with the Columbus Buggy Company to make racing his business. He made this change with characteristic thoroughness. Knowing the nerve-racking grind of racing and its drain upon the physical resources of drivers, he decided that his best investment in himself would be complete nervous and physical stability. He would adopt the abstemious habits of prize fighters in training: no smoking, no drinking; early to bed and early up; lots of exercise and no fancy foods. He enrolled in the severe school of self-discipline, and never played hookey until after he reached France as a soldier in 1917.

In quitting the C.B.C. Rick gave up his beloved racing car and joined a flying squadron of second-rate professional drivers that staged speed contests in Nebraska and Iowa. It was decidedly a small-time start, but he reasoned that nothing was lost by hopping on a coach in the middle of the train instead of waiting for the lounge car at the end. One might miss the train that way, he figured. As things turned out, he caught the wrong train, for the squadron was not approved by the Contest Board of the American Automobile Association, the judge and jury of authorized auto racing. He learned about the unsanctioned status of the squadron just too late and had quit it when the Contest Board caught up with him and, despite his pleading of innocence, fined him $1,000 and ruled him off the tracks of A.A.A. meets for one solid year. This was in December, 1912. That year, he did not believe in Santa Claus.

Rick's speed wagon had been fixed by the A.A.A. and there was no appeal. He had quit his job as C.B.C. branch sales manager, and he was too proud to go back; but he could not race for a whole year. What to do? He mulled the situation over for several days, then packed his belongings, paid up the rent for his furnished room, and went to the railroad station.

"Give me a ticket to Des Moines, Bill!" he said.

"Hi, Eddie!" grinned the ticket agent. "Round trip?"

"Nope! I'm going one way."

This time Eddie caught the right train.

In Des Moines he went straight to Fred Duesenberg, who had taken on the job of building three special racing Masons under the sponsorship of William Sears, the Dodge agent in that territory. Sears' interest in motors was on the speedy side. He wanted to claim a stake in the five-hundred-miler at Indianapolis; and, to that end, he financed the building of the three Mason specials in a small shop behind his salesroom.

At Duesenberg's suggestion, Eddie went to Sears and told him his story: how he had started in the automobile business in Columbus; how he had served as trouble shooter and salesman; how he had driven in speedway and dirt-track races; and how he had been ruled off the track by the A.A.A. And he got a job as mechanic at three dollars per day. Quite a comedown from $150 per month or more, but Eddie the Strategist felt that the temporary reduction might well turn into a long-range gain.

Despite wearing hours and ceaseless toil, which included nights and Sundays, the cars were barely ready in time for the 1913 Indianapolis race. Duesenberg was a genius who never compromised with perfection: everything had to be made by hand; everything had to fit and mesh like the parts of a fine watch. You might say he made four-wheeled watches that ran against time. The struggle for perfection took more time than Sears had anticipated. Come havoc and high water, he wanted his cars in the race. Duesenberg advised against it—a brand-new type of car, he pleaded, was bound to have bugs in it; but Sears insisted. The outcome was that the cars were pushed into a freight car to be painted and polished as the train puffed slowly eastward.

The Mason cars reached Indianapolis a few days before the race; but trial runs showed them to be so full of "bugs" that they might well have won first prize as entomological exhibits. As racing cars, they were not in the money.

After the race, while Duesenberg and his men disinfected the Masons with their tool kits, Sears tackled the job of lifting the A.A.A. ban on Eddie. His lever was the argument that Eddie should have a chance to drive in the Independence Day race in his own home town, Columbus. N. J. Ruggles, head of the Columbus Automobile Club, and a member of the A.A.A. Contest Board, took up the fight. Reinstatement came only a week before the race, a two-hundred-miler on the old Columbus Driving Track. Eddie was pleased in more ways than one; but his chief pleasure was that his teammate in the race would be Ralph Mulford, one of the giants of speed. Mulford, a devout Baptist, sang in church choirs in a fine tenor voice and never raced on Sundays; but he was a fearless driver and stepped on the gas. They called him "Smiling Ralph" because of his affable and cheerful ways. His driving technique was flawless. Eddie, who up to now had had little but a heavy foot and a will to win, learned many fine points from Mulford, a coolly scientific Doctor of Speed.

The technique of the team was about the same as that employed by Eddie and Frayer against Oldfield. Eddie was the lead man, the speed bait which the competitors had to try to swallow. From the moment the race started, he would set a killing pace designed to wreck and ruin drivers who fell into his trap. His pay was not much, only $50 a week and a percentage of the winnings. Still, although his was a "suicide mission," he often survived long enough to speed into the prize money.

Before the 1913 racing season ended, he had landed from first to fourth in more than a dozen meets. The money he won, he sent home. But money was not all his mother received from him. That telegram, "Don't believe what you read in the papers," came to Mother Rickenbacker time and again.

In a race at Galveston a tire blew out while Rick was driving at ninety miles an hour. Instead of leaving the rim, it became a club and struck paralyzing blows on his left arm and shoulder. The arm was becoming numb when Eddie O'Donnell, his riding mechanic, stuck his arm out and took the blows until Rick could stop the car. Both had serious arm and shoulder lacerations, and O'Donnell had a dislocated shoulder.

From St. Paul, Rick sent another "Don't you believe it, Mother!" telegram. In a five-mile race he lost control of his machine in trying to pass Louis Disbrow on the far turn. It made a triple somersault as it shot into the air, and landed upside down after crashing through a fence; but Rick's personal Providence tumbled him out of his seat as the car began to turn, and he landed on the track, badly shaken but unhurt. Scrambling to his feet, he cleared the track of ragged pieces of fence knocked loose by his car, nail-studded boards that menaced his fellow contestants. He then limped around the track to the Mason pit in front of the grandstand. When he got there, the crowd rose and cheered. And it was a good, heart-warming sound.

Again, from San Antonio, Rick sent his mother a "Believe it not" wire. This time, he had installed a neck-saving gadget on his car. It all began when he felt that he was being ruled out of the track record time trials. He claimed that he had beaten Disbrow to a standstill. He asked for a chance to prove it again—and got it.

It had rained the night before. Rick got the pole position, which was wet and soggy. He cut in on the curves to save time and distance, so far that he hooked his right front wheel in a groove. Getting out of it too fast, he headed toward the outside, swung back, and finally hooked his wheels in the mud, went end over end three times, and landed upside down. But, since St. Paul, he had anticipated such a spill like that. To guard against injury, he had made a special cowling of the steel rim of a buggy wheel. Because of its shape, it made a very strong buffer. When he saw that he was going to turn over, he ducked under it. The car rolled over three times, but the gadget held up and he came out with no more injury than a dislocated shoulder. It was the only time he had any injury that was at all noticeable in his entire racing career. But from that day on everybody in the racing business had a steel hoop like his under the cowl, and it saved a lot of drivers from harm. If the cowl had not been on his car that day, chances are he would have been killed or seriously injured.

Ralph de Palma's comment in a hotel lobby after the race sums up the place Rick held in the hearts and minds of the men with whom he competed:

"Eddie never knows when he is beaten. He is the most daring and withal the most cautious driver in America today, and before many meets he will strike a gait that will send some of us veterans back to reciting our deeds of the past."

Louis Disbrow was in the circle, and he paid the young driver the same high compliment: "The nerviest and the most unerring of them all."

Eddie Rickenbacker's indifference to danger made him a favorite with the public. He was the same sort of favorite as the heavy, hard-hitting slugger in the prize ring. There was only one rule in his book:

"Give her gas, and keep going."

At Cincinnati that summer Eddie coasted up to the pit with an engine so hot for want of oil that it would not start again. Several mechanics took turns at starting it, but their cranking was fruitless.

At last Alex Sloan, the meet manager, shouted: "It's no use, Eddie. The motor won't start. You are out of the race."

"That's what you think," yelled Eddie. He jumped out of the car, swung the crank—with the heavy and obstinate engine at the end of it—as if it had been a 1905 Ford. *Bang!* The engine barked, and once again he was off. He came in a strong fifth.

By September, he had rolled up a record of victories of which even a veteran might have been fairly proud. De Palma was right when he called Eddie an up-and-coming youngster who made speed, money, and friends. An article in the Sioux City *Tribune* on September 2, 1913, described him as "one of the popular young men in the speed world who should be at the top in another year or two —a good talker, although he differs from other drivers in preferring not to talk about himself."

Eddie was building up a good name everywhere he went, and thereby hangs a story. J. Alex Sloan, who admitted being the "Greatest Little Manager on Earth," believed his name was too long.

Time and again Sloan showed Eddie press clippings with his name misspelled all the way from Richenbacher to Rackenbocker.

"Your name will kill you, Eddie," the manager would howl. "Nobody with a handle as long as that can get anywhere in this business."

"It's good enough for me," Eddie insisted.

"You can't make it stick in people's minds," ventured the dirt-track psychologist. "Call yourself Rick or Back. Any kind of a two-cylinder name. Take my tip, boy, and get rid of your straight-eight moniker and whittle it down to newspaper size. It's too long to get in print."

"The trouble," answered Eddie, "is that it is not long enough!"

"Long enough! What do you mean?"

"Well, instead of being just Edward Rickenbacker, there should be a middle name!"

From that time on, Eddie spent much of his spare time writing the letters E and R with a space in between them. And, in the space, he would insert, one by one, the various letters of the alphabet to see which gave the best flow from E to R. After much experimenting, he decided on V.

Now he had a middle initial, but it did not represent any definite name. In cities he went to, he would study telephone books and city directories for names that began with V. At long last, he selected the name Vernon. It was a good enough name, as names go, but Victor would have fitted him better.

Toward the close of the 1913 season, he had gained considerable racing maturity, not only through self-analysis and experience, but also through contacts with the colorful and frequently spectacular men who made up the roaring-road fraternity.

In a profession where everyone is rated for what he is as a man, Eddie was held in high regard by all levels—from grease monkeys to speed kings. The veterans liked the tall, lithe young man with the happy disposition and ready laugh who did not have much to say. He was a good fellow, but he was all business. Before and after races, he was forever tinkering with his car and was always coated with dirt and grease. He seldom mixed with the crowds; he never sought conversation but, on the other hand, he always had a cheerful answer whenever anyone spoke to him—and the infectious Rickenbacker grin usually went with it.

Rick wore well when he lost. But, what was even more important, he wore even better when he won. He never whined or crowed. The fact that he neither smoked nor drank, and kept early hours, worked in his favor with the old-timers, too, for the barnstorming circus type of fire-eating, ditch-jumping, house-wrecking daredevil had not yet arrived in auto racing. To be sure, the drivers pushed their cars without mercy, but the contest was in speed and human and mechanical endurance alone. They pushed their speed wagons until these fell apart, or the tires exploded, or the engines dropped out.

It was a fast and furious competitive game then as it is today—a keen, clean hard-hitting sport that has never been tainted. No one has made any accusations against it in all of its history. The hazards, then as now, were so great that a "fixed game" was not worth the candle; and everyone realized that that was so. The men had a keen respect for one another. They would fight on the track for position, naturally, but not in a dirty way; again, because of the hazard. It was just as dangerous for the driver who tried to take an unfair advantage as it was for the racer who might be the victim of it.

One trouble with automobile racing some three decades ago was that the teams had to have backers or angels with well lined pockets. There were two kinds of teams: those financed by rich individuals, and those supported by the firms that built the various racing cars. While the Mason team had made a fine showing in 1913 and burnt up plenty of tracks, the drivers had also scorched plenty of engine parts and tires. The result was a change in management which brought the rebuilt Mason cars out under the Duesenberg name early in 1914 with Eddie as manager of the team. Part of his job was to run the three sleek, long-snouted Duesenbergs on a frayed financial shoestring.

Chapter X

Eddie drove his last race in a Mason car in the American Grand Prize race at Santa Monica in February, 1914. Bad luck still hovered over him. He rolled out of the race at one hundred six miles with engine trouble. A few days later, he left for Des Moines, where Duesenberg had set up shop under his own name.

The Duesenberg team line-up in 1914 consisted of three cars, two of one hundred horsepower and one of ninety. The first two were driven by Ralph Mulford and Rick; the third, by Tom Alley. Again Eddie went to work as a factory mechanic, but this time without any wages: Fred Duesenberg had no financial angel to underwrite his pay roll—so, he had no pay roll.

This year the cars would be ready for the five-hundred-mile race; and the bugs that had fluttered forth the previous year would be wholly absent.

One morning early in May, when Eddie came to work, he found a small black kitten imprisoned on top of the hub of the right rear wheel of his car. She had crawled through the close network of wire spokes but could not get out again. She cried piteously.

Eddie had now developed an elaborate system of superstitions. He not only swore by the feet of rabbits but had a veritable museum of good-luck charms in his pockets, ranging from balloon-bellied Billikens to birthstones and elephants. To him the black kitten spelled good fortune. He called her Lady Luck. He fed her, made a box for her to sleep on; but she preferred the driver's bucket seat in the car. She went with him on all his test runs, and soon they were inseparable companions.

One of the new features of the Duesenberg Eddie drove in the 1914 Indianapolis five-hundred-miler was a small rather deep box just behind the driver's seat. And in it, as the race got under way, sat Lady Luck, purring as loudly as a feline racing engine, her whiskers flat against her small pointed face, for she loved speed and the taste and feel of cold high-speed air.

If Lady Luck had been a little larger and therefore more power-ful, she might have brought Eddie more luck than she did. As it was, he completed the race but way back in tenth position.

After the race, Eddie made ready for the next event, the Fourth of July race at Sioux City, Iowa. Then he went to Columbus, taking Lady Luck along. Of course, Mother Rickenbacker made both her son and the kitten welcome. She was interested when Eddie told her about Lady Luck. She was concerned when her son un-folded his hard-luck story of endless breakdowns that had kept him from reaching the really important prize money. On top of that, Eddie told her he had spent most of his savings in financing Duesen-berg and was almost down to his last dollar.

"Hang it, Mother! We've got to win the Sioux City race. We've got to snag that $10,000 purse for first place. If we do, we're on Easy Street! If we don't, we're sunk! At this moment all the cash of the whole team is these seven silver dollars."

A few hours before Eddie was to leave for Sioux City, Mother Rickenbacker came down from the attic.

"I just happened to remember," she said with an uneasy smile, "that among the things I took along when your father and I left Switzerland was this book of old Swiss legends."

She handed her son a small, dog-eared, paper-bound book. It was printed in French, a language he knew a little of during his childhood but had forgotten with the years.

"What about it, Mother?" he asked.

"Well, as I remember," she replied with a chuckle, "there is a sure-fire charm in it for hunters and horse racers and, since you place such faith in good-luck charms, you might want to try it."

"Would I!" exclaimed Eddie. "You bet, I'll try anything! What is it?"

"Oh, it is rather complicated. Here, let's sit down and study it out."

According to this ancient Swiss success formula, you had to capture and kill a bat, cut its heart out, tie the heart to the ring finger of your right hand with a red silk thread. If you did that, both luck and opportunity would break down your door to get at you.

That night, Eddie caught a train for the West. He had a lower berth for himself and Lady Luck. All went well until Lady Luck fell to yowling and woke passengers up. The complaining buzz-buzz of the Pullman porter's bell sounded like a four-alarm fire. At last he came and laid down the law that kittens should ride in baggage cars and not in Pullman sleepers.

Eddie roared that he would be triple-dyed if Lady Luck was going to travel in the baggage car. In the end he sat out the night with Lady Luck in the smoking compartment. For that privilege, he gave the porter one of his seven precious silver dollars.

Rick arrived in Sioux City chock-full of confidence but not much else. Certainly he was low on funds, only six dollars in his pockets: six dollars to cover living costs for himself and six other men—two drivers and four mechanics—for the ten days until the race. After that? Well, after that he would have the $10,000 grand prize! He would be in clover.

Tom Alley and Ralph Mulford were Rick's fellow drivers. Faithful Eddie O'Donnell was his riding mechanic. The race was to be held on the new Union County Speedway, a two-mile oval track on gumbo ground—gumbo being a dry, brittle type of soil rich in stones that range in size from pebbles to rocks as large as tennis balls —but much harder.

The prizes were $10,000, $5,000, and $2,500 for first, second, and third position at the end of the 300-mile run. Because the Duesenberg's racing stamina was unknown, and because Rick was a hard-luck rider, he was not a favorite before the race. The "wise money" was on track-smoking Bob Burman and cigar-puffing Barney Oldfield. Rick himself discounted these two and regarded Spencer Wishart in the thundering Mercer as his greatest threat. Unless he could keep Wishart at heel on the turns, his light car would go down to defeat.

The Duesenberg team, with only six silver dollars to its name, could not afford garage expenses and hotel bills. So, Rick wangled free space for his three cars under the grandstand. Cots were also placed there for the drivers and mechanics. He made a deal with the wife of a near-by farmer to feed his teammates for a dollar a week per man—on credit, of course, payment to be made as soon as Rick cashed the $10,000 first-prize check. For himself and Lady Luck, he arranged room and board at another farm at $1.50 a week. On the same terms of payment.

Now, all Rick and his merry men had to do was to win the ten grand. They worked hard to improve their chances, but he figured that not a single chance should be overlooked.

There was that bat!

He told the boys who always gathered around racing camps that he wanted a bat—a live one—and that one would be worth two bits. Money was no object.

The night before the race, two things happened.

Lady Luck took "French leave." She went over the hill and far away with a tomcat. This was a bad sign, and gave Rick the jitters. Besides he had grown fond of Lady Luck.

Then a boy showed up with a shoe box containing a large bat. It was ten o'clock, and our hero suddenly realized, to his horror, that he had forgotten all about the red silk thread. What to do? The charm might not work if it was not executed exactly right. So, he got into his car and drove eight miles into Sioux City. It was late, and the bigger stores were closed; but after much searching he found a small shop on a side street. There he bought a spool of red silk thread.

It was midnight when Rick got into bed, and after only four hours' sleep he got up, killed the bat, cut it open, took out what he believed to be its heart, and tied it to his finger. Then he went over to the track to make ready for the grind.

The race began about noon, and from the very start it was a rip-roaring contest. Drivers strained to surge ahead on the early laps, wheel to wheel and hood to hood. The flame-spouting engines sped around the track, rumbling, swaying, weaving; and, as the race roared on, the track became like the furrows of a plowed field. From the madly whirling wheels streams of gumbo shot up—solid squirts of stone and gravel and clods of sun-baked earth. They blinded drivers and slashed their hands and faces.

Also, as the race roared on, tires exploded. Engines rattled loose.

One by one, more than half of the contestants dropped out. Among them were such formidable contenders as Oldfield and Burman, favorites of the expert observers. Wishart, the man Rick feared most, stuck to him like his shadow.

But the gumbo—the gumbo was getting Rick as well as every one else. Whenever Wishart burst into the lead, the stuff would smack into Rick's car like coal coming down a chute. Well, toward the end of the race, the oil pressure began to go down. Why didn't O'Donnell, his riding mechanic, pump it up? Rick kicked him twice, the signal for more oil pressure. But O'Donnell did not respond. Another two kicks. Nothing happened. As he came out of a turn and hit the straightaway, Rick took his eyes off the track long enough to steal a look at the mechanic. He was out. O'Donnell had been hit on the head by a chunk of gumbo big enough to knock him cold. Rick had no way of knowing if the mechanic was dead or just unconscious. There was no time to stop and investigate. The car had to run as long as the engine ran. He was rounding into the 148th lap. If his engine would only hold out—four miles more— and he would win—he had to win—had to win—had to win. Give 'er gas!

There was Wagner now. He snapped the checkered flag—sign that Rick was on the last lap. Once more around, and—oh, baby! —victory. Ten thousand smackers! Give 'er gas!

Eddie O'Donnell? Dead or alive? No time to find out now. Nothing he could do even if he could find out. Give 'er gas!

The engine began to heat up. No oil. It was smoking. It was red-hot. Hold up, old girl, keep rolling—one mile more—half a mile —a quarter. Give 'er gas! Gotta win! He was going to make it! There was the finish line ahead and coming up fast. He could almost coast in now if the engine quit. It began to knock. Knock —bang—slam! Over its pounding he could hear Wishart pushing up from behind. Give her gas, burst her cylinders wide open, crack her up, but get her over that line—first! Give 'er gas! Let 'er burn!

The line!

He was over it. He was in. Then a terrific bang! The car swerved wildly like a furious animal before he brought it to a stop.

The engine gone?

No, just as he crossed the finish line, one of his tires exploded.

Forty-nine seconds after Rick pulled in, Wishart thundered up. Mulford came in third, driving Tom Alley's Duesenberg. Tom had been blinded by flying gumbo and had to quit. So Mulford, whose engine had fallen by the wayside earlier, took Tom's car and position in the race.

Slowly, it dawned on Rick that this meant total winnings of $12,500 for the team. First and third! Not bad!

Both Alley and O'Donnell recovered swiftly. It was a great day for the Duesenberg, and it was a great car. In that long grind, Rick had not lifted its hood once. He had stopped only twice—for oil and new tires.

The check for the winnings would be presented the next day, but Rick decided to enjoy immediately some of the comforts it offered. After the races, he and his teammates went into town and took rooms in the best hotel. Chances are that they all celebrated the victory in the same way: went to their rooms, enjoyed the luxury of soaking in a hot and soapy bath, then had dinner in bed—and deep engulfing, unworried sleep.

As he downed a hearty dinner, Rick sent for an evening newspaper. He got a copy of the Sioux City *Tribune*. Its front page carried a screaming seven-column head: "Rickenbacker Captures First Place."

After he had read the article, Eddie went to the wall telephone, asked for Western Union and sent this telegram to his mother:

You can believe what you read in the papers tonight and tomorrow. Love and kisses.   EDDIE

Eddie slept that night the deep and pleasant slumber of the just and the solvent. The next morning, he whistled "Too Much Mustard" as he shaved and dressed, while he thought how fine it would be to have a batch of his mother's fried corn-meal mush floating in a sea of maple syrup.

Having dressed, he went down into the lobby and headed toward breakfast when someone shouted his name. He looked around and saw Fred Wagner, the starter, looking long-faced and solemn.

"I'm terribly sorry, Rick."

"Sorry about what?"

"You didn't win yesterday," said Wagner mournfully.

"Like fun, I didn't! You can't fight the timer and the clock, and they both counted me in yesterday afternoon."

"Yeah," deplored Wagner, "but last night they counted you out."

Eddie looked at him through slit-lidded eyes as he drew his lips in a thin line across his teeth—the Rickenbacker fighting face.

"Tell me the whole story, Fred," he finally said, "so I know where I stand and where to start."

The story was that, after dinner the night before, Wishart had thought things over and decided that he had been credited with one lap too few. If true, this made him the victor in the race. He demanded a recheck. It began that night, and about 2:30 A.M. the recheckers decided that Wishart's claim was right and he had won the race and the $10,000 first prize.

"There it is, Eddie!" said Wagner. "I know what this means to you. But there's nothing I can do about it."

"Maybe *you* can't, Freddie, but *I* can! If they can check the timing tape for Wishart—they can check it for me, too."

A little while later, the tiresome job of checking the timing record was begun again. In the small hours of Monday, when the checking was well toward the end of the race, Eddie pointed triumphantly to the record and roared:

"There, that's it! That's where Spence blew a tire and I went by him while he was in the pit!"

Wishart, who was present, banged his heavy fist on the table.

"By gosh, Eddie, you're right!" he cried. "I remember now. I was part of a lap ahead of you, and, by the time I got rolling, you were just that much ahead of me!"

"Right!" agreed Eddie.

"I don't see how I could ever have missed it," observed Wishart penitently. "It's your race, Eddie, and no question about it."

But all this checking and counterchecking took some eighteen hours. When all the issues were finally settled, Eddie wiped his brow and said:

"Fellows, this has been the slowest race on earth. It took me a day and a half to win first place twice in a three-hundred-mile race!"

News of the Sioux City race and its repercussions went by wire all over America and by cable to every corner in Europe. The fact that Eddie's name was German became doubly interesting when Lautenschlager, the German speed ace, captured the famous Grand Prix of France. This, incidentally, is the place to record the fact that American sports writers, with their love for nicknames, had dubbed Eddie the Big Teuton, Baron von Rickenbachor, the Dutch Demon, the Speedy Swiss, and other German-sounding sobriquets too numerous to mention. Those were the invasion days of foreign racing cars and foreign drivers on American tracks. The name Duesenberg had a foreign flavor; so did Rickenbacker. Presto, Eddie was given a German tag, and it stuck. Just how thoroughly it stuck is illustrated by John C. Burton's poem in the *Motor Age* of July 9, 1914:

> All Germany is on a spree
> And other lands is scorning;
> The Teuton clan now leads the van
> While France is wearing mourning:
> One, two and three in the Grand Prix,
> First also at Sioux City—
> Just quaff your beer, don't shed a tear;
> The Dutch ask not for pity.
>
> Great Kaiser Bill has had his fill
> Of Pilsener and lager;
> He loudly boasts and drinks deep toasts
> In praise of Lautenschlager;
> Across the sea a victory
> Has led this peace-plan knocker
> To plan to knight in his delight
> That Deutscher, Rickenbacker.

Accompanying the verses was a drawing of a smiling Kaiser Bill who held a racing car in each hand. The poem drew attention not only in this country but in England. An elderly clerk in Scotland Yard clipped it and filed it in an envelope marked: "Rickenbacher, Edward, also known as E. V. Rickenbacker."

That file was to grow with the years and come to sudden, unexpected life shortly before Christmas, 1916—but that is in the future.

The victory at Sioux City seemed to bring about a change in Rick's luck. During a three-day meet in Galveston, he landed in the money twice. But from there on, race after race, track after track, it was the same old Rickenbacker story: out in front at the start of the race, and out in the pits before he reached the finish line. There were exceptions, few but important. He won where it counted, but not often enough. The race-going public loved him, but love did not fill the pockets of Eddie and his teammates.

Eddie drove his last major race in a Duesenberg at Elgin. He gave up a car he had come to love because he thought it was time for him to move on to other cars and learn more. By now, the race track had become a testing stand to him rather than just a merry-go-round for the brass ring of Speed King. He had driven several makes of racing cars since that first clumsy Frayer-Miller, and he had learned much about engines, construction, balance, design, fuel consumption, brakes, and tires—but he wanted to learn more. There were the Stutz, the Mercer, the Peugeot, the Blitzen-Benz, the Maxwell—just to mention a few. He wanted to try them all. After looking the field over, he decided on the Peugeot. It had speed, endurance, and balance; but it had something else that fascinated him. The new Peugeot had four-wheel brakes. He made a deal with the Peugeot agency in New York to drive one of its two racing cars in the Point Loma three-hundred-mile road race at San Diego on Thanksgiving Day. Wild Bob Burman was to handle the other Peugeot.

Eddie did not win that race: he was out after 108 miles with engine failure. Still, this particular trip to the coast was to be of unusual significance. He formed a friendship with Glenn Martin, who had just begun building aircraft after several years of experimenting. Martin had been an auto salesman and racer, so that they had a strong point in common. Eddie's attitude toward aviation had not changed much since his Omaha days. Like most people, he regarded the airplane as a deathtrap. The ever-rising mortality rate of exhibition fliers turned the average American against the airplane as a means of transportation. The World War in Europe was still too young to have brought military aircraft in imposing numbers and decisive performance.

Eddie was primarily attracted to Martin's plane because of his interest in engines. He wanted to know the differences, if any, between aircraft and automobile motors. Martin showed him and, incidentally, took him aloft on his first flight. He liked it, but was not stirred by any urge to be an aviator.

As Father Time gave 1914 the checkered flag at the close of the year, the A.A.A. issued the annual list of National Championship standings. It revealed that the boy from Columbus who had been coming up from behind so bravely and so full of determination stood sixth on the roster of America's Speed Kings. Sixth! With 754 points! He had begun the year in twenty-seventh place with only 115 points to his credit.

Yes, indeed, in one year Eddie Rickenbacker, against keen competition and heavy odds, had come a long way, the hard way.

The opening event of 1915 was the Point Loma Road Race at San Diego, staged over a seven-mile dirt road that had some of the up-and-down-and-around features of a roller coaster. Although the race did not take place until January 9, Eddie Rickenbacker shipped his car west early in November. He went by way of San Francisco, where he signed up for the Grand Prize and Vanderbilt Cup races to be run in February and March as features of the Panama-Pacific Exposition.

He predicted, without reservation, that his Peugeot would win both races. This prediction proved 100 per cent accurate. From San Francisco, he went to Los Angeles to put his mile-eating steed in trim. One thing that gave him considerable pause, in planning the race strategy, was that he would be passing his repair pit only once every seven miles during the three-hundred-mile event. This meant that the system of signals worked out between racers and their pitmen would not function with the frequency it did over a one-mile or two-mile speedway. Again Eddie the Strategist went into executive session. He came out with a weird but workable device which consisted of twin sets of masks and helmets connected with each other by heavy rubber speaking tubes—one for himself and one for his mechanic. This improved on the crude and some-what limited signals by means of which driver and riding mechanic usually communicated with each other.

Before the contest, while having the car overhauled in a garage near the old Alexandria Hotel in Los Angeles, Eddie began to doubt if his luck would hold out long enough to let him finish the race. Up to that moment, he had forgotten all about the heart of the bat that had ridden with him to victory in Sioux City. Perhaps it was time to get another. He let it be known that he was in the market for a live bat. On January 1, a boy brought him one and collected a dollar for it. Around the corner from the hotel was a small bird store whose owner Eddie had come to know. Taking the bat to the store, he explained its importance as an instrument of victory, and pledged the man to look after it.

Now, confident that the first prize was as good as his, Eddie took his outfit to San Diego and began practicing. The car ran smoothly and fast; the new speaking tube enabled him to talk with his mechanic above the roaring engine and humming tires. Things looked rosy, indeed.

The afternoon before the race, he went by train to Los Angeles and reached the bird store about eight o'clock only to learn that the bat had died the night before. He returned to San Diego with unhappy forebodings.

"The race is lost—the race is gone," was the thought that pounded through his head. "The race is lost—the race is gone," was the song the pounding car wheels seemed to repeat mile after mile after mile.

The next day, Rickenbacker's Peugeot led the field after an almost rocketlike start. Up to the halfway mark of the contest, the slim powerful product of French engineering genius was not marked by any car's dust. If the auto could stand the pace, it would finish first. But, suddenly, it began to buck and bang. Eddie pulled up to the side of the road with a grim smile. For him, the race was over: a broken connecting rod. For weeks after this damage was repaired, the Peugeot continued to act up, and he finally turned it over to Henry Miller, one of California's leading automotive engineers and racing-car builders, to put into shape.

Meanwhile, Paul Hale Bruske, glib-tongued manager of the brand-new Maxwell team, invited Eddie to join his outfit and become a teammate of Barney Oldfield and Bill Carlson, who had already signed up. The car did not have a particularly good reputation at that time. For one thing, it ran on kerosene instead of gasoline; and it had a great deal of carburetor trouble. However, Bruske assured him that this trouble had been licked. Both Oldfield and Carlson seemed to have faith in the Maxwell, and their attitude decided him. He signed up. So, instead of driving a sleek Peugeot to victory in the San Francisco exposition races, he sat at the wheel of a low-slung Maxwell. The strategy was the old "Rickenbacker Razzmatazz," of which Oldfield had been the first victim. Eddie was to drive at a man-killing clip as speed bait for the rival pilots. Carlson was to follow at another pace, while Oldfield in their wake was to spurt to victory at the proper time.

On the day of the Grand Prize, it rained so hard that almost all of the sixty thousand spectators had raincoats or umbrellas. Not to be outdone, Eddie bought a large beach parasol and spread its protecting dome over himself and his mechanic as he slithered over the mud-slick course. He drew a laugh but not the prize, dropping out at 218 miles with engine trouble. His luck in the Vanderbilt Cup race at San Francisco a few weeks later was no better: out at 28 miles with engine trouble. In both races, the Maxwell rolled to the pits because its carburetor did not perk.

Oh, yes, he had been right in November when he predicted that the Peugeot would win both races. The little French car that had given him so much trouble ran with the speed of a scared antelope in both races, with Dario Resta at the wheel. Giving up that car after such a brief trial was one of the biggest mistakes Eddie ever made. In that Peugeot, Resta not only sped to victory in race after race throughout 1915, including the Chicago five-hundred-miler, but also soared to championship position at the close of the year with winnings that totaled some $36,000.

After the San Francisco races, the members of the Maxwell team served notice that, unless the cars were adapted to use gasoline, they would quit. The Maxwell people yielded and turned the cars into gasoline burners before the St. Patrick's Day races at

Venice, California. As usual, Rick sat way out in front and seared the track for the opposition until a stone ripped his crankcase wide open and forced him out; but, thanks to his blasting, his team-mates landed first and second. Next, a road race at Tucson, in which the same technique brought the Maxwells in first, second, and fourth. Shortly after this race, Oldfield left the team and Ernest A. Moross took over its direction.

Moross had gone from bicycle racing into automobile barn-storming on the dirt-track circuit, and his prime possession was the old but still formidable Blitzen-Benz with which Wild Bob Burman had set numerous records. He had a touch of the circus in him and advertised Eddie as a daredevil speed-star who zipped around tracks in the old B.-B. in exhibition drives but battled for prize money in Maxwells. By this time, Eddie had learned to understand the Maxwell car. He had found its weaknesses, and corrected some of them; he had discovered its strong points, and played up to them.

On May 16, after much hurrah and fanfare, Eddie drove the B.-B. in a mile match race in his home town, finishing second; and he won a twenty-five-mile race in a Maxwell. He drove with un-usual caution that day, because his mother was among the spectators and he did not want an accident to spoil her pleasure. The last and main event of the day was a hundred-miler in which he set out to establish a record. After seventeen miles he was blinded by a cloud of dust. He skidded, hit the fence, crashed through it, and wrecked his car beyond immediate repair. His first thought, on realizing that neither he nor his mechanic was hurt, was: "What will Mother say?" Jumping out of the wreckage, he ran to the grandstand only to learn that his mother had gone home just before the accident "to get supper ready."

From Columbus Eddie went to Indianapolis to prepare for the Memorial Day race—which was, as ever, the main target in his racing year—after arranging with his brother Albert to capture a bat and ship it to him alive a few days before Memorial Day. The bat arrived. On the morning of the race, Rick rose about four o'clock as usual. Closing the windows of the room and the transom over the door, he lifted the lid of the cigar box and found the bat huddled in a corner. He thought it was dead and lifted it gingerly; but the animal was only playing possum and, in an instant, was out of his hand. It made a swooping dive to the crack at the bottom of the door and was gone. "Well," said Eddie to himself, "that isn't going to stop me from winning. I have another bat up my sleeve."

The bat up his sleeve was a brand-new stunt designed to stop wasting precious time on tire changes. In those days, the Indianapolis Speedway was a brick track, rough and dry for the first hundred miles or so of the driving. After that, oil dripping from the cars and rubber wearing off the tires formed a film that made the track not only smooth but even slippery in spots. He decided that if he could manage to save tire wear in the first hundred miles he would have a vital time factor in his favor—the time required in replacing worn-out rubber. After some heavy thinking, the remedy came to Eddie the Strategist: a secret design for squirting oil on the two outside tires while running at full speed. A gallon of oil was placed in a pressure tank hidden under the mechanic's seat, with two copper tubes running under the frame to positions opposite the right front and rear tires, which took the brunt of the pressure on the turns. Mornings, before the race, when no one was around, he tested this system out. He found that when oil was splashed on his tires just before the turns the rubber would stand up longer under the strain and he could take the turns at speeds up to ten miles an hour above his ordinary curve pace.

Eddie knew that his new design would be protested if it were discovered before the race. So, that day, he brought his car into place at the very last minute and, as a further precaution had two of his pitmen lean against the right wheels to hide the small tubes that jutted out from under the frame. When the cars broke formation at the end of the first lap, Rick gunned his engine and spurted forward. He maintained top pace during the first hundred miles and was a lap ahead of every one else when a crankshaft bearing burned out for lack of oil. O irony, where is thy sting? Plenty of winning oil on the tires but none in the crankcase!

The secret? Oh, yes, the secret came out when the technical committee examined his auto and wanted to know about those oil-dripping tubes on the side of the car. Eddie grinned and confessed.

The committee then and there recommended a ruling which banned that form of tire-saving in races.

During the summer and early fall of 1915, Eddie the Strategist began to realize that planning that increased the efficiency of his pitmen would be just as much of a factor in winning races as a heavy foot on the gas. It was really at this point that he began work on the system of head-and-foot driving that was to take him high into the championship brackets.

Among his mechanics in those days was short, fat, and jolly Harrison Van Hoven, a Sioux City boy who threw over a secure business because the only world for him was the speedway. Van joined the Maxwell team in San Francisco and became closely attached to Eddie during the spring and summer months. From an average riding mechanic, he developed into a truly remarkable pit manager. The two worked out a system for complete service during a pit stop, which included gas, oil, water, and four new tires in fifty-nine seconds. Van Hoven drilled his pitmen to cut this seemingly irreducible time to forty-nine seconds by eliminating every waste motion and lining up tools and supplies on the pit counters.

Eddie was rather unhappy when the fleet Peugeot won first place in the Chicago five-hundred-miler with an average speed of ninety-seven miles an hour while his own Maxwell came in third with ninety-six miles an hour. But he was captured by Harry Grant's British Sunbeam, which made the whole run without once stopping at the pits. That, to him, was a wonderful feat, and he made up his mind that the Sunbeam was a car he would know more about some day.

Sioux City, where Rick had climbed out of financial and mental depression the previous year, was next on the schedule. The main threat to his title as King of the Gumbo was not Spencer Wishart but Eddie O'Donnell, who had been his 1914 riding mechanic. O'Donnell was now the head man of the Duesenberg team, and, although they remained close friends, it would be a fight to the finish.

For Rick, it was a happy finish. He came in first, but O'Donnell and two other Dusenbergs came in second, third, and fourth. The two high-speed Eddies and Van Hoven celebrated their victories by downing round after round of their favorite beverage—heaping, frothing, frosted chocolate malted milk sodas.

That evening a reporter came to Rick's hotel room and asked him to comment on the news that he was out of a job.

"Quit your kidding, Willie!" laughed Rick.

"I'm not kidding. Here's a statement from the Maxwell people in Detroit. It just came in over the A.P. wire."

Grabbing it, Rick learned that, after the meet in Omaha two days hence, the Maxwell Company would fold its tent and steal away from the dirt tracks and speedways of auto racing.

"All I know is what I see in the papers," he said with a forced chuckle. This was bad news and he did not quite know how to handle it.

"Why do they quit with you on the top of the heap?" asked the reporter.

"I know why," cut in Van Hoven. "The Maxwell people quit because, with Rick driving, the cut-out can't keep up with the car. I have heard—on good authority, too—that the Maxwell people are afraid that, the way Rickenbacker drives their car, the back wheels won't be able to keep up with the front wheels, and they will have to build it in two sections, one known as Ricken and the other as Backer."

The plain fact was that the Maxwell owners had lost interest in racing, and Rick headed straight from Omaha to Detroit, where he wound up his affairs with them.

He was far from broke—in the nine days from June 26 to July 5 he had won $18,500; also he had an idea that might make his future more secure and his income even higher. Without much trouble, he talked Carl Fisher and Jim Allison, chief owners of the Indianapolis Speedway, into buying the Maxwell cars and placing him at the head of the team on the basis of a percentage of all winnings. Having known him from his early racing days, Fisher and Allison gave him a free hand in recruiting and conducting the team, and insisted on only one point: all the drivers and riding mechanics must be single. No married men! Rick subscribed heartily to this. He knew from experience the burden of loss borne by the wives of drivers and riding mechanics killed on the roaring road. He also knew that men who had wives or sweethearts lacked the freedom from fear of men who had no family ties.

It took time to transfer ownership of the Maxwell cars and rebuild the team, and, until September, Rick had little opportunity for racing. But on September 18 he drove what many observers call the smartest race of his career. It was the hundred-mile race at Narragansett Park, Rhode Island, and in it he made a history-making twenty-five-mile spurt that carried him from among the stragglers to leading position.

The cheering, howling crowd saw Eddie Rickenbacker's Maxwell—a black asteroid on wheels—surge forward in the swirling firmament of speedway stars. It passed them at a clip so fast that it seemed as if these giants of the racing universe stood still. What the public did not see was the tires on the Maxwell; and thereby lay a bit of brilliant scheming. It began on the day of the first trial runs. The track had an asphalt surface and was banked very gently at the turns. Eddie figured that he could win the race if he maintained an average of seventy-eight to eighty miles an hour. Having proved he could maintain that average, Eddie the Strategist looked for an edge. He found it in the size of his tires. Big, heavy tires would last longer than small, light ones, and by using them he could go through the race at that speed without making a change. This went against the common practice, which was to use the lightest and smallest tires practical, because of the greater speed they afforded. In other words, it was a matter of gambling track speed against pit delays.

Of course everybody watched everybody else and, particularly, everybody had an eye on Eddie. His friendly rivals feared his skill in pulling speed rabbits out of his racing helmet. Therefore, when he decided to use the big heavy tires he went out of his way to make everybody think that he was going to use the small light ones, and never let big tires be seen on his car or in his pit; but six of them were carefully hidden in a garage in Providence. Only at the very hour of the race, with all the cars in place at the starting line, did he switch from small to big tires. Exactly a minute and a half before the starting gun, a truck braked to a quick stop near Eddie's No. 1 Maxwell. Mechanics piled out. Some pushed jacks under the car. Others loosened bolts on the wheels. Still others had new tires ready.

Sixty-three seconds from the time it drew up, the truck drove away, and Eddie's speed baby had a new set of shoes—big black shoes. But it was too late for anything to be done about it by other drivers. That was how Rick pulled down the $4,000 prize that afternoon.

Before the 1915 racing season ended, Eddie won in several other meets, including third at Sheepshead Bay, New York. When the A.A.A. compiled the championship standings for the year, the former Dutchie of the Horsehead Gang stood fifth among the speed kings with 1,785 points and prize winnings of $24,000. Among the records he established that year, by driving skill and human and mechanical endurance, were the following:

One-mile circular track, Providence: 45 4/5 seconds.
One hundred miles on a one-mile circular track, Providence: 86 minutes, 2/5 second.
Two-mile dirt, Sioux City: 1 minute, 5 seconds.
Two-mile speedway, New York: 1 minute, 3 4/5 seconds.
Three hundred miles on a mile-and-a-quarter track, Omaha, at an average of 93 miles an hour.

Chapter XI

~~~~~~

As 1916 came up, Eddie Rickenbacker grew more determined than ever to use the speedways as testing grounds for ideas that he might use in producing the Great American Car and, at the same time, as sources of some of the capital he would need to make it. But the research engineer in Eddie did not supplant the racing driver or moderate his headlong rush toward the finish once the race began. He was still spectacular and fast; still the man out front who led the procession as long as his car lasted.

Neither fame nor growing income had changed Eddie's personal habits. Ten o'clock was his taps; smoking and drinking were taboo; regular exercise was on the must list. He knew that checks could not be drawn on the Bank of Energy without making deposits, and he was a faithful and large depositor. He was now twenty-five years old and no longer the boy-wonder of motordom; but, without losing the energy and drive of youth, he had added experience which strengthened his judgment and ability to analyze. In a racing car and out of one, he was two different fellows. Behind a wheel, he had snap, dash, quickness of decision. Elsewhere, he was slow-spoken, quiet, ready to listen. In a profession where well dressed daredevils usually wore checkered caps, attention-getting suits, two-color fancy shoes, loud ties, and screaming socks, Rick went in for the quiet garments of a young, successful businessman. On the track, he continued to be all business. After the race, he went to whatever hotel room he called home. He avoided crowds and personal publicity. Usually, he would eat in his room with a few close friends.

Eddie was a popular target for engagement rumors. A heavy crop of leap-year stories involving him was harvested in 1916, and he received leap-year proposals from girls all over the country. To each, he sent a copy of that clause in his contract which banned wedding bells for Maxwell drivers.

Among those who wanted Eddie to race up the road of romance to the finish line at the altar was Irene Tams, a motion picture actress who, in March, was in Florida making a picture. She telegraphed:

Some people say that they regret the state of matrimony was ever admitted to the Union. I love speed and admire endeavor. I am so interested in your welfare that, if you will cease racing, you may consider this a leap year proposal. Are you game? Wire me, Seminole Hotel, Jacksonville.

When Van Hoven saw the telegram, he went to the Indianapolis office of the film studio that had the actress under contract and got a photograph showing a handsome young woman with a huge mop of wavy hair, large eyes set wide in a small oval face. The eyes had the intense and compelling stare made fashionable by the great screen "vamps" of the era; but the gaze was not compelling enough, and Eddie replied in a night letter:

Your most generous telegram received, and am very grateful for same. Sorry indeed that I cannot at this time see my way clear to give up racing. My sentiments are as follows: I much prefer to travel with Herr and spell it with a double *r*, for a woman is only a woman, but my soul mate is a racing car.

Under his contract Eddie was to receive 75 per cent of all winnings, while Fisher and Allison were to get 25 per cent. Fisher and Allison put up the money for the purchase of the cars, as well as for replacement parts, repair equipment, and an operating fund. Rick, on the other hand, was to meet all maintenance, travel, operating, and salary expenses out of his share. For a fellow who had landed in Sioux City in 1914 with only six silver dollars, Rick had done very well indeed. Neither Fisher nor Allison did things by halves. They established a generous fund for Rick to draw against— and he needed money for the novel and ambitious scheme he had thought out to corner the prize-money market in American auto racing.

To begin with, the cars were virtually rebuilt. New stream-lined bodies, with fishtail rear ends and spear-shaped fronts, to cut down wind resistance, were installed. The drivers' and mechanics' seats were lowered to bring down the point of gravity and reduce air resistance. These changes added almost five miles an hour to the speed of the Maxwells.

During the long winter months while this work went on, Eddie the Strategist figured out a way of taking part in every one of the sixteen major events of 1916. This meant dashing hither and yon to a dozen tracks scattered all over the country. He did this by splitting his team in two. He made each unit self-sustaining, from personnel to parts.

Under A.A.A. racing rules, each car was allowed only two men out of the pit for servicing during the race aside from the driver and his riding mechanic. In the pit, there was a pit manager and a crew of mechanics depending, in number, on the number of cars in the team. Two pit mechanics were allowed for a one-car entrant, and one additional mechanic for each additional car. Eddie planned to increase his prize-winning mileage by creating two teams of two cars, three drivers and four mechanics. He obtained two railroad automobile cars for permanent use that year. Each was fitted out with enough spare parts to build two new machines, and special tools and workbenches for making parts when needed. Long, waterproof extension cords were on hand to bring electricity to the freight cars. The plan was for Eddie and Van Hoven to ride the high rail from city to city for the most important races. Under this program, they were to cross the United States four times in four months, and they did.

In Van Hoven, Eddie had a pearl above price. Almost as round as a Babbitt bearing, Van had more energy, kind words, and ready humor than two average men. His brother was the vaudeville headliner known as the Mad Musician. Van had a touch of the zaniness that made his brother famous. When things went wrong during a race, Van lifted the morale of the men by his rapid-fire monologue of misshapen sentences. When he laughed he closed his eyes and opened his mouth, and his two hundred pounds shook like jelly. But, while he was fat and funny, Van was also a fast and efficient mechanic. There was no fat behind his eyebrows. It was all lightning-swift gray matter.

Van had also worked out a new and comprehensive, yet simple, signal system between the pit and the drivers. With chalk and a large blackboard he could tell a driver, in code, to speed up or slow down, inform him how far ahead or behind he was in the race and who drove the car in the dust cloud ahead or who was coming up like thunder from behind.

Believing that races were won both on the track and in the pit, Eddie gave Van Hoven a free hand—so much authority, in fact, that he even had the power to tell the Boss what to do. Frequently the Kewpie-like Van Hoven would tear into tall, muscular Eddie with right- and left-hook expletives that reminded the former of the C.B.C. dealers in Dallas. Yes, indeed, Van was a stout feller in more ways than one; especially in the obscurity of the pit where internal fortitude counted most.

During those winter months of 1916, Eddie Rickenbacker wrote his first book, "The Book of Rules"—a complete textbook on how to operate an automobile racing team on the road, in the pit, on the track, and the safe and sane way of life for hard-working drivers and mechanics. It unmasked Rick the daredevil driver and revealed, instead, a 100 per cent Safety-First Fatalist. The book contained sharply defined rules for the guidance of his helpers. His pit men and mechanicians could not make a mistake if they followed his written instructions, and no rule was broken a second time, for he punished the offender by making him memorize the entire code.

Evidently recalling his mother's warning that we arouse in others the attitude we feel toward ourselves, Rick began with this comment:

"Always conduct yourself as a gentleman. If you do not, you not only reflect discredit upon yourself but also upon automobile racing, the means by which you gain a livelihood.

"In case of accident, see that the victim receives the most expert treatment. Take him to the best hospital. Engage the best doctor. Don't spare expense. Money is cheap compared with a human life.

"Before the start of a race, get ready to ride instead of gossiping, fooling, and playing to the grandstand. See that you have an orange and gum in your pockets and two pairs of goggles. Examine the car carefully. You can't go back for forgotten articles or rectify mistakes after the starting bomb explodes."

"The public can't be damned. You've got to give them a show for their money or there will be no money for you," was another Rickenbacker axiom.

The book closed with a bluntly worded bit of advice: "If you don't like the way we do business, if you don't like your teammates, don't grouse and don't go around with a long face. Quit this job and get another one somewhere else. I want you to remember that practically everything I have been able to accomplish is due to my willingness to work at any kind of job I could get until I could better myself. I am naturally proud, but I do not let pride get in my way in the matter of making a living. From my earliest boyhood, I have had a great deal of self-confidence. If my racing job should end, I would take the first thing I could find in the way of employment. My feeling about the matter is that, in case I should have to start with a spade or a shovel, in a short time I should be bossing the gang, and that would put me in a position for further promotion. My first objective would be to get a job of some kind at any price, and then fight my way up.

"The trouble with a lot of people is that they are not willing to begin anywhere in order to get a fighting chance. They are all dolled up with a lot of fool pride which is constantly holding them back. My advice to such a fellow is: Throw away that false pride. No honest work is beneath you. Jump in and demonstrate your superiority. Once you get on the pay roll, make up your mind to master everything about your own job, and get ready for the job at the top. Your particular task is merely one end of a trail that leads to the driver's seat. That is my philosophy of success. It works, I have tried it out."

The members of the Rickenbacker team were working so hard in getting ready for the 1916 season that Eddie thought they might crack under the strain. To be sure, they had a double incentive: first, enthusiasm for the job; secondly, a share in the winnings. Even so, he looked around to find something that would reduce fatigue. He found a cue in a Sunday edition of the *New York Times*. It was a short dispatch from Vienna announcing that an Austrian physician had tested the truth of the maxim that music soothes the savage breast by playing phonograph recordings of soft waltz music for shell-shocked German soldiers. The music tended to quiet them.

If waltz music was a sedative for war-weary soldiers, thought Eddie, lively fox trots and marches should stimulate work-weary grease monkeys. It would not cost much time and money to find out. He bought two victrolas—one for each team—and a library of records. He told the Indianapolis music store where he bought them that he wanted "something inspiring and easy to listen to." Favorite tunes were Sousa's marches and fox trots such as Daddy English's "I Love You, California." The records served their purpose. Late at night, whenever fatigued heads began to droop and tired hands started to fumble, on came the music with a lively tune that soon set the pace for the tired mechanics.

Even as Eddie Rickenbacker's ability to show Dan Cupid his challenging exhaust started a newspaper controversy, so his musical mechanics caused wide discussion. Music-while-you-work has been taken up since 1916 in many fields of activity; but then it was revolutionary and stirred up a great deal of discussion. Unmindful of praise or criticism, he and his teammates put on the records; and often as not, when they were working at night in a speedway pit, some one would yell from a neighboring outfit: "Hey, you Maxwells, put on a louder needle so we can hear better!"

Nearly all the weight of Eddie's added responsibilities as team boss went into his feet. He stepped more than ever on the gas, kept his eyes on the finish line, letting the devil take the hindmost. The nerviest piece of driving of his career was staged in his pursuit of the $10,000 stake in the Metropolitan Trophy Race at Sheepshead Bay on May 13, 1916. Some superstitious people regard thirteen as an unlucky number, but Eddie always thought it a good omen. Two men were killed in that one-hundred-fifty-mile event, and he barely escaped destruction with them; but, instead of letting up on his speed, as some of his rivals did, he roared to victory through a smoke-filled danger zone at one hundred ten miles an hour.

Before the race started, Rickenbacker knew that he was in superior company, opposed by cars that were faster than his. This meant that he had to push his car hard throughout the race and drive as fast as he dared on the turns. Resta was there with his Peugeot,

Limberg and Devigne with Delages—all fast and skillfully driven cars. From the start of the race, lap after lap, Rick, Limberg, Resta, and Devigne were bunched together like a cluster of grapes. Passing the grandstand on the thirteenth lap, Resta was leading; Devigne came next, then Rick, and lastly, Limberg. Coming into the turn, Limberg shot past his competitors with a scorching burst of speed. He ran ahead of the group, but he also ran out of luck; a tire let go, and the huge car shot into the air. Out of control, it hit an iron fence post at the top of the embankment. Limberg and his mechanic were thrown out, and both died. The right rear wheel was sheared off and wobbled down the slope of the gigantic saucer. Rick saw it miss Resta by inches. Now the other rear wheel, attached to the axle but knocked loose from the car, began to slide downward, as did the rest of the machine. The two sections bracketed Rick's car front and rear, and he missed disaster by seconds. Having learned to use his eyes as if they had been high-speed cameras, he noticed two things: neither driver nor mechanic was in sight at the top of the embankment, and no parts of the wrecked car were strewn on the track. This knowledge was to prove priceless. Of the four drivers clustered together when Limberg broke away, Rick had been the last; and he was the only one who could know that the track was clear when the oil and gas in the wrecked car caught fire at the bottom of the saucer and put a thirty-foot screen of thick black smoke across the track. Naturally, the other drivers slowed up before driving into the smoke screen; but Rick, knowing there was nothing in it to fear, pushed on at full speed. Frantic speedway officials tried to flag him down, slow him up—but he just grinned and stepped on the gas. By the time his rivals realized that the smoke-filled track was perfectly safe, he was two laps ahead of the procession; and they never caught up with him.

With victory at Sheepshead Bay to his credit, Rick headed for Indianapolis, confident that this year—*this year*—he would win the prize he coveted most of all. Short-wave radio was in its cradle in those days, but he decided to take the radio baby out for a ride. He set up an observer with a short-wave sending set in the center field, and had a receiving set in his car. The idea was that the observer was to keep him informed of the positions of the other contenders.

It was a good idea, but the baby was too young: engineers did not know how to shield against spark-plug and magnetic interference, so that the plan did not pay out. Nor did his hope of winding up in the big-money pay-off. After twenty-five miles a connecting-rod bearing burned out, and he had to quit. That burned-out bearing was one of the greatest pieces of luck Rick ever had. As his car limped to the pit, the all-important knuckle on his steering wheel broke. Five minutes earlier, the results could have been fatal to both driver and mechanic.

Two weeks later came the three-hundred-mile race at Chicago. Again he had high hopes; again, they were blasted. After one hundred and twenty-three miles of furious driving, he was out with a broken valve. But one thing this Chicago race produced was a story of Eddie Rickenbacker as a racing driver as seen through a pitman's eyes—the only one ever written. Oney Fred Sweet, of the *Chicago Tribune,* had succeeded in worming his way into a pitman's job. Here is his piece:

Four abreast, accompanied by a dull roar, the twenty-one cars have crossed over the painted white line and are passing the pits. The horns of ordinary automobiles along the track's edge begin to toot; that portion of the 90,000 spectators seated in the grandstand begins to cheer. The great international auto derby is on!

Those of us in Eddie Rickenbacker's pit keep our eyes on number 7 as she goes past. Number 7 is Rick's car. She thunders before us in the front row, second from our end. We follow her course until, at the far side of the track, she appears like a flea climbing the limb of a tree. The cars of red and yellow and white and blue are stretched out now and their engines are emitting noise and smoke with increasing vengeance. A tenseness has come over our pit. The kidding has ceased. The cars are already passing us again.

"Twenty-five, twenty-three, seven!" megaphones our pit caller, announcing the order of the cars as they pass, and the two clerks beside him get busy at their long score sheets. Van Hoven, our pit manager, refuses to be bothered further with what he terms my fool questions. It is enough, he feels, that Rick should let me join the team at the last minute. First prize means $12,000!

What a morning it had been for me!—a morning spent along the row of galvanized iron garages that reminded me of a row of stables in the old horse race days. Jockeys and swipes then; drivers and mechanics now. It had been no easy matter for me to get acquainted with the bunch in Eddie Rickenbacker's garage. I really had not felt like one of them until I had donned a one piece khaki suit, turned the peak of my cap to the back of my head and smeared my face with grease. All morning we had been engaged in oiling and painting and adjusting the half dismantled car as she stood quivering with artificial life.

Rick himself had not been so distrustful of me as the rest. They had called him "Rick" as he first appeared in the garage doorway, and I had quickly taken the cue. A tall, thin youth was Rick. He was probably twenty-seven years of age. Maybe he wasn't that old. The lines in the breeze-beaten faces of these speed demons are apt to be deceiving; De Palma is gray and he is but thirty. Rick had listened to the story of the others about my persistently hanging around and I had explained to him hurriedly how I desired to work in his pit that afternoon and change tires or help take care of anything that might go wrong with his car during the race.

The leading cars have just finished their tenth lap. Rick goes by either first or second most of the time taking turns at supremacy with Resta. Each car has its pit; each pit has its team of five men. The pits are like trenches, separated from the elevated wooden track by a concrete wall and separated from each other by a board fence.

I wonder if I will be able to do the right thing and do it quick enough when Rick pulls into the pit. I wonder if I have remembered all the rules which he has so carefully dictated for his men. I open the homemade book of rules and shuffle through the pages. Knowing nothing about cars, I skip the instructions which have to do with checking up the various parts of the mechanism previous to a race. But here is the warning against losing one's temper. Here is the page that cautions against bragging or kicking, with the pararaph at the bottom advising pit men to be sure to get to bed early at night.

Near the front of the book I find these typewritten lines: "Above all, I want my men to keep cool during any pit work, regardless of trouble, and there must be harmony in the pits during a race, regardless of personal feeling." One entire page of Rick's book of instructions is given over to a general rule which orders his team to get injured drivers and mechanics to the best hospital in town in case of accident.

I realize from what I have heard during the morning that this rule about hospitals is apropos. Of the eight boys in Rick's team at the Vanderbilt races in Frisco a year ago February, five have since met tragic death on the tracks.

Rick is depending a lot on his team in the pit. He knows how much they have to do with his success. I have come to the conclusion that all these star drivers are good executives and that to succeed in racing one must have something more than the mere nerve to drive fast.

But Rick is surely driving fast. He is hitting it better than a hundred miles an hour. Half the time now he is setting the pace. Over in the grandstand the band is playing "My Mother's Rosary," the strains reaching us but faintly in the pits. The sun sizzles down upon us. I can understand better now what Rick's fast driving means, because of some of the things he told me over in the garage.

"When I'm in a race," Rick told me, "I realize that I am traveling through life in an awful hurry. You can't tell what steel will do and I'm always conscious of the fact that something may happen to dash me into eternity. We drivers are all fatalists. Once last summer when I blew a tire going at a hundred miles an hour and my car turned over three times, I stuck to the wheel until the last turn, consigning myself to the worst, yet holding fast so that if it wasn't meant to be my time to go I would be doing what was expected of me.

"You've no idea how the breeze forces a fellow's cheeks back and distorts his face when he's going good and fast. And you take this track out here; it's as smooth as a boulevard when you're going at sixty miles an hour, but when you get up to 105 it feels like a rough road beneath you. I always relax on the straightaway and put on tension at the curves. When seven cars are coming around a curve wide open and one of 'em blows a tire, the whole seven are pretty apt to pile in a heap, and when you see a driver skidding on the curves you can count on it that he's nervous.

"When I'm going fast, the steering wheel constantly jiggles in my grasp, but it wouldn't do to hold it still. With every lap a man tires just a little and his brain fags along with his body; many's the time my mechanic beside me has to kick me to keep me waked up. The position we have to take in the car is not a comfortable one, though of course I bandage myself thoroughly before a race to keep my insides from jumping and giving me acute indigestion."

They have just made the twentieth lap. The crowd is growing more and more enthusiastic. The weather is ideal for a gala day. The sun is beginning to sink and the grandstand is beginning to throw long shadows across the track.

A car pulls into a neighboring pit.

It is the same car in which Bob Burman was recently killed. The faces of the driver and the mechanic in the car are black. The mechanic waves his right hand over his shoulder to indicate that it is the right rear tire that needs changing. The old tire is off and the new one is on in twenty seconds of time—a frayed, sick, worn-out tire, the old one is. "Go on!" yells a pit man before he has hardly removed the jack from the new wheel, and the car is off again at a terrible speed.

They speak in the pit of "changing tires," but it is really entire wheels that they change. I practice at lifting one of the wheels in our pit so as to be as handy as possible in case Rick should need it. The wheel weighs seventy pounds, but Van says that I should be so interested in helping get it over the concrete wall when occasion arises that it will seem no heavier than a feather. We have over fifty wheels in reserve, and along the top of the concrete wall Van has laid out all sorts of tools to be used in emergency.

"Keep Rick behind Ralph; let Resta go," yells Van, and he commands me to draw the number "12" with a ring around it on the pit blackboard. Van is making use of me in the signal work. I have already familiarized myself with part of the secret code. The number "12" with a ring around it means "You are going at 1:12." A zigzag line means "Something is dragging under your car; if you don't know what it is, find out immediately." We have twenty-five signals in all, but they can be combined to form at least a hundred different messages.

Though traveling like a rocket, Rick catches the signals and answers them with certain nods of his head.

Laps follow each other so fast that it does not seem possible the two mile track can be circled so quickly. Yet there are three hundred miles to go before the race is done—enough distance to carry the drivers across many states were they traveling in a straight line. Fifty times the cars have passed us like bullets out of a gun.

"She don't sound right," I hear Van comment. He is referring to Rick's car. Those in the pits have their ears primed for any message the car may give as she whirls by.

"I thought we had all the 'bugs' out of her," says Van, "but if I'm not mistaken there's a 'cuckoo' showing up. You never can tell when a car's going to turn to cheese!"

Yet Rick stays in the lead with Resta. It looks to me as if Rick would win the race and the $12,000 purse. I begin to wonder if he is ever going to be obliged to pull up to the pit. I want to do the right thing when he does pull up. I fight with my nerves to keep cool for the occasion.

At the close of the sixty-first lap Rick does pull in. I leap over the wall of the pit with the rest. Rick climbs out of the car and removes his helmet and goggles. There are deep red lines on his smeared face where the goggles and helmet have pinched. I begin to jump around like a jack rabbit in an effort to do something to help. I do not realize that Rick's chances for winning any part of the $30,000 purse have gone glimmering. He turns toward me, laughing.

"I guess maybe I didn't make Resta hurry," he jokes, slapping his knees with his hands and doubling over like a mischievous boy.

Even at this demonstration I have no other thought but that he will soon return to the race. I continue to jump around the car with a wrench in my hand.

"The valve's broken," explains Rick, still smiling. "I knew at fifty miles that she was gone, but I stuck on to make things as merry as possible. Looks to me as if it was going to be a nice day if it don't rain."

"If you'll show me where that valve is," I offer, "I'll—"

Rick grabs the wrench out of my hand and lays it among the other tools along the top of the concrete wall.

"Do you mean you're out of it for good?" I gasp. "Well, you certainly take it cool."

"I hope I do," answers the youth from Columbus, Ohio. "If I didn't I wouldn't be much good in this game. The valve's gone and that's all there is to it. I'm going over to the garage and change my clothes."

The tenseness in our pit evaporates with the elimination of our driver. The strained looks of the mechanicians and the megaphone caller and the signal man and the clerks fade, and they begin to kid each other again. We remain in the pit, however, until the last lap has been finished, and Resta, worried by Rick's tactics until he was out of the contest, has driven across the white line—winner.

From Chicago to Des Moines, first and third. To Sioux City, victory for the third year running. They called it now the Rickenbacker Race. Minneapolis-St.-Paul, out. Omaha, second. Kansas City, out. Tacoma, first. Cincinnati, out. Indianapolis Harvest Race, out. Astor Cup at Sheepshead Bay, second. Chicago, third. Harkness Trophy at Sheepshead Bay, out. Vanderbilt Cup and American Grand Prize at Santa Monica, out and out. Thus the months of the year turned with the speed of red-hot racing tires.

First, second, third, out, out, and out again. Third, first—and out. Victory and defeat. Hairbreadth escapes. Dull routine breakdowns. Blood-tingling conquests. The gate to fame just down the road. The Grim Reaper waiting! He is always waiting—for some other fellow! But he is waiting. Yes, but so are gold and glory!

Rick's last race in 1916 was run on the Pacific coast on Thanksgiving Day. It was also the last race he would ever enter; but all he knew was that he had ended his connection with the Maxwell team and agreed to go to England and help rebuild the Sunbeam racing car in preparation for heading the Sunbeam team in this country in 1917.

In California that November, Rick had made many new friends. Among them was a young flying Captain in the Army Signal Corps named Henry H. Arnold, whom he soon learned to call "Hap." And one day, when he was driving from Los Angeles to Santa Monica, he saw an Army airplane stalled in an open field while a man in uniform tinkered aimlessly with the engine. Rick brought his car to a stop, went to the plane, and said, "Got trouble?"

"Yes, engine trouble," replied the flyer, who wore a major's leaves.

"Perhaps I can help you. I know a little about engines."

"Glad to have you try," answered the pilot, who introduced himself as Major T. F. Dodd.

After nosing about a bit, Rick discovered the engine had spark-plug trouble. He put it in shape, and the plane took off; but Dodd and he were to meet again.

Soon after Thanksgiving Day, Rick received a cable from Louis Coatalen, head of the Sunbeam Motor Car Company, closing their deal and asking him to come to England at once. It took but an hour for him to pack his bags and jump on an eastbound Santa Fe train. As the cars snaked across Arizona, Rick got to thinking of his C.B.C. days in that region not so many years ago. He recalled the rabbit's foot, his first good-luck charm. He thought about the heart of the bat. He remembered the time he almost got hurt when he did *not* walk under a ladder in Iowa. As he debated the issue of good and bad luck, he emptied his pockets of the weirdest collection of charms ever carried in the clothing of one person: lucky elephants and four-leaf clovers; Billikens and tail buttons of rattlesnakes; rabbits' feet and other charms in dozens. He had almost half a hundred tiny luck tokens of one kind or another, accumulated through the years and carried around in one suit after another. Suddenly, he felt disgusted with the whole idea of lucky charms. He went into the toilet, dumped them into the bowl, and consigned the lot to the wind of the speeding train by pulling the chain.

At the close of 1916, when the A.A.A. championship list was

published, Rick stood third with a total of 2,910 points. In three
years, he had skyrocketed to that point from twenty-seventh place.
His total winnings in 1916, after all expenses, salaries, and per-
centages were paid, amounted to almost $40,000. Yes, he was
drinking the rich milk of contentment; and yet it had a trace of
bitterness, in his failure to come within reach of victory at the Indianapolis after six successive years of trying. He did not mind
missing out on the money, but the Memorial Day event was to him
not only the peak of the racing year but also a milestone in the
forward march of automotive engineering.

He had a feeling, which the years have confirmed, that the five-
hundred-miler would give birth to a great industry. He was really
underestimating its productive value, for with the coming of age
of the automobile in America the assembly lines of the vast automotive industry sent out millions of cars, to which the oil and rubber
industries contributed, and nation-wide highway construction resulted.

Rick kept his own counsel about his trip to England to join the
Sunbeam people. He stopped in Columbus to say goodbye to his
mother, went to Washington to get his passport, and, on December
15, boarded the liner *St. Louis* for England.

The black thunderheads of war were creeping across the Atlantic
as the year 1916 drew toward its end. The United States, although
still neutral, was approaching the day of decision to enter the conflict. Meanwhile, German U-boat commanders halted its ships and
scrutinized their cargoes, and English sea patrols searched them and
questioned their officers. "Neutral" German sympathizers in the
United States asserted that England's interference with American
shipping and mails was illegal. The English, on the other hand,
realistically maintained that strict measures were necessary for their
own safety and preservation.

Therefore, as the *St. Louis* steamed over the bleak winter route
to Europe, its passengers wondered just what sort of adventure they
might run into. The passengers were very few, but among those who
hoped that U-boats would leave the *St. Louis* alone were Major
William Thaw and two other American pilots in the famous La-

fayette Escadrille. As active belligerents, these flying fighters ran
grave risk of arrest by any submarine commander who might board
the *St. Louis* and inspect its passenger list. Major Thaw and Eddie
Rickenbacker found a common interest in speed and engines; and
now, for the first time, Rick felt an interest in both the war and
aviation. In a way, he envied the Lafayette Escadrille pilots their
stunning blue uniforms of the French Foreign Legion, their thrilling
existence; but racing cars were still the center of his life. Thaw
hinted that he could do worse than join up with the Escadrille, and
Rick answered that he would think the matter over. Debating the
issue with himself, he decided it would be best to remain neutral as
long as Uncle Sam continued to straddle the fence.

Even as Rick sought the company of Thaw and his fellow
pilots, two middle-aged prosperous businessmen tried to cultivate
an acquaintance with him. One was named Immermann, the other
Goodyear; and both were in the wheat business in Chicago. Immermann complained about the trouble his German name had made
him in getting a British visa on his passport. Rick reported similar
trouble—he had been told in Washington that the name Rickenbacker might expose him to spy hunters in England—but laughed it
off. However, unguarded words showed pro-German tendencies in
Immermann and Goodyear; and he began to suspect them of being
not exactly what they seemed to be. They were very curious about
him, and always tried to get him to talk about himself. Rick found
this rather tiring but did not let it spoil his first ocean journey, which
ended in Liverpool several days before Christmas. As the ship entered
port, the usual officials came aboard and took their places at tables
in the ship's salon, and all the passengers stood in line to have their
papers approved—all except Goodyear and Immermann. They had
vanished completely. Rick submitted his passport to a choleric-
looking official with bleary slate-blue eyes and a droopy mustache
who looked at it and then looked at Rick.

"What's your name?" he bellowed.

"Rickenbacker," answered Eddie, disgusted. "It's right there!
You can read it on the passport if you don't believe me!"

"I can read all right," roared the official; "but you can't always
believe what you read on a passport these days."

"But I'm an American citizen!"

"We'll find out about that, *Herr* Baron von Rickenbacker. I'll bet a farthing that you're a ruddy German spy. . . . Here, Sergeant Wallace!"

"Aye, sir," answered a long-nosed, heavy-set six-footer who had a bowler on his head and shoes with bunion blisters on his large flat feet. "Come with me," he commanded Rick, and led him, seething, to a room on A deck. At a knock a voice answered, "Come in!" and they entered a cabin to find Immermann and Goodyear.

"So they got you too," laughed Rick.

"No, my friend," replied Goodyear, "but we got you! So you're an American, Herr Rickenbacker. Born in Columbus, you say. Well, my friend and I are Scotland Yard inspectors, and we've picked you out for what you are—a German spy trying to sneak into England from a neutral country."

"We catch you fellows all the time!" cut in Immermann. "You might as well own up. You'll be executed anyway, but it saves a lot of trouble."

Rick realized that he was in a serious jam. He argued. He gave his whole life history. But the two Scotland Yard men looked at him with flat, unfriendly eyes.

"We know that song by heart," said Goodyear.

"But, if I were a German spy, would I call attention to myself by using a name like Rickenbacker?"

"Certainly! You Germans are all sold on this deep-thinking stuff. And this flagrant use of your German name is part of the plan to curb our suspicions."

"Right you are," chimed in Immermann. "But we can play the same game. You don't think that my name is what you think it is, eh, Baron von Rickenbacker?"

"Where do you get that Baron stuff?"

"Out of the dossier we got from London. Oh, they know you in London, they do. The Wild Teuton, the Happy Heinie, the Baron, the Daredevil Dutchman—we have it all here—posing as a racing driver to establish an innocent identity."

"Smart enough at that," conceded Goodyear.

"But not smart enough for Scotland Yard," triumphed Immermann.

"Oh-h-h!" groaned Rick. And he tried to explain the love of

American sports writers for nicknames. He made no impression whatever upon the inspectors. Presently Goodyear cut off further argument by banging the table and shouting to the policeman.

"Come on, sergeant—let's be going to work."

They stripped their suspect to the hide. They rubbed lemon juice and other acids on his skin to bring out any secret writing. They searched his pockets and ripped the seams of his clothing. They probed the soles and heels of his shoes. They questioned him by the hour. They sifted his baggage through a fine mesh. They gave him no access to his fellow passengers and would not permit him to get in touch with Louis Coatalen at the Sunbeam works. At long last, when all the passengers had left the ship, they told him he would have to remain aboard the *St. Louis* until sailing time and would not be permitted to set foot on English soil.

Rick protested against this ruling.

Sergeant Wallace took a deep puff on his pipe and drawled: "It's better than a cell in the Tower of London, eh?"

That floored Rick. The next few days went slowly, and Christmas promised to be mighty bleak. Goodyear and Immermann, who were regularly assigned to the *St. Louis* to scan its passengers for spies and had caught quite a few, also remained aboard. On Christmas Eve, with the aid of the ship's captain, Rick talked the two inspectors into letting him spend that night and Christmas Day in Liverpool at the Adelphi Hotel—provided he would take the Scotland Yard men along and pay their bills. An hour later, he was in a three-room suite at the Adelphi with Immermann and Goodyear. They had dinner in the room, and Eddie tried to get Coatalen on the telephone; but the only man in England who could help him could not be located.

Although it was a raw night with spurts of rain and a well honed wind, Rick decided around nine o'clock to go for a walk. Both the inspectors protested but agreed in the end, and out they went. The streets of Liverpool were empty and dark, except for feeble blue shafts of light at the corners. Stumbling through the murk, Rick and his guards reached the mouth of an ink-black alley—at least that is what he thought it was. Yielding to a sudden impulse, he ducked and ran as fast as he could. Why? He did not know. He

THE RICKENBACKER "HAT-IN-THE-RING" CAR.

EDDIE RICKENBACKER WITH PURSUIT PLANE IN WHICH HE FLEW TO ACEDOM IN THE 94TH SQUADRON
(SHOWS HAT-IN-THE-RING INSIGNIA), FRANCE, WORLD WAR I.

heard the Scotland Yard men yell. They only called once or twice, and he expected them to shoot. But no shot rang out. He put on more speed, only to run full tilt into a solid, unbroken wall. He had run up a blind alley. That was why the detectives had let him go! That was why they had not fired a shot.

For some reason, Rick's guardians took his unsuccessful attempt to escape as a huge joke. They returned to the hotel in good humor, and he provided them with some Christmas cheer. All was well on earth, and there was good will among men, but Goodyear took pains to drag his bed across the only door that led out of the suite—there was no escape by the window.

Santa Claus came to Rick early the next morning in the form of a telephone call from Coatalen. It assured Inspector Goodyear that Rick was a bona fide American and not a German spy. Goodyear replied that he was glad to hear it but had no authority to release *Mr.* Rickenbacker. Thereupon the manufacturer must have pulled some wires, for instructions quickly came from London to release the prisoner. In short order, Rick was on the train. He reached London long after dark. There were no porters at the station, but he finally got a pushcart and took his trunk and bags to a checkroom. Then there was no cab to be had.

It was one of London's foggy nights, blacker than coal. Rick asked directions to the Savoy Hotel and started out only to find that, in the fog, the only way to keep straight was to walk in the gutter and pat the curb now and then. Every time he bumped into a person he would ask for the Savoy Hotel and try to follow the directions.

"You go around this corner—turn here—then you turn again—and go there," said voices in the fog. Hopeless hours of this.

About midnight he bumped into a thin little man. Again he asked: "Do you know where the Savoy Hotel is?"

"Certainly."

"If you'll lead me to it, I'd be glad to pay you whatever you think is fair."

The man said, "Take hold of the tip of my stick, and come along."

As they stumbled through the darkness Rick told his guide that he was a stranger in a strange land, that it was his first visit to England and that he had been trying since nine o'clock to find a place that was supposed to be "just around the corner."

"But it is," exclaimed the Englishman. "Here's the Savoy, right in front of us!"

Rick wanted to reward him, but the man would not take a dime. He said that the fog did not bother him a bit—he was totally blind.

In the hotel, Rick asked for a room, any kind of room.

"Have you registered at the police station?" asked the clerk.

"No, I didn't know I had to."

"Well, we can't give you a room until you do."

Rick was fighting-mad but curbed his temper. "Look, I did not come to England to fight." Then he explained all the trouble he had had, and added: "Unless you give me a porter to take me to the police station and bring me back, I'll lay right down here on the floor and go to sleep, and you can have the cops come here!"

The clerk laughed and rang for a porter who took Rick to the police station. He registered, was fingerprinted, and returned about four o'clock to the Savoy, where he went to bed. He was awakened at the crack of dawn by airplanes roaring overhead, which proved to be English training planes and not German raiders.

About noon, Coatalen arrived. They decided that Rick should go to Wolverhampton at once to work on the 1917 Sunbeam racing cars, and he went to the plant before dinner. He was immediately captivated by the new design, which promised a fleet-wheeled vehicle able to do one hundred twenty-five miles an hour, not in spurts but in steady, hour-upon-hour driving. It was interesting work transforming this dream car from blueprint to reality, and he would have been thoroughly happy but for the fact that he was under constant observation by Scotland Yard and Military Intelligence operatives. Every morning and every evening he had to report at a police station. Week ends, he would go to London and stay at the Savoy, where his Sunday morning slumbers were always interrupted by planes flying down the Thames from Brooklands Motordrome, which had been changed into an Air Force training school. But it was an alarm clock he learned to like. On hearing the hum of plane engines, he would hop out of bed, rush to the window, watch the formations with eager eyes and decide that perhaps it would not be such a bad idea to join up as a student aviator. Then he would remember Scotland Yard and conclude that any effort he might make to enlist in the Royal Flying Corps would be interpreted as part of an elaborate German spy plot.

At Wolverhampton, where the Sunbeam Company made aircraft engines, Rick got acquainted with pilots who had been over the front. He learned much about airplanes and found that, under the surface, the feeling in England was bitter and pessimistic. The Allies were fighting with their backs to the wall. Only their hope that America would come in and save the situation kept them going. The steadfast and courageous spirit of the British found a response in him. The feeling against Germany and what it stood for—instilled in him by his father, but dormant since childhood—came to the top as an active, conscious force.

Chapter XII

~~~~~~

It was at this time—after a few weeks in England—that a new Eddie was born: Rickenbacker the Crusader. His immediate impulse was to join up then and there, with the Lafayette Escadrille perhaps; for by now he wanted to get into aviation. On further thought, he concluded that it would be better to return to America and take part in the preparedness movement that was rising, but not fast enough. Uncle Sam would join the Allies sooner or later, and Rick wanted to fight under his own flag.

January went its course, and Eddie felt, with greater issues in the balance, he was wasting time working on racing cars. The thunderheads of war now hung in solid masses over the Atlantic. On February 1, 1917, a friend in the American Embassy warned him to pack up and return to America.

"Germany has just issued notice," the friend said, "that it will sink all merchant vessels, enemy or neutral, in British waters. There is a five-day period of grace for Americans to get out of England before the submarines start torpedoing on sight."

Virtually every American in England and France sought to go back home, and steamer space was at a premium. Eddie tried to find any kind of accommodation. No luck. The five days of grace ticked off. On the last day, a telephone call came from Liverpool. It was the captain of the *St. Louis*: Was it true that the *Herr* Baron von Rickenbacker was going home to be the Crown Prince of America? The captain was sailing that evening and had a bunk for him if he could make it. Did he want it? Eddie most certainly did. All right, get aboard the *St. Louis* and see the purser, said the captain.

That afternoon, a Sunbeam racing car with Eddie at the wheel and Coatalen as mechanic and navigator made a record-breaking run from Wolverhampton to Liverpool. Not once did the needle on the speedometer go below sixty, and most of the time the speed of the car was over eighty miles an hour. They reached Liverpool a good hour before sailing time.

As Eddie walked toward the gangplank, a heavy hand fell on his shoulder. He looked around, and there was Sergeant Wallace who had searched him on his arrival.

"Aha, so it's you again," he said in a strong nasal Liverpool water-front accent.

"Holy Moses," exclaimed Eddie, "you here!"

"Aye, that I am. And you won't be going aboard until we've had a good look at your baggage."

"Well, let's get at it then."

"Don't be impudent, my man," drawled the sergeant. "It won't be quite as easy as that, you know. There's always the Tower of London for the likes of you."

He made a thorough search of Eddie's baggage and person. Finally, he told him that he might go aboard with his personal baggage, but that all books and papers, including Sunbeam drawings and specifications, would have to remain in England. Having no choice, Eddie gave them to Coatalen. Boarding the ship, he was hailed by a steward: "Are you Mr. Rickenbacker? . . . Very well, sir, you are to go to Cabin A at once. I'll show you the way."

In the cabin, there were the same two Scotland Yard men. They greeted Eddie cordially, but that did not change their procedure one whit. After an ordeal lasting almost three hours, which delayed the sailing of the ship, they finally told him that they had nothing to hold him on.

Worn to a frazzle, Eddie left the cabin and entered the ship's main salon. There sat Gene Buck in a big chair next to a small table, drinking tea and eating dainty sandwiches. Eddie, who knew Buck rather well, scooped up the sandwiches, stuffed them in his mouth and gulped them down.

"Why don't you eat the plate, too, Eddie?" laughed Buck. "Stick around. There's going to be some excitement. There's a dangerous German spy aboard, and I hear that they've got him down in Cabin A. They'll probably shoot him."

"Yeah, I know all about it. That dangerous German spy is me. When the firing squad comes, tell the boys I've gone to bed."

Eddie remained in New York about ten days, then started westward, stopping over in various cities. Wherever he went, he preached that America would soon be in the war with all its resources of men, money, and munitions. He had always made it a point to be friendly with newspapermen, from owners down to space writers. Now, in his new role of crusader, he used these wide connections to give out interviews and to prompt editorials on America's duty to come to the rescue of the nearly defeated Allies in Europe. Journeying slowly across the country, he noticed, at each stop, a vaguely familiar face. It was a tall, thin, very blond man with a military bearing, who might be Scandinavian, German, or English, but hardly American.

Eddie pulled into Los Angeles at the very time when the news exploded of Germany's offering California to Mexico in return for joining in the fight against the Allies. This news put him on the front and editorial pages of newspapers up and down the Pacific coast. One day, he was in the lobby of the Alexandria Hotel with Van Hoven when the tall, thin blond man came up and was about to speak.

Eddie cut in: "Well, when is Scotland Yard and British Army Intelligence going to find out that I am not the Crown Prince of America? You've been following me, haven't you?"

"Quite, old boy," said the stranger. "However, I was just about to tell you that I have reported to my government that your German name means nothing; that you are exactly what you appear to be: a loyal patriotic American citizen, with decidedly anti-German bearings."

"Thanks," replied Eddie. "I am grateful for the bill of health. I hope you have enjoyed trailing me?"

The Englishman gave a broad wink: "Really, old chap, it's been wonderful seeing America and all that—there's really something in a name, what?"

"Yeah," Eddie laughed. "Come and join me with Van Hoven and Priscilla Dean at lunch, and I'll tell you about Alec Sloan, who warned me that Rickenbacker was too long a name to stick in anybody's mind."

One project Eddie had worked on across the country was the

recruiting of a corps of flyers in the United States Army, somewhat along the lines of the Lafayette Escadrille, from automobile racing drivers, riding mechanics, and pitmen. He had first put the plan forward in New York a few days after his return from England, and the *New York Times* of February 18 presented his idea in an interview under the two-column headline, "Flying Corps of Daring Racing Drivers Plan If War Comes," stating:

War would put a damper on automobile racing for the coming season. There is a movement among racing drivers and their mechanicians to enter the flying corps of the United States Army if this country should be drawn into the war. Eddie Rickenbacker, who recently returned from a two months' stay in England, where he found that aviation had enlisted the services of many men formerly connected with motoring, is the sponsor of the plan. Rickenbacker said:

"If war is declared I will enlist at once for aviation work. I have already had some experience. I leave for the West tomorrow, where I shall see many of the boys and at once put the matter up to them. I think many of them are looking at it just as I do. War would practically put a stop to racing and we have a training that our country would need in time of war. We are experts in judging speed and in motor knowledge. This is also true of the mechanicians, and I am sure we could all quickly qualify for aviation work. I expect to get up a body of not less than fifty of us who will volunteer if war is declared."

One of the things that struck Rickenbacker forcibly was Uncle Sam's utter lack of aerial preparedness. In the early spring of 1917, the Army had fewer than half a hundred planes, fewer than three dozen pilots and fewer than a thousand mechanics and other troops in the flying section of the Signal Corps. The United States had to start from the very bottom in building aircraft plants, constructing planes, and training air and ground crews.

On his tour around the country, Eddie won promises to enlist in his proposed unit not only from such outstanding racing drivers as Ralph De Palma, Earl Cooper, Eddie Pullen, Ray Harroun, and Ralph Mulford, but also from many famous exhibition flyers including Deloyd Thompson and Art Smith. The group was to be known as the Aero Reserves of America.

Full of enthusiasm, he brought his plan to the government. He

was referred to Captain Walter G. Kilner, commander of the Army
Aviation School at Mineola, Long Island. Captain Kilner listened
politely and referred him to Brigadier General George O. Squier in
Washington, head of the Signal Corps. General Squier greeted him
pleasantly enough and turned him over to several officers. To them
in succession Eddie expounded his idea that racing drivers, with
their knowledge of engines and high-precision speed, would make
above-average flyers. Although William Jennings Bryan had recently
said that every cab driver was a potential combat flyer, the Signal
Corps officers turned Rickenbacker down flatly and definitely. They
believed that knowledge of engines and speed might be a handicap
in a pilot rather than an asset, causing fear instead of confidence.

Failing in his first effort, Eddie tried to enlist for flying training
on his own hook.

How old was he? . . . Twenty-six and a half! Rather old!

What was his education?

Six and a half public-school grades and the International Correspondence School course on automotive engineering.

No college training whatever?

None! But he knew all about motors, he was an expert at judging speed and distance and had instantaneous mental and muscular
coordination.

Sorry! Application denied on grounds of inadequate experience
and education.

Eddie was thoroughly defeated. He had run his race for a cause
he believed in deeply, and he had lost. As a realist who never
groused over water that had gone over the dam, he did not sulk or
brood when aviation turned him down. He went back to his old
love, the racing car, until the day when something else might turn
up. Eddie the Strategist had a hunch that some day soon lightning
from the thunderheads of war would strike in his direction, and he
wanted to be ready. That he might be hurt was completely beyond
his consideration.

Restrictions dictated by war made it impossible to ship the Sunbeam cars out of England as planned, and the Indianapolis five-
hundred-miler was canceled soon after the declaration of war in

April; but Edide made a deal to drive a Mercedes at the Memorial
Day race on the new Shelbyville Track near Cincinnati.

On the evening of May 23, he came into his hotel from the race
track after a long day of trying to learn the characteristics and
moods of the Mercedes. He was told that Major Burgess Lewis of
the Army General Staff had been trying to reach him by phone.
Would he please call the major at once at Governors Island, New
York. When Eddie got his call through, Major Lewis asked:

"How would you like to go to Europe on a secret sailing as a
driver on General Pershing's staff?"

"I don't know, but I think I'm all for it! Let me chew it over.
Call me back tomorrow morning about seven o'clock."

When Lewis telephoned the next day, Eddie answered that he
would like to go but needed ten days to drive the race and wind
up his private affairs.

"Let me put it this way," cut in Lewis, "If you are not in my
office at Governors Island tomorrow morning, you don't go!"

"O.K.," laughed Eddie. "You've talked me into it. I'll be
there!"

Dropping everything, he took a train to Columbus and spent
an hour with his mother. He told her that he was on his way to
New York but not that he was going to enter the Army and sail
for Europe.

On the train, Eddie began to worry. What if they should discover that blind spot in his eye? He decided to take a chance and
say nothing. He passed the Army physical examination with ease,
put on the uniform of a sergeant, and sailed presently aboard the
old *Baltic*. On the ship were General Pershing and his staff, the first
contingent of the A.E.F. to sail for France.

The accommodations aboard the *Baltic* for buck sergeants were
far from luxurious. With other soldiers, he was sardined into the
very bowels of the ship. The food was cold, the quarters dank and
dark and stifling-hot. Eddie complained to a top sergeant who had
space in a pleasant second-class cabin on an upper deck.

"Get yourself another rocker or two," said the top kick, "and
you'll travel in style like me!"

"Who'll I get it from?" asked Eddie.

"Search me, soldier. From Black Jack himself—if you can."

Eddie knew that he would not have a chance that high, but he learned that Major Dodd was aboard. Without asking permission, he barged into the major's office-cabin, introduced himself as the man who had fixed the engine of his plane in California, and stated his case. Dodd grinned.

"Don't you know, sergeant, that in the Army promotions come only through meritorious service? How do you propose to win the promotion?"

"That's what I brought you along for, major. You know that I'm Johnny-on-the-spot when it comes to fixing engines."

Both roared. The next day Rick was a staff sergeant, entitled to a second-class berth.

As the *Baltic* steamed toward Europe, General Pershing and his staff spent endless hours working on the strategy and tactics that would carry them to victory.

In his narrow cabin behind a tightly sealed and thoroughly blacked-out porthole, Eddie the Strategist was planning the campaign that would carry him to his private objective—aviation; for he had not the slightest intention to drive staff cars in France for General Pershing or anybody else longer than he had to. In France, he thought, far from the rigid requirements of Washington, he might work his way into the Air Service and, eventually, win his wings. That was why, on a moment's decision, he had thrown all his racing plans to the winds. That was why, although a leading contender for the 1917 racing championship, he had been willing to become an obscure Army chauffeur.

Book Four

World War I

ACE OF ARMY FALCONS
1917–1919

Chapter XIII

~~~~~~

One morning, life in the corridors and cargo holds of the *Baltic* began to pulse rather early. Land had been sighted in the night, and now a long ragged coast line lay ahead. At first, the soldiers thought they were looking at the shores of France. But soon word got around that they were heading into the Irish Sea for Liverpool.

This time the Scotland Yard men were not on hand—which amused Eddie as he recalled his previous visits to Liverpool. However, learning that long-nosed, flat-footed Police Sergeant Wallace was on duty in the wharf office, he could not resist the temptation to stick his head in and say: "Remember me?"

The sergeant's eyes had the calm indifference of those of a long-dead codfish. He grunted: "Aha, so you're back again, eh?"

"Yeah—and this time my uncle is with me!"

"So." The policeman stepped into the trap. "And is his name *Herr* Rickenbacker, too?"

"No," shouted Eddie gleefully, "his name is Uncle Sam."

"Better be careful," growled the sergeant, "or you will yet wind up in the Tower of London!"

Eddie only slammed the door and galloped back to his unit. However, the prediction proved correct. Eddie, on his arrival in London, was taken to the ancient Tower where so many heads had fallen under the executioner's ax, and was placed in a small room with solid walls and a tiny iron-barred window. There he slept on a straw pallet, with his fellow staff drivers lodged there by military orders. After a few days in London, the unit proceeded to Paris.

The reception to General Pershing and the first contingent of American troops arriving in France was most impressive and soul-stirring but need not be described here. Eddie drove in the procession through the streets of Paris, lined with tens of thousands of men, women, and children who laughed, cried, cheered, prayed, waved the American flag, and shouted: "Vive Pershing! Vive l'Amérique!"

He was present also at the speaking of the most famous phrase in World War I history (so long falsely attributed to General Pershing, who placed the wreath on the tomb of Lafayette) by Lieutenant Colonel Charles E. Stanton, a member of the A.E.F. staff: "Lafayette, we are here!"

General Pershing's first headquarters was at the Crillon Hotel. Almost from the outset, Eddie was assigned as staff driver to Major Dodd. Those were busy days. American aviation had to start from the bottom rung. The French and the British had hoped that the United States, in short order, might produce an air service of thousands of planes and pilots, tens of thousands of mechanics, plus additional thousands of planes and engines for the Allies; but production in the United States grew slowly, and the training of air and ground units took time. So plans were worked out to give American fighter pilots combat training in French pursuit planes and to equip United States Army fighter units ready for combat with French Nieuport fighter planes.

Some steps toward cooperation with the French in air expansion had been made by Colonel William Mitchell, who, as chief of the aviation section in the Army Signal Corps, went to France on a special mission before the United States entered the war. Mitchell had a well coordinated plan prepared, which General Pershing endorsed when he arrived, calling for an extensive A.E.F. aviation training program. It fell to Major Dodd, rushing from one corner of France to another, to choose sites for training fields and visit French aero squadrons at the front for the study of equipment and selection of instructors. Although Eddie hinted broadly that he had joined the Army as a staff driver in the hope it would lead him through the back door into aviation, Major Dodd gave him no encouragement whatever. On the contrary, his attitude was: "Why turn a good driver into a poor aviator?" It was really not a question, but a statement.

Realizing that he had no chance whatever of getting off the road and into the air with Dodd, Eddie turned speculative eyes upon

Colonel Mitchell. But he had been around A.E.F. headquarters long enough to know that Mitchell was highly mercurial and had to be approached just so. Since Army regulations do not prescribe any procedure for sergeants to deal with colonels direct, all he could do was bide his time after Sergeant Blank, his roommate and boon companion, and driver of Colonel Mitchell, refused to trade jobs because he liked his job too well.

Eddie the Strategist was stumped; but Lady Luck came to his rescue on a bright morning in the early part of July as he was driving Major Dodd's olive-drab Cadillac over the wheel-churned road to Verdun. He had just driven through Epernay when he came upon a big twin-six Army Packard pulled up beside the road. There was only one such car in all France—given to General Pershing's staff by James Hazen Hyde, an American millionaire who lived in Paris— but the only man who used it was Colonel Mitchell.

Dodd ordered Eddie to stop and help if he could. He found Sergeant Blank poking ineffectively under the hood while Colonel Mitchell stood looking over his shoulder, his brow creased with annoyance, and glancing every other second at his wrist watch. Impatience radiated from him like quills from a porcupine. He bristled when Eddie saluted and asked Blank what the trouble was.

"These blankety-blank drivers know nothing about cars," Mitchell growled to Dodd.

It reminded Eddie of that morning long ago when he had been sent out to fix Mr. Firestone's car. He prayed for the same kind of luck. All Flake knew was that the car would not run. Eddie tried to start the engine, but the powerful motor merely popped, spat, pooped and died. It looked to him as if the trouble came from water and dirt in the flow chamber of the carburetor. It was a matter of only a few minutes before he had the chamber cleaned out, and— the engine ran like a charm.

"You seem to know something about automobile engines, sergeant," said Mitchell with a pleased grin (when he was in a genial mood, the sun itself could not radiate more warmth than he).

"He ought to," cut in Dodd. He told the colonel about Eddie's position in private life. "I'm pretty lucky, eh, Billy, to have such a wonderful driver?"

"You mean you *were* lucky you *had* such a driver," snapped Mitchell as he looked at Dodd with cold blue eyes. "Driver!" he said abruptly.

"Yes, sir."

"You drive Major Dodd where he wants to go—and you, Sergeant Rickenbacker, will drive me from now on. Let's go!"

Thus Eddie became staff driver for Colonel Mitchell, who liked high-powered cars and tire-blistering speed no matter how bad the road. The peppery colonel was a constant traveler, always on the go, always in a hurry, always probing into places where he had no right to be. Once, during the siege of Rheims, Eddie drove him into the very heart of the shell-plastered city to confer with some French officials. After the meeting, one of them took him and Eddie down into the famous wine cellars which stretch under certain parts of the city like runways and nests in an anthill. They saw endless rows of wine casks and hundreds of thousands of dust-encrusted bottles in cellar after cellar.

Suddenly their guide said: "Do you know where we are, colonel?"

Mitchell shook his head.

"We are about a quarter of a mile behind the German lines."

"What!" exclaimed Eddie in a hoarse whisper. "Then why don't the Heinies dig down? Or don't they know about this?"

"Oh, they know about it," was the answer, "but the firm that owns these cellars is half French and half German. So there's a gentlemen's agreement not to destroy the wine supply or ruin the cellars."

It was late in the afternoon when the small party climbed out of the wine cellars. As they passed the battered cathedral, Colonel Mitchell decided he wanted to see it, and entered the great edifice. It was ruined by repeated shelling; the roof was gone, and there was a brand-new hole in the floor, made by a six-inch shell, a dud that a priest had just dug out.

"Do they shell you often?" asked the colonel.

"Every afternoon at five o'clock, messieurs," said the priest.

"Every afternoon," repeated Mitchell as he looked at his wrist watch.

"At five o'clock," added Eddie as he glanced at his.

"Oui, oui. And you can set your watch by it."

"Hadn't we better get going, colonel?" cut in Eddie. "It is one minute to five."

Mitchell nodded. The car was barely under way when the first shell came screaming over. Others followed. Eddie stepped on the gas with a heavy foot and was well out of Rheims before the barrage really got under way.

His opportunity to plead admission to the Air Service for training came one day on the return to Paris from Issoudun, which had been selected for the United States Air Combat School for Perfection Training in Pursuit Tactics. Here the cream of American youth was to come from preliminary flying schools in the United States and France for training before getting a course in gunnery and going to the front. On that summer day, the great Perfection School at Issoudun was still a dream. It was only a broad and bare expanse of land. However, leveling it off for flying was to start soon, and plans were under way for railroad tracks, sidings, barracks, hangars, and machine shops.

On this occasion Eddie was driving Mitchell in a fast French car he had "borrowed" for him. It was the Renault that had won one of the great road races just before the war broke out. Next to flying, Mitchell loved fast and flashy cars. He had the idea that Eddie had obtained the French racing car to please him. Well, perhaps he had. But, at the same time, Eddie saw his chance to extend his knowledge of automobiles, all toward the day when he would build the Great American Car.

As they sped over the smooth road to Paris, Eddie said to Mitchell, who sat in a bucket seat at his side:

"What do you think my chances are of getting into aviation, colonel?"

"Oh, I'd say that they are almost next to nothing. Dodd told me about you and your ambitions to fly. Forget them, Eddie. Stick to the job you know—driving."

"Yes, sir." Then, after a pause: "Would you mind if I put in for transfer to the Aviation Service?"

"Persistent devil, aren't you? Sure, go ahead! But I'll block you.

When the war is over you'll come home a live driver, and that's better than staying here as a dead aviator."

It was a glumly respectful sergeant who drove into Paris, dropped Colonel Mitchell at his headquarters in the Elysées Palace and wove through heavy traffic at high speed to his own barracks at Epernay. There was black fury in his heart toward the one man who could help him get into the Air Service but, deliberately, stood in the way for reasons that appeared selfish. Other men could drive staff cars as well as he. As he entered the barracks, he found Sergeant Blank prowling through his stuff.

"Just looking for some writing paper, Rick."

"Sure, help yourself," answered Eddie.

Something about Blank's attitude puzzled him and made him think back. Always asking questions. Always nosing around. Could he be a spy? Nonsense! But maybe a spy hunter with Rick as his quarry? Also nonsense. But then he thought of Bill Nye, high in the United States Secret Service, who was in Paris. Nye was a great auto racing enthusiast, and Eddie had formed a friendship with him back home before the war.

As soon as he could, he called on Nye and placed the whole spy story before him, from the time of his arrival on the *St. Louis* in Liverpool. Checking into the matter, Nye found that Army Counter-Spy Intelligence actually had Eddie on its books as a man to be watched. The informer had been a Police Sergeant Wallace in Liverpool. Sure enough, Blank was a counter spy. From that time on Eddie, out of sheer orneriness, ran the poor driver-detective ragged. With a curdled sense of humor he concocted plots and situations that kept the man alert and on the move day and night. Soon, Blank was replaced by other spy-hunters but it was easy to spot them.

Eddie reported his spy status to Colonel Mitchell, who regarded it as a huge joke. By this time, well toward the middle of August, a warm friendship had sprung up between the two men, on the solid foundation of mutual respect.

One day they were coming up from Tours in a new Hudson Super-Six when a bearing burned out on the main street of Vendôme and the engine gave up the ghost. They walked to the one garage in town only to learn that it had no bearings in stock.

As Mitchell began to berate all cars and drivers, Eddie asked the garageman if he had any Babbitt metal. Yes, and he had a blowtorch. Mitchell watched with speechless fascination while Eddie made a rough mold out of sand and water, melted the metal in the flame of the blowtorch, poured it into the mold, and cast a bearing. It was a crude bit of casting, but Eddie trimmed the black metal ball down to the proper size and filed it smooth. He put it in the place of the burned-out bearing, and before dark the Hudson was rolling toward Paris once more.

For a long time, on the way to Paris, Mitchell sat silent; then he cleared his throat and said: "I didn't know you were such a good mechanic, Eddie. I guess a man who is resourceful enough to make his own bearings might make a good airman."

Eddie's heart began to pound a little faster.

"Wouldn't surprise me at all," continued Mitchell, "if something happened to that application of yours for transfer into the Air Service."

What little space there was between the accelerator pedal and the floorboard vanished entirely as Eddie's joy went to his feet and the big car seemed to take wing.

A day or two after this incident, Eddie was marking time outside Signal Corps headquarters when a snappy-looking young officer with wings on his tunic came up to the car. It was Captain James Miller of the First Aero Squadron.

"Hi, Rick!" he shouted. "Fancy meeting you here!" He slapped the sergeant on the back.

"Hi, yourself, captain," grinned Eddie, delighted to see an old friend. "Where have you been, and what are you doing?"

"One thing at a time, boy," answered Miller. "I've just come from Billy Mitchell. He ordered me to Issoudun to build the new flying school they're putting up there. I'll need an engineering officer, and you're just the fellow I'm looking for!"

"Says who?"

"Says Mitchell!"

"Well, I don't know," parried Eddie. "I don't know anything about flying, Jim."

"But you can learn, can't you?"

"Learn? Who? Me! Quit kidding me! It means too much to me. I came over here to get into flying, but I don't stand a chance."

"And why not?"

"Well—for one thing, to come down to brass tacks, I haven't got enough education."

"Don't worry about that, young feller," said Miller gayly. "Billy Mitchell will take care of that. You go and report to Doc Grow for your physical examination, and we'll start pushing papers around to get your orders through."

On the way to Dr. Grow's office, Eddie began to sweat with apprehension. His old eye deficiency, the dancing spot before his vision, arose to haunt him. But he passed the eye test without trouble.

"Colonel Mitchell spoke to me about your case, Rickenbacker," said the medico. "I notice that you made a mistake on your application blank with respect to the year of your birth. See?"

Eddie looked at the form. It gave October 8, 1890, the right date of his birth.

Dr. Grow continued: "That would make you twenty-six years old, and twenty-five is the age-limit for pilots." He winked as he changed the date to 1892. "That'll fix it."

Eddie was released from duty as a staff driver. He received his commission early in August and on the 25th of that month he was ordered to Tours to enter the Primary Flying School. He looked very tall and straight and proud as he paid his final visit to Signal Corps headquarters. He wore the best tailored tunic in all Paris, the best cut riding breeches, and the best polished boots. His overseas cap rode precariously on his left ear; and on his shoulders, golden as the autumn sun, were the shining bars of a brand-new second lieutenant. That day, his life was full to overflowing. There was just one empty spot: the place over his breast pocket where a pair of wings would soon find roost.

On the evening of September 1, Eddie wrote to his mother from Tours that he had started flying training that day. Knowing that she would worry about his going into aviation, he added that planes were much safer than racing cars because there was lots of room in the sky and no fences to run into.

In getting the feel of an airplane, Eddie had the troubles other students have. He began by controlling stick and rudder too strongly, so that, if he had had his way, he would have landed either fifty feet over or fifty feet under the ground. But the record shows that after seventeen days at the school and only twenty-five hours of flying training—including cross-country and basic combat acrobatics—Edward Rickenbacker won his wings and also promotion to first lieutenant.

As Eddie left Tours for the Precision Training School at Issoudun he preened his mental wings as he dreamt of becoming a soaring combat Falcon. That dream was to be realized in time, but first he was to wallow for many weary months in the mire of Issoudun, not as a Falcon but much like the soul mate of a mud hen.

The fall rains came early and often that September of 1917. When Eddie arrived at Issoudun, the field was a huge expanse of mud. Buildings were going up, but only a few constructors' shacks and the huts occupied by officers and men had floors to keep out the ooze, walls to keep out the wind, and roofs to keep out the rain.

Captain Miller, as engineering officer, had an unlimited bank account to buy anything he needed. But Eddie soon discovered that the trick was to find out what he needed and, harder yet, to find what he wanted, at any price. The first contingent of precision students was to arrive about November 1. Eddie's first task was to buy millions of dollars' worth of airplanes. Old stuff, discarded by the French, was all he could get. More millions went into machine tools, parts, and other equipment. Mechanics had to be brought in and organized.

All things came in a thin trickle, excepting the rain, which came in torrents. The story goes that the weather was so bad at Issoudun that the ducks not only ceased flying, because of poor visibility, but also stopped walking, because of the mud. Still the work went on.

About this time Eddie received a helpful letter from his mother. She expressed great concern about Eddie soaring around in the sky in airplanes and cautioned him to "fly slowly and close to the ground." This gentle and well meant warning gave Eddie a moist laugh that did him a great deal of good.

In October, Captain Miller was shifted to another command.

His place was taken by Captain Carl A. Spaatz—Toohey Spaatz who, a quarter of a century later, was to be Uncle Sam's Boss Bird-man against the Germans under General Eisenhower. If the spy-hunting police sergeant in Liverpool had come to Issoudun at that time and read the roster of officers, chances are he would have turned in a five-ply spy alarm. The commanding officer was Herr Spaatz; the engineering officer was Herr Rickenbacker; the adjutant was Herr Widenbach, the assistant adjutant was Herr Tittel and the transportation officer was Herr Spiegel. Since they had more work to do on the ground than they had in the air, they called themselves the Kaiser's Flying Carpenters.

In due time, the first class of potential pursuit pilots arrived from the States, neat and nifty youngsters, full of ambition. They came in tailor-made uniforms, Sam Browne belts, handmade boots and cus-tom-made caps. Most of them were from rich families, fresh out of Harvard, Yale, and Princeton, or at any rate fresh. To Eddie they were a strange breed of cats, for in his automobile and racing days he had wasted little time on college boys. All his contacts had been with men who worked as he did, and he did not understand these young men any more than they understood him.

Whenever he went among the youngsters, he could feel walls of vigorous dislike. He tried to convince himself that he did not care. This effort failed, because it was not true. He did care, but he tried to bury the knowledge under the rough and driving manner of an uncompromising taskmaster. He would show them who was boss! He would put calluses on their hands, blisters on their feet, aches in their backs, and hate in their heads. Let them hate him! What did he care?

These spirited boys, who had come to France to fly and fight as crusaders for Democracy, found themselves, in batches of a dozen, scores, or hundreds, digging ditches, laying hangar floors, construct-ing latrines, making roads, picking up rocks by the bushel from the runways; and they did this back-breaking work under the disdainful eye and lashing tongue of First Lieutenant Rickenbacker. They did not call him that, however; the names they had for Eddie in those days will never run from molten lead into cold type. They hated Rickenbacker, the Hun. They hated all Huns, and that included

Spaatz and Widenbach and Tittel and Spiegel. In the privacy of their windy barracks, the boys swore that their "Hun officers" were German sympathizers, and that the heavy work they had to do was part of a deep German plot to break their morale as well as their backs.

The men who attended that first class at Issoudun passed through a crucible where all the dross was eliminated from the pure gold of gallant manhood. They became the first and finest combat fliers of Uncle Sam in World War I. In time Eddie Rickenbacker was to understand and love these men as brother knights of the flaming skies, even as they were to hold him in warm-hearted esteem; but in that fall of 1917 at Issoudun, Rick, to them, was a hateful answer to the Kaiser's prayers.

At long last, construction jobs were completed; the runways were ready; and flying classes got under way. Since Rick had enrolled in that first student group on the day he arrived, he was Number One on the list; but actually, he was not even at the foot of the class. His duties as engineering officer demanded some fourteen hours a day of continuous labor in hangars and machine shops. Hence, he was not able to take advantage of the regular periods of flying practice and classroom instruction. Instead he would listen when he could to the French instructors, and would jump into a plane and "perfect" himself whenever he had a few minutes. In this way he passed through the various stages of training until he came to "stunt" work in the small Nieuport scout. This was not as easy as it sounds. To be sure, he had watched the instructors' attempts to show the students how to do a perfect tail spin. He also looked on as embryo fighter pilots tried the vrille, and some of those spins had fatal endings.

Having made up his mind to do a tail spin or die in trying, Rick started out one afternoon on his own. For fear of being seen by instructors and ordered down, he flew some twenty-five miles north of the aerodrome to a large wooded area. There, at an altitude of ten thousand feet, he tried to whip up courage to pull the plane into a stall, cross his controls, and slide off into a spin. For about thirty solid minutes, he sailed along, shut his motor at different intervals, pulled up to the stalling point, got cold feet, straightened out, and opened up his motor again. Finally he headed home, a failure in his own estimation. He hated himself and he felt more alone that night than ever in his life before. Throughout the night, his failures worried him. Before he went to sleep, he decided to spin after his day's work was done the next afternoon.

On arriving over the same spot the next day, Rick followed the previous day's pattern of indecision for about fifteen minutes. Then angrily he pulled the ship into a stall and crossed his controls. He fell off into a spin and made a complete circle; but, as he swirled about, Rick decided that the age-old proverb "One good turn deserves another" does not apply to tail spins. Straightening out, he started for home satisfied with his progress. As the days went along, he added a turn a day until a tail spin meant no more to him than taking a speedway curve at breakneck clip.

After the spin came the loop, or rather an attempt to loop. After a long dive, Rick stuck the plane up into a zoom, with the control stick in his lap. But he failed to shut off his motor at the critical point in going on his back. The result was, with motor wide open and the stick back in neutral position, he flew upside down until tools and loose equipment rained past his head out of the cockpit. This brought him to attention. He shut off his motor and returned to normal. That was his first try at looping. Other tries followed and soon he was able to loop with the best of them.

Shortly before Christmas, Rick handed the students the finest present they could hope to get; namely, a hearty laugh at his own expense. On a Sunday afternoon, the school's rather formidable football talent was staging a game on the field. Nearly all the high-ranking officers of the A.E.F. came down from Paris to see it, and many prominent French and English officers went along as their guests.

In the middle of the game, Rick came hedge-hopping in a Nieuport from Tours. Thinking what he did about "college boys" and "A" letter-men, he decided it would be fun to break up the game. As he roared over the field, he hauled his ship up to almost five hundred feet, did some spins and rolls, zoomed up, came down in a loop, the bottom of which almost went through a goal post. Next he coursed up and down the improvised stadium and drove players and spectators off on the double-quick. On landing he was ordered to report to (now) Major Spaatz. That day the daredevil pilot almost lost his commission. Any other man would have lost it, but Lieutenant Rickenbacker was so valuable as an engineering officer that the major decided not to "break" him. He was lucky to escape with a thirty-day grounding and a strong dressing-down.

Thirty days when he could not fly—thirty days lost in his struggle for combat training! The sentence almost broke Rick's heart. Thirty days of humiliation for that Heinie taskmaster whose many and hated names shall be unprintable—Major Spaatz had clipped his wings. The students almost died laughing.

But everything comes to an end. A laugh! A course at Issoudun! On January 15, 1918, the students thumbed their noses at Rick as they left for the School of Aerial Gunnery at Cazeaux. But Rick, in Dutch—Student Number One of Class Number One—remained as engineering officer with his wings, if not snipped off, at least so confined that they were useless.

The moment departure orders were posted and Rick discovered that his name was not on the Gunnery School list, he called on Major Spaatz. Eddie asked if the omission was due to an oversight. No, it was not. Was it because he had dusted the football field with his Nieuport? No, the reason was that, as an engineering officer, the lieutenant was too valuable to be spared. Eddie protested that his assistant was just as able in that job, but Spaatz was adamant. The answer was, No!

This sat pretty hard on Rick. He had joined the Army to get into combat aviation. He had learned to fly and mastered the basic principles of fighter technique. And now, just as he had a good start toward the aerial front, he was doomed to play nursemaid to a bunch of training planes in a school for fighters. Or was he? Out of the blue, Eddie the Strategist came down in a power dive loaded with a red-hot idea. Acting on it without delay, Lieutenant Rickenbacker went over to the post hospital and called on Captain Goldwaithe, the post surgeon. He said that he wanted two weeks of hospitalization, first because he felt run down, on the verge of flu (the medico took his temperature and found it in the red) and secondly because his absence in the hospital would give his assistant a chance to show his mettle. Then he revealed to Captain Gold-waithe that it was all part of a plan to show Major Spaatz that he was not irreplaceable as an engineering officer.

The next two weeks Rick spent as a patient in the hospital while his assistant did a bang-up job. When he was released from the hospital he went straight to the commanding officer for a showdown. After cooling his heels some ten minutes, he was called in. Spaatz acknowledged his salute sternly and handed him a piece of paper, which Rick read twice. He literally tingled with joy. It was an order directing him to proceed to the Gunnery School at Cazeaux. A slow smile melted the frost on Toohey Spaatz's craggy features as he said :

"I'm onto your game, Rick! If you feel that badly about going, I don't want you around here."

"Thanks, Toohey, and goodbye," shouted Rick as he barged out of the door, breaking the panel as he went.

At Gunnery School, Rick was no record breaker; and there was no reason why he should be. The fact that he took to airplane pilot-ing quickly is explained by his long knowledge of engines and their moods, plus his extensive training in coordination of mind and muscles while in swift motion. In shooting, Rick's only experience was a hunting trip out of Tucson, on which he had fired a shotgun at a rabbit and gone head over heels doing it; but he tackled the gunnery course with grim earnestness. Eventually he managed to hit stationary and moving targets with rifle and shotgun, and scored a fair degree of accuracy.

Next came aerial machine gunnery, a phase in which many of the students won the tragic *croix de bois* (the wooden cross over a new grave) by crashing after going into a spin or stall too close to the ground.

Rick came near scoring his first victory at the Gunnery School by shooting down two French pilots. They were aboard an old Caudron towing at the end of a three-hundred-foot rope a cloth cone which he used as a target on his first aerial machine-gun lesson. There were a hundred rounds of ammunition in the Lewis machine gun mounted on the wing top of his plane. According to plan, he dived on the target and blasted away. His bullets were gone in the twinkling of an eye—and so was the target. Almost instantly there was not any target plane either. The old Caudron was diving for safety as if Richthofen and not Rickenbacker had it in his gun sights. When he landed, two irate French pilots came sputtering up to Rick, waving hands, popping eyes, shrugging shoulders, shaking heads, and spraying words.

At last one of them, in broken English, said as he pointed at the collapsed target cone lying some distance off on the ground : "It is zat which you should shoot at, and not zis sheep—for I am ze pilote! You shoot apart the target rope ten feet behind my sheep. You almost keel me!"

Rick, red-faced and unhappy, stammered his apologies, and the pilots, mollified and forgiving, returned to their towing job—but with a five-hundred-foot rope between the target and the "sheep."

The gunnery course lasted some three weeks. When it ended, Rick went to Paris and called on Colonel Mitchell to report his progress, hoping to expedite his orders for the front. Paris, at that time, was agog with rumors about the impending American miracle of aviation production. Twenty thousand of the greatest planes ever built—so the story went—would soon blot out the sun over Germany and Austria. Just wait until April. Not only planes from America, but hard-hitting, quick-firing machine guns, great bombs, and other paraphernalia were on the way to insure Allied air supremacy immediately and forever. Rick took these rumors with a grain of salt and a few beers or cocktails. By this time he had established a new set of habits that suited the circumstances of war. To find relaxation, he joined the merry-making night patrol of the boulevards; he crammed his evenings with shows and parties; he took up smoking and went in for beer, wine, and cocktails.

At the age of twenty-seven, Rick sowed his wild oats, but on a strictly rationed and regulated basis. In switching from strict tee-totaler to gentle drinker, he decided that action over the front and alcohol do not mix any more than oil and water make a blend. He made it an iron rule never to take any kind of alcoholic drink, even beer, at any combat base to which he might be assigned. His drinking was done while on leave and stopped a full twenty-four hours before he returned to duty.

Rick marked time in Paris some two weeks before he was ordered to join the 94th Pursuit Squadron. He bade farewell to Paris on March 4 and headed gayly for the war.

But the time had not yet come when he was to join the gallant fighters of the air. The 94th and the 95th together were receiving advanced combat training at Villeneuve, some twenty miles behind the lines. Major John Huffer was in command of the 94th, while Captain Miller, Rick's first commanding officer at Issoudun, headed the 95th. The pilots in the squadron were mainly the same flock of students who had been spurred and lashed by Rick at Issoudun, and their attitude toward him was one of hostile indifference. On his arrival, Lieutenant Rickenbacker was put into Flight One under Captain James Norman Hall, who had won fame in the Lafayette Escadrille. Rick was given a brand-new "baby" Nieuport, a tiny one-seater fighter, fast for its day. The squadron consisted of some twenty planes and pilots, plus about two hundred enlisted mechanics. This meant that each plane had a permanent crew of three men.

None of the new pilots in the 94th had been in combat or even near the lines, up to that time. To be sure, soon after the squadrons moved in, a French pursuit pilot came over from a near-by French squadron with orders to escort the new flyers on trial combat flights. He took two of the men on a mission but had barely climbed aloft when he noticed that the Americans had no machine guns on their planes. Abruptly landing, he left his charges taxiing on the field, took off in a mad rush, and never came back. Strange as it may seem, Uncle Sam's two new fighter squadrons had neither guns nor flying instruments—none of the tools of war. America was not producing as rapidly as had been hoped, and in equipment France and England were close to the bottom of the barrel.

On Rick's first night at the 94th, Captain Miller invited him over to the 95th for dinner. There he met a man whose influence on his combat career, although brief, was to be overwhelming: Major Raoul Lufbery, whose name is written in flaming letters on the stormy and crimson skies of aerial war. Leading ace of the Lafayette Escadrille, with seventeen victories to his credit, Lufbery had been assigned to the American squadrons as morale builder and combat instructor on flights across the lines. He had reached Villeneuve a few days before and had heard about Rick from both Miller and the pilots. This was plainly shown by his words of greeting that evening.

"So you're Eddie Rickenbacker, eh?" Lufbery said in his slow, dry way. He had a heavy French accent. "Miller tells me that in America you are a wonderful racing driver; but the boys say that over here you are a low-down slave driver."

Eddie laughed as he took a guarded inventory of one of the greatest air fighters of all time.

"Luf" was a short, stocky man, with mild eyes and a gentle mouth. He was soft-spoken, sober-minded, and affable. From the very start, the two found much to like in each other. Both had come up in life by dogged effort. Lufbery was born in France and was left with a grandmother when his father migrated to the United States. At twenty-one, he went to join his father in Connecticut; but the elder Lufbery had moved without leaving a forwarding address. Raoul never found him and had to shift for himself in a strange land.

He wandered all over the country, working at anything that turned up; then he drifted to the Orient, and ended up as a mechanic for a barnstorming French aviator. And it was as a mechanic that he came into World War aviation. In time, he became a pilot and flew to the very top of aerial acedom. Naturally, the rolling stone who had become a shooting star found kinship in Eddie, whose struggle for wings had been as bitter as his own.

When Eddie joined the squadron it had been raining cats and dogs for days; but toward sunset on March 5 the sky cleared up, and Lufbery announced in the mess hall to all the pilots that if the next day dawned blue he would lead a three-plane formation from the 94th over the lines. While they waited for him to select his two wing men, not a man stirred. Eddie prayed that he might have a chance to go.

"Rick," said the major casually, "you and Doug Campbell will be ready to leave with me at 8:15 tomorrow morning."

Douglas Campbell grinned. Eddie tried to appear nonchalant as he replied, "Yes, sir." The other pilots crowded around with bittersweet advice, and one thoughtful fellow cautioned him to crash behind our lines if the Huns shot him down. He said it would give him great pleasure to put the *croix de bois* over his grave. The boys had not forgotten their sharp-tongued taskmaster at Issoudun. To be candid, most of them had hoped to forget him forever—never to see again their first "enemy" in the war. If an unpopularity contest had been held in the squadron that night, he would have won it hands down.

The next morning, Campbell and Rick were at the hangar when Major Lufbery showed up on the dot of eight o'clock. First he gave a few instructions to Campbell, then he turned to Rick and said, "Stick close to me, and keep formation!"

With that, he climbed into his own plane, snapped on his goggles, gunned his motor, and took off. Campbell followed suit; next, Rick opened his throttle and nosed into the air. His heart was thumping, but it was heavy too. This was his first flight into the realm of combat. Some pilots did not come back. Would he? He cast a last, longing glance at the flying field as the wheels of his plane began to skim the ground. With the wind in his teeth, he tried to catch up with Lufberry and Campbell, but his plane was a slow-poke and continued to straggle in the three-plane formation. Soon they approached the German lines, and Lufbery, his only salvation, was at least a mile ahead. Rick worried: his plane was dropping behind, and he did not have a gun to defend himself with. But, just as he felt that his guide had forgotten all about him, Lufbery suddenly made a virage and took up a position a few hundred feet away, as much as to say: "Don't worry, my boy—I have an eye on you." Again and again this occurred, when Rick fell too far to the rear.

He found it difficult to execute the endless corkscrew turns that Major Lufbery rolled off with ease. Soon, however, he was so absorbed in his attempts to follow these gyrations and at the same time keep within shouting distance of his companions that he did not check on where he was going. The formation had been aloft about half an hour when Rick, during a short breathing spell, had a chance to look below. His heart popped straight up between his tonsils. He was flying over the stage of war—and what a spectacle! A world of battered trenches, parapets, and millions of shell holes that pitted the surface of the earth as far as he could see. Not a tree, not a

fence, not a house was left standing. Nothing but ruin and desolation. Beneath him lay the blood-drenched earth of no man's land.

To Rick, the devastation was appalling. Horror got the best of
him for a moment. He wondered what Campbell was thinking and
supposed Major Lufbery was far too used to the scene to think twice
about it. He would have to get used to it too. Just at the moment
when he recaptured control of his emotions, he realized, with even
greater horror, that he was getting airsick in the effort to follow
Lufbery's corkscrew turns and neck-breaking twists. Feed-the-birds!
That must never happen. He would be laughed at. He would never
live it down. He visualized what would happen when he got back
to the field—if he ever did—and grew cold with the thought of
it. He set his teeth and prayed that he might fight the sickness off.
He decided to look straight ahead, fly dead-level, and concentrate on
taming the upheaval within him. It worked.

The threat of nausea had barely been vanquished when he was
startled by an explosion that seemed to be only a few feet behind
him. The concussion caught his plane and made it roll and toss, out
of control. The terror of the situation drove away the last lingering
thought of sickness. More explosions and more shocks set his plane
rocking. What could it be? Twisting his neck, he saw half a dozen
huge black puffs of smoke a short distance behind and below his
plane: he was being shot at by antiaircraft batteries. The black puffs
were eighteen-pound shells of shrapnel fired at him by the most
accurate German battery in the sector. He had been told about this
battery, near the town of Suippes. Right! There was Suippes, just
under his left wing: he saw it clearly. So this was the famous Archie
fire?

To his last day, Rick will remember how scared he was, and how
enraged he felt at the old-time fighters who had told him never to
worry about Archie. Shells were bursting all around him, too close
for comfort, and he wanted to live through it if only to paste some of
those smart-aleck pilots in the nose. They had said pish and tush—
antiaircraft guns were a joke. He had been fool enough to believe
them! Now he knew better. He was scared stiff.

Never had Rick so appreciated the comfort of having a friend
near at hand as he did when Major Lufbery swung alongside him.

Almost subconsciously, he followed the major's changing pattern of flight and gradually realized that each move was a direct word of encouragement. Lufbery's plane seemed to speak to him, to soothe his feelings, to prove that there was no danger so long as he followed the wise leadership of its pilot. Soon his alarm passed away. He began to watch the blossoming of the black puffs and grew used to the volcanic upheaval after each explosion. Soon, and almost subconsciously, he met the plunge and slither of the plane with gentle pressure on stick and rudder, which righted his craft and straightened its course. Elation swept over him as he realized that he was not going to be sick and had no fear of the bursting shells. He had had his baptism of fire! A warm glow came over him as he realized that his long dreamed and long dreaded initiation was over. He had been under fire and emerged unafraid. He had lost all fear and uncertainty. This was war, and war was his cream dish. Let the Archies bang and blossom. He liked it. Let the Huns come shooting. He would knock them down. He was floating on a crimson cloud of cockiness when he discovered that Major Lufbery was swinging homeward. He glanced at the clock on the dashboard. Almost ten! They had been out nearly two hours, and the fuel supply would soon be gone. The battlefield gave way to country unscarred by war. Snow still filled some hollows, for a heavy storm had raged over the Toul region but a few days before.

In time, the three planes landed and taxied toward the hangar, where all the pilots and mechanics waited to hear the details of the flight—to learn how two beginners had faced the German music. Rick and Campbell tried to show bored indifference. Oh, yes, there had been quite a bit of Archie over the Hun batteries at Suippes. Sure, it had been fun to watch the gunners waste their ammunition and ride hobbyhorse on the black puffs. Afraid? Nonsense! Archie —pish and also tush!

Had they seen any planes on the mission? No, not a plane. The day was pretty rough, you know. Both friend and foe had remained on the ground.

At this point, Major Lufbery broke in and asked Rick and Campbell what they had seen in the air, if they had not sighted any planes. There was a touch of acid in the sound of his little chuckle.

MOTHER RICKENBACKER IS FIFTY-FOUR YEARS OLD WHEN SHE MEETS HER SON, CAPTAIN EDDIE RICKENBACKER, ON HIS RETURN FROM FRANCE, WORLD WAR I.

RICK AND GENERAL BILLY MITCHELL, 1934

The two young pilots repeated that they had not seen any other planes in the sky.

"Just what I expected! You're all as blind as bats!" was the major's wry comment. "Listen, boys! This is what you should have seen: A formation of five Spads crossed under us before we passed the lines. Another flight of five Spads went by about fifteen minutes later. You didn't see them, either? And they were less than five hundred yards away. It was just as well they were not Boches, eh!" Lufbery laughed unpleasantly, and continued: "Then there were four German Albatrosses two miles ahead of us when we turned back. And there was a Hun two-seater only about a mile away, about five thousand feet above the lines. So there were no planes, eh? You ought to look about a bit when you get into enemy country. You live longer that way!"

At that time Rickenbacker and Campbell thought that the major was trying to take some of the conceit out of them. But after weeks of experience over the front they realized how true his comments were.

"No matter how good a flyer you may be," added Lufbery, "and no matter how perfect your eyesight, you have to learn to watch out aloft before you can observe things either on the ground or in the air from a plane. That kind of sight is called 'vision of the air,' and you can only get it from experience. No pilot ever has it when he first comes to the front. But he does not stay alive very long unless he gets it. First sight means first shot!"

With this, the major went over to Eddie's Nieuport, and asked: "How much of that shrapnel did you get, Rick?"

Rick almost chuckled at Lufbery's trying to make him out a hero for the benefit of the listeners. Imagine his surprise when the major poked his finger into one shrapnel hole in the tail. Another slug had gone through the outer edge of the wing, and a third fragment had passed through both wings not a foot from his head. "Holy Moses," he thought, "I've been hit!" He went pale, and the story goes that he stayed pale a good thirty minutes after this interview. At any rate, a whole week passed before Lufbery invited him on another shell-defying flight over German territory.

This first flight toward combat had a threefold effect on Rick.

To begin with, it gave him the aerial self-sufficiency a combat pilot must have. Secondly, it took away the cockiness that had led many a hot pilot to a premature chilling in the cold, cold ground. Lastly, his ability to laugh at himself and show that he was human and not just a rough, tough racing driver in Army uniform tended to break down the wall between him and the pilots who had hated him at Issoudun. Amazingly, he swung in no time at all from being the most unpopular man in the 94th to being one of the best liked companions-in-arms. But it had taken some hot shrapnel to do the trick.

Chapter XIV

~~~~~~

Much rain, many clouds, and no visibility kept Uncle Sam's young birdmen more or less grounded during the next two weeks. With the weather too thick even for veteran pilots, there was little flying anywhere along the front. But when the ceiling lifted enough Rick would go up for flying and gunnery practice. This won the warm approval of Lufbery, Hall, and the other old-timers who had been assigned to help build up the combat spirit of the untried American fighter pilots.

"Know how to use your guns," Lufbery would say. "You may be the finest flier in the world; but unless you can place your shots where you want to your flying ability counts for nothing."

While our aviators were waiting for weather, Germany was crouching for a leap that was intended to carry it to the French coast, blocking the Channel ports to ships loaded with United States troops. This drive was begun on March 21 and became an immediate threat to airdromes close to the crumbling Allied lines. On March 30, the 94th and the 95th were moved back to Epiez. At that time, the squadrons still lacked machine guns and flying equipment. This deficiency was corrected during the first week of April. At the same time, orders came for the 95th to go to Cazeaux for gunnery training. This left the 94th in sole possession of the field, and its members swore to make the most of their opportunity.

But the weather continued bad—bad enough, at any rate, to keep green pilots grounded. The boys gritted their teeth when more experienced English and French pilots went aloft among the clouds. To build up their morale, they decided to adopt a challenging squadron insigne. Huffer proposed Uncle Sam's stovepipe hat. Lieutenant Walters, the squadron medico, got the idea of "throwing the hat into the ring" as an invitation to battle. Both were adopted.

Lieutenant Wentworth made the design. It was painted on all the 94th's planes, and thus the world-famous hat-in-the-ring insigne was born.

On April 10, without having fired a shot, the 94th retreated again, to an old French airdrome two miles from Toul and only some eighteen miles from the steadily advancing German artillery and infantry. Soon after this move, wind and the weather improved, and every type of flying activity increased on both sides.

Always regarding thirteen as a favorable number, Eddie predicted that April 13 would bring a change in his luck. As it happened, on the evening of April 13, the first war flight order ever posted by an American squadron commander to a unit of American pilots was put on the 94th's operations board. It stated that Captain Peterson and Lieutenants Chambers and Rickenbacker would patrol the lines the following morning at six o'clock. At an altitude of sixteen thousand feet, the patrol was to run from Pont-à-Mousson to Saint-Mihiel and back for a period of two hours. Captain Peterson was designated leader of the flight. Lieutenants Douglas Campbell and Alan Winslow were ordered to stand on alert at the hangar from six o'clock until ten in case of an enemy bombing raid or a sudden call for action against intruding enemy planes.

After dinner Captain Peterson gave Eddie definite orders to lead the flight if anything happened to him, and to continue the patrol until the time was up.

Try as he might, Eddie could not get to sleep that night. He thought over everything he had ever learned or read or heard about pursuit fighting. He imagined Huns coming at him from every direction. He visualized the various ways he would bring them tumbling down. At last he fell off to sleep only to dream of battle. Just as he was shooting down the last of a batch of Boches, an orderly woke him up. It was five o'clock, and a wonderful morning. At breakfast he and Chambers told Campbell and Winslow to keep a sharp lookout, for they intended to give the Germans a big buzzing and knock a few of them down. The quintet went to the field to find a mist so heavy that the ground was completely hidden a short distance away. Captain Peterson sent Chambers and Eddie up to investigate at fifteen hundred feet. Away they went. After circling the field two or three times they saw Captain Peterson climb up to join them. They continued climbing, but at sixteen thousand feet the captain's plane headed back to the field.

"Motor trouble," thought Rick. "Well, he told me last night to carry on in case he dropped out. It is my show now! Come ahead, old boy—we'll bag a Heinie, maybe!" He turned around and saw Chambers following—probably scared green, for this was his first flight over the front.

They picked up the valley of the Moselle and proceeded blandly upon their way. They would probably have kept on to the Rhine but for a sudden burst of black which revealed that they were flying over German guns. Having been shot at by Archie before, Rick felt an utter contempt for it. But this was Chambers' first exposure to anti-aircraft fire, and, as he admitted later, he thought it was all over with him. At any rate, he sheared in so close that their planes nearly collided. But in no time at all he caught the spirit of the thing, and both pilots proceeded on their way disdainful of the shell bursts from below. Four times they made the trip up and down the lines under continuous Archie fire, but without seeing any planes in the sky. Then Rich decided the time had come to turn home.

To his horror, he discovered the entire landscape to the south was blanketed by fog. Under it, somewhere, was the field upon which they must land in a short half-hour before their gas was gone. Now he knew why Captain Peterson had gone back to the field: not because he had engine trouble but because of the ground fog. Cold chills ran up and down his spine as he contemplated the various kinds of mishaps that might be in store for Chambers and himself; and yet there was nothing for it but a dive through the thick fog.

Rick nosed his plane into the woolly stuff. He lost Chambers immediately and only hoped that he had not come in directly behind his own plane. Flying by compass in a gentle dive, with his eye on the altimeter needle, Rick flattened out at one thousand feet, for he remembered that there were high hills in that sector, hills covered by tall trees some of which might crop up ahead any moment. But no menacing shadows rose in the fog. Again, and gingerly, he went into a glide and crept nearer the earth. Suddenly the world turned from gray to soft color. He was out of the fog, barely over the tree tops of level country. To the right he caught a brief glimpse of a highway and a railroad track that seemed familiar. He circled for a closer look and was overjoyed when he recognized a landmark near Commercy. He put about and, flying only a hundred feet above the ground, went straight toward Toul and his squadron's airdrome. He felt quite chesty over his homing instinct; but his pride in himself died abruptly when Captain Peterson gave him a piece of his mind. Then he asked about Reed Chambers: nothing had been heard from him.

Rick walked over to headquarters to make out his report. He had barely begun writing when the telephone rang.

The operations officer answered the call. "Quick," the officer yelled. "Two Boche planes over Foug! Sound an alert!"

Almost on the instant two Nieuports dashed off the field: Campbell and Winslow, who had been standing by all morning for a chance nobody had expected them to get. Before Rick could reach the hangars a mechanic shouted: "A German crate has just crashed! It is burning like a blowtorch!" Rick stopped and turned toward the German plane, which was burning rapidly at the edge of the field, but then a new series of shouts aroused his attention. On his right a Boche machine came nose-down through the mist to make a rough landing not five hundred yards away.

The entire squadron was agog with a babel of shouting, excited voices. When the hubbub died down it was discovered that the first German plane had been downed by Alan Winslow, who had bagged it within three minutes after leaving the field. The second Hun was forced down by Douglas Campbell. It crashed in the fog before the pilot discovered how close he was to the ground.

These were the first two enemy aircraft brought down by any American squadron. Neither of the German pilots was seriously hurt. Questioning revealed that they had gone up to attack two Nieuports flown by Hat-in-the-Ring pilots between Pont-à-Mousson and Saint-Mihiel—Rick and Chambers, neither of whom had seen the two Germans—and were ready to shoot when the Yanks dived into the fog. Lost in the wool, they tried to find their way home to Metz, flew over the Toul field, and were thinking it might be their own until Winslow and Campbell attacked them. Had the stage been set and the plot written, this start for the 94th could not have been improved upon. To make the day perfect, Chambers telephoned about noon that he had landed some distance away but would be in before dark.

Rick resented the Fate that had brought Winslow and Campbell credit for the very Huns who had been sent up to do battle with Chambers and himself. The competitive urge that had pushed him to the front as an automobile racer, now drove him on to win high place in air combat. His ambition was not only to lead in ridding the skies of German planes but also to be the number one man of the number one squadron. He did not think in the self-centered terms of an individual; his habit of teamwork was too ingrained for that.

He wanted the team to win, but he was determined to lead the team in victories. Hence he had the never-resting urge to equal and exceed Campbell's and Winslow's victories. Lufbery's slogan was, "You can't shoot Huns in the hangars!" and Eddie made that his slogan too. He went on patrols whenever he could during the next few days, always looking for a chance that did not come. Four days after the two Germans were downed, he was sent up with Campbell to find a Boche reported by the French. Again he got lost in low-hanging clouds. On getting out, he found himself over Nancy, far from the German lines. Poor navigation. On April 23 when he was on "alert" he was sent up to chase a Hun off the lines near Saint-Mihiel. Instead, he came very close to shooting it out with a French Spad he mistook for a German plane. The Hun, meanwhile, got away. Poor observation. By now, Eddie appreciated the value of Lufbery's advice to acquire "vision of the air." He resolved that from that day on he would strive to see all and know all when he went into air combat.

Our bold lieutenant had a chance to stick to this decision six days later when he was heading toward the lines to put a Rumpler photographic plane out of business. The heavens were overcast, and the German seemed to hang on a skyhook right under a thick puffy cloud. Eddie was ready to hurl himself on his victim when a sixth sense told him that he was falling into a trap. Sure enough, tearing out of the cloud cover came a German fighter ready to send him crashing. But the German had reckoned without Eddie. Instead of serving as a ready target by diving, he gunned his engine up, zoomed, swung over and, a second later, sat on the German fighter's tail. Again he was ready to shoot. But, once more, his sense of caution overcame his lust for conquest. He looked around and saw two planes diving at him from the German lines. He was outnumbered and, what was worse, outmaneuvered.

Deciding that he who fought and flew away might live to fight another day, Eddie left his intended victim and put on full speed to escape the two newcomers; but they hung on as if they had been glued to him. Try as he might—climbing, spinning, circling, diving, looping, and lamming—he could not shake them; the newcomers followed as if they were kites tied to his string. Cold sweat spread its chilling dew all over his rising gooseflesh. What were these Germans up to? Why didn't they shoot? Ah, suddenly he knew! They wanted to herd him behind their lines, force him down, and take him prisoner to learn about the Americans at the front. Never! Never would they take him alive! Step on the gas, Eddie—catch that cloud bank if you want to get home. Presently, it loomed right before him. Now, he was in it. He churned around in the sheltering cloud. Whenever his protective vapor blanket turned light, indicating the edge of cover, Rick would shy away. Finally his gas was getting low and he had to take a chance. Timidly he ventured out of the cloud and looked around. Not a plane in sight. With a grateful prayer, he headed home and landed. He had hardly killed his engine before the hangar when Douglas Campbell and Charles Chapman came up.

"Say," called Chapman, "what was the idea of all of those fancy acrobatics, Rick?"

"Yeah," added Douglas, "we didn't mind doing a war dance with you under a clear sky—but, boy, when it comes to flying into clouds to do stunts, I draw the line!"

Rick smiled as if he had known all along that Campbell and Chapman were his two "pursuers"; but under his breath he swore that he would try to develop better air vision. If he had not taken the two Nieuports for Boche planes, he would have downed the Hun

fighter who was framed in his sights. Those were trying and bewildering days for him. He tried not to show his feelings, but,
what with getting lost, and rushing into battle against French
pilots, and fleeing from his fellow pilots, he was far from pleased
with himself.

Eddie's internal, and strictly private, morale was at its usual low
on April 29, when he woke up about dawn and looked through the
windows for a hasty survey of the sky. As always, it was raining. It
kept on raining all morning; at lunch the sun broke through, and
his hopes began to rise. Being on "alert" duty with Captain Hall,
from three o'clock to sunset, he was ready to take off on a moment's
notice. Their ships stood wing to wing, noses into the wind. At five
o'clock, French headquarters at Beaumont telephoned that a German two-seater observer had just crossed the lines and was flying
south. Within the minute, Captain Hall and Eddie jumped into
their seats, and mechanics swung the propellers to start the engines.
At that moment a sergeant ran up with orders to hold the flight
until Major Huffer joined them.

While they waited Eddie scanned the northern sky and picked
up a tiny speck against the clouds above the Forêt de la Reine. He
began to fidget in his seat. The major was not yet in sight; the
motors were turning over, and everything was ready. Pointing out
the distant speck, he pantomimed for permission to start before they
lost sight of their victim. To his joy, Captain Hall nodded. On
signal, ground men pulled the blocks away from the wheels; two
motors roared as Hall and Rick opened up their throttles, and both
machines swept into the blue. Wing to wing, they climbed swiftly
and thundered toward the distant Boche.

Rick was on Hall's right wing and, off to his own right, in
the direction of Pont-à-Mousson, he could still see their unsus-
pecting quarry. Still, try as he might, he could not induce Captain
Hall to turn in that direction. He dipped his wings, darted away,
and tried in every way to draw attention to the target. Hall doggedly
flew straight north. In desperation, Rick decided to take on the
Boche alone. Within five minutes, he overhauled the enemy plane
and maneuvered himself into an ideal position just under its sheltering tail.

The plane was a large three-seater machine, and a brace of guns poked their noses out to the rear over his head. With fingers closing on his trigger, Rick decided to dash upward and yanked his stick back. Up he zoomed until his sights began to travel along the length of the fuselage overhead. Suddenly his eyes caught a curiously familiar device: the French circular cocarde painted brightly under each wing!

Intent on the kill, Rick had not thought of looking at the plane's nationality. He was thoroughly disgusted with himself and swung abruptly away, but found some satisfaction in the startled surprise of the three Frenchmen aboard the craft. They had never seen him. At any rate, his stalking had been good.

Now he looked around for Hall and found him cavorting in a thick barrage of black shell bursts across the German lines, halfway to Saint-Mihiel and a mile or two inside Hun territory. Evidently the captain was waiting for him, because he was killing time by teasing the Archie gunners, doing loops, barrels, sideslips, and spins over their heads. At last he came out of the Archie area with a long graceful dive, swung up alongside Rick, wiggling his wings as though he were laughing at him. A moment of this, and he set a course toward Pont-à-Mousson.

Presently, Hall changed direction and headed up into the sun. Rick followed, wondering what was up. He scanned the sky in every direction. Oh, yes! Over to the north a plane was coming toward them at about their own altitude. He knew it was a German Pfalz the moment he saw it. Hall was still climbing into the sun, carefully keeping his position between its glare and the oncoming Hun, and Rick clung closely to his companion. The German fighting plane kept on, unaware of danger. Now Hall swung into a screaming power dive, Rick at his side, with at least a thousand feet edge over the enemy.

Rick tried to figure out what the Hun would do. He might try to outdive their craft, for the Pfalz was a wonderful diver and their Nieuports, although faster climbers, had a sad little habit of stripping their wing fabric when diving too fast. Rick decided to keep altitude when Hall attacked, and try to get into position to cut off the enemy's retreat. As he changed his line of flight to execute this plan, the German saw him, and began a furious climb with Hall already halfway to the attack. Rick swung into his planned position just when Hall began firing. Chances are that the Boche had not seen Hall's Nieuport until that very moment.

Abandoning the battle, the Pfalz banked around to the right and started for its own side of the lines, just as Rick had expected. In a flash, he was on its tail. Down, down they sped with throttles full open. Hall came on somewhere in the rear. Rick was gaining upon the Boche every instant, waiting for dead-eye range. He fired the first shot at one hundred fifty yards.

With pounding heart, Rick saw tracer bullets cut a streak of living fire into the Pfalz's tail. Raising his nose slightly, he sent the fiery streak like a stream of water from a garden hose, into the cockpit. The erratic weaving of the Hun showed the plane was out of control. At two thousand feet, Rick pulled out of his dive and watched the Boche crash on the edge of a woods just inside the German lines. He had brought down his first enemy plane.

Tickled pink by the victory, Hall pushed his plane about in incredible gyrations through a furious blooming of shells from the ground. Rick was ready to call it a day and zoomed out quickly from the machine-gun and rifle fire; but his companion continued to do stunts over the Archie batteries for ten minutes. Finally Captain Hall finished his war dance and they swooped down on their airdrome. As they climbed out of their planes the entire squadron of pilots and mechanics came streaming across the airdrome toward them. The French had telephoned in a confirmation of Rick's first victory.

The death of Charles Chapman, shot down by Germans on May 2, sobered Rick's elation over his first victory. This was the Hat-in-the-Ring's first loss in combat, and, although it doused the fire of jubilation within the squadron over three victories in three weeks, it also lit flames of revenge. Up to now, the new pilots had fought the Germans without hate—now vengeful fury added its sting to their aggressiveness. On May 6, the 95th Squadron returned from Gunnery School, and a friendly rivalry for top honors soon began between the two units, in which eventually the 27th and 147th squadrons shared. The four squadrons together formed the First Pursuit Group.

One of the greatest mishaps of the 94th, which formed a link in the chain of events that carried Eddie Rickenbacker to stardom, occurred on the morning of May 7. Flight One, consisting of Captain Hall as leader and Lieutenants Rickenbacker and Green, had taken off on an alert to head off four German planes that had crossed the lines and were flying south. Rick got one of them, Green got another; but Hall was seen to fall behind the German lines. His wing had seemed to collapse, and the plane was surrounded by the black blossoms of Archies as it went down. With Hall gone, Rick was made leader of Flight One. He was not particularly happy over the assignment, because his flying blunders during April were still fresh in mind and he believed American pilots in general were then undertrained and overconfident: like himself, they had much to learn about air combat. He determined to do what he could to improve not only himself but also Flight One as a whole in the science of aerial warfare.

Eddie's closest friend in the squadron was Reed Chambers, and the two would sit up all night trying to figure out new ways of beating the Hun to the draw. One morning they took off long before dawn and climbed to eighteen thousand feet behind the German lines, where they became separated. Eddie met and attacked a flight of three Albatrosses, shooting one of them down at thirteen thousand feet. The remaining two swung upon his tail to polish him off. As Eddie yanked the stick back to grab some altitude, he heard an explosive rip and saw his top wing lose its canvas covering. The plane went into a spin. Swooping around it, the Germans pumped lead as fast as their guns could shoot. Luckily, the helpless Nieuport made a poor target.

As he sat pulling and pushing at stick and rudder without any response, Eddie thought that this was the end. His mind turned toward Columbus and entered the little living room, where his mother sat reading a newspaper with a headline clear across the page: "Rickenbacker Killed by Hun!" He yelled as if his voice could defeat not only death but time and space:

"Don't you believe it, Mother. Don't believe what you read in the papers! I'm not going to die!"

Feverishly he pulled and shoved again on the stick. Again he kicked the rudder bar. No response. With nothing to lose, Rick decided to violate all the rules for getting out of a spin. He took feet and hands off the controls and pulled the throttle wide open. The engine roared, and a miracle happened. The ship not only came out of the spin but flew level and, as luck would have it, straight toward the French lines less than ten miles away. He passed through Archie outbursts at three thousand feet, untouched. Mortars, machine guns, and rifles banged away at him from the German trenches. No bullet hit him. Now he was over no man's land. Presently he soared across the Allied trenches and made a rough but safe landing on a shell-pitted field.

As the result of this encounter, Eddie was credited with his second victory. The plane he had shot down on Hall's last flight had not been observed to fall, hence it did not count. A few days later, Eddie nailed his third official victory. He was on his way to acedom.

But a bitter lesson in the briefness of aerial greatness came to Eddie on May 20 when he and Walter Smyth returned empty-handed from a patrol to learn that Major Lufbery's plane had been shot aflame almost over the Toul airdrome. The horrible part was that Major Lufbery had jumped to certain death rather than endure the torture of fire. In those days parachutes were not used on the Allied side, except by balloon observers; they were, however, coming into use among German fliers. Luf's death depressed both pilots and mechanics, for he had been deeply loved by all.

Spurred on to revenge Lufbery's death, Eddie and Campbell scored their fourth victories on May 28 when they tackled two Albatrosses guarded by four Pfalz fighters. Two days later, during a furious dog fight, Eddie downed still another enemy, without credit because no one on the Allied side saw the plane fall. The very next day, Campbell sent his fifth Hun crashing. He was an ace. Eddie's private journal showed six planes downed, although the official scorebook gave him only four; his figures showed that Campbell, who was wounded a few days later and invalided home to America, actually had seven notches on his gun grip.

The deaths of Lufbery and the other pilots in the 94th and 95th squadrons affected Eddie as they affected his fellow pilots. Life was uncertain. The man you laughed with at breakfast might never come back from patrol to laugh again. Eddie learned that it was dangerous, not only to the emotions of the individual, but to the morale of the organization, to form attachments that went too deep. Be hail fellow well met. Drink and be jolly with one another on leave. Fight together with the will to win over the front. But don't, thought Rick, let friendship root deep in the heart, for any day death might uproot it. Although he tried hard, Eddie never attained this hardboiled indifference to the death of a comrade. To him it was one of the greatest horrors of war. To protect himself, he made few real friends in the squadron; but there was one boy who won his way into Eddie's firm friendship—Walter Smyth, whose unchanging good nature, alert mind, steadfast courage, and unusual flying ability endeared him to Eddie like a younger brother. Even as Lufbery and Eddie had been almost inseparable in the early days of the Hat-in-the-Ring, so Eddie and Smyth now became a Damon and Pythias of aerial combat.

From time to time during those spring months, strangers would come to Toul and engage Eddie in conversation. Some of them liked to get off into dark and solitary corners and whisper how easy it would be to get lost on a flight into Germany and land there, or how simple it would be to drop important messages on early-morning patrols. It was all part of the game of spy hunting. Eddie was still on the suspected list. However, instead of being angry Eddie regarded these experiences as good, free fun. The visitors came until his third victory. After that he saw them no more. Evidently counterintelligence was finally satisfied that he was a loyal American and not a German in disguise.

Late May brought some drastic changes in the American air command. Brigadier General Benjamin D. Foulois became Chief of Air Service, First Army, and Colonel Mitchell was placed in charge of aviation in the First Army Corps. At that time, too, German plans for a thrust toward Paris were coming to a head. In order to obtain as much information as possible Boche observation and photographic aircraft made almost constant patrols. The photographic planes were, in particular, a thorn in the side of the Allies, but Rumpler No. 16 became a personal insult and challenge to Lieutenant Rickenbacker.

It all began innocently enough on a sunny June morning over Toul. Eddie was making a routine patrol when he saw a Rumpler sailing alone and stately high in the sky, taking photographs of the Toul railroad yards. Swiftly as he could, he swung his Nieuport into the sun and began to climb, ever careful to use the glare of the sun as a covering shield. As the Rumpler came closer, he saw the figure 16 painted in black on an orange background on the plane's dark body, which also displayed a Rising Sun insigne.

"I'll set your sun for you," he thought as he roared upward and saw the pilot sitting quietly while the observer used his camera. The Rumpler had two forward-shooting guns manned by the pilot and a swivel-mounted gun in the rear cockpit fired by the observer-photographer.

Having gained the altitude he needed, Eddie yanked his engine wide open and swooped upon No. 16. Through his sights, he saw the finely executed lettering. He shifted rudder, jiggled his stick a bit, and brought the observer into focus. Forward his gun muzzle traveled until it pointed straight into the pilot's cockpit. The distance between the two planes shrank with swift velocity. At one hundred yards, he pressed the trigger—a bullet or two ripped out. Silence! The gun had jammed. Circling off to be out of the Rumpler's gun range, he began to break the jam with the one-pound copper hammer which all pilots carried on a thong around their wrists. He was red-hot over the failure of his attack. Meanwhile Rumpler 16 was heading east. As soon as Eddie got his gun going, he went after the Boche in such a flaming fury that he did not see two Albatross planes swing onto the tail of his Nieuport until a hair-split second before it would have been too late. Having no confidence in his gun, he outflew the two Heinies, reached his own lines and got home.

White with rage, Eddie taxied toward the hangar eager to seek out Abie Karp—a short, thin little man with a Brooklyn accent and a heart of twelve-cylinder loyalty, whose duty it was to keep the gun in shooting trim. The armorer was where he always was when Eddie came in, right alongside the slowly rolling plane.

"How many this time, lieutenant?" he called out, panting as he ran beside the plane. "Any luck at all, Eddie? How's the gun?"

Eddie cut the engine and glared. "This gun couldn't shoot holes in a Swiss cheese, Abie, and you know it. If that gun isn't doing its stuff tomorrow morning, I'll—I'll—"

"But that gun was as good as I could make it, Eddie," protested Karp. "I tested every part, I gauged every bullet and cartridge!"'

Eddie softened, and slapped him on the back. "Well, maybe there's something wrong with the gun, Abie. But I want it fixed by tomorrow morning."

Shortly after dawn Eddie came into the hangar to learn that the gun was beyond quick repair. He saw Lieutenant Smyth's plane, asked as to its ceiling, and was told about twenty thousand feet. He also noticed that it had two guns instead of his one. Getting aboard the ship, he headed toward Metz. He had an idea Rumpler 16 would be aloft again, and he wanted to be to the east of it in the light of the sun.

Right as rain, the photographic plane was there. Again Eddie stalked his quarry. This time he planned to climb above it, make a straight dive. As he figured it out, the Rumpler would try to throw him off by spinning or diving. In that case, Rick would zoom up and plunge after it. The plan was good, only it did not work. Instead of going down the Rumpler pilot pulled up, and as Eddie shot under him bullets sang around his head. A quick and startled look revealed something Eddie had never read about in the book of air war: a machine gun sticking out of the floor of Rumpler 16. Realizing that he had no monopoly on strategy, he turned away briefly, then remembered Lufbery's advice to bore in and punch, and swung toward the Boche only to pull away again! This time *both* his guns jammed! He hammered one gun into life, but the other was out. Meanwhile the Rumpler, as contemptuous of the Nieuport as a ram of a ewe lamb, completed its photographic business and nosed home. When Eddie bored in with one gun, the observer gave him as good as he dealt from the floor gun and the regular tourelle weapon in the rear cockpit. After a running fight of forty minutes, Eddie realized he would soon be out of gas—over Hun territory. He swung westward, ran out of fuel, failed to reach his airdrome, but landed in a field near Toul. He was safe but, hang it, so was the Rumpler!

Stealing a ride home on a truck, Eddie found two new Vickers machine guns mounted on his Nieuport. How Abie had corralled them, only the Lord and he knew. The next morning, June 6, he took off again in pursuit of Number 16 and found it at twenty-two thousand feet over the railroad yards. To save his soul, he could not rise one foot above twenty thousand; and after a brief exchange of shots he turned back. He knew that his harmless presence was welcomed by the Rumpler since, as long as he was circling around it, Allied antiaircraft guns would not reach their probing fingers in its direction.

Abie listened to Eddie's explanation when he landed, and said:

"Trouble is, lieutenant, you haven't enough ceiling with full tanks. Bet you could push her up to thirty thousand feet without a gas load."

Pilots and mechanics who stood around laughed at the gibe, but Eddie felt too out of sorts to make any comment whatever. His head ached, and his ears ached, and he felt rocky and uncertain. He must have looked ill to the squadron flight surgeon, who called him in, found he was running a temperature, and ordered him to Paris on a three-day sick leave.

Rick did not find the gay and confident Paris of two short months earlier. The Hun hordes were only thirty miles away. Streets and boulevards swarmed with homeless and hungry refugees—desperate, fear-stricken people who were on the very point of riot—a danger that was removed only when the American Red Cross performed the miracle of providing them with food and shelter.

Chapter XV

~~~~~~

On returning to the squadron Eddie found two items of good news. General Foulois had visited the field and, impressed by the inadequacy of the flying equipment, had promised new fast high-flying Spads in place of the obsolescent Nieuports. And another victory had been added to Eddie's official score. This was now five Boche planes, and he was an ace.

The glory of acedom did not go to Eddie's head, but it did go to his blouse and his breeches. Billy Mitchell's uniforms designed from "moonlight" regulations, had caught his fancy from the beginning, and now he had some uniforms made that would have put Hollywood heroes to shame. The Beau Brummell in Rick had a rather late blooming. In his racing days, Eddie's appearance was almost clerically austere; now, he had large patch pockets on his tunic which fitted his tall, slim, well set figure as a shell fits its egg. He wore a strictly irregular English Royal Flying Corps cap with United States insignia. His riding breeches had an arrogant flare and were of the finest whipcord. He sported handmade French high-laced boots and swung a colorado-claro Malacca cane on the field and off it.

Eddie's pickings in June were slim, because most of the German aircraft had been moved into the more active Soissons-Rheims sector where the enemy advance had forced a deep salient.

When he was not flying, Eddie, wanting to know all the angles, would go to the front by motorcycle, talk to artillery and infantry men and get their viewpoints; he interviewed balloon observers for the same purpose. And he learned more about air-ground relationship that most pilots knew in those days when air fighting was too new to have a chapter in the book of strategy and tactics.

On the 26th of June, orders directed the entire First Pursuit

Group to move to an airdrome at Touquin, some twenty miles south of Château-Thierry. The group was to patrol the Soissons-Rheims sector. The 94th had barely established itself at its new base when Eddie came down with fever and was confined to the station hospital. His head echoed with an anvil-ringing ache, and the dull throb in his ear became an acute stabbing pain, but, fearful he would be invalided out of combat and sent home to America, he voiced no complaint.

In the hospital, Eddie Rickenbacker had plenty of time for some badly needed self-orientation. He had passed overnight from civilian to military life, and his evolution from a driver on General Pershing's staff to aerial acedom had been both swift and violent. Strange new values had entered his life, and lifelong standards had been swept aside. It was all confusing and unreal. Indeed, an over-all fog of confusion cut down Eddie's inner vision almost to zero.

Throughout that week, he made a point-by-point study of every cog that meshed in the wheels of aerial warfare. He analyzed himself, his fellow pilots, and his enemies. He thought about the weaknesses and limitations of planes, engines, guns, and equipment. Out of this meditation came a pattern of approach to his problem that was just as definite as the plan he had made in the old days before every race.

Aerial action was limited by the speed, climb, dive, and combat capacity of the plane; but its maximum performance could be assured by thorough overhaul and inspection on the ground and constant care aloft. Respect for the limitations of the craft would make it more reliable in a tight corner. As for gun jams? Well, honing of breech and breech parts would help. But jams were also caused by oil freezing at high altitudes. If there were only some way of heating the guns! That was worth thinking about, and so was the scheme worked out by Willie Coppens, the Belgian ace, who fired flaming rockets into the gas-filled bags of observation balloons. A few rockets in the side of that Rumpler 16—that would have fixed it for keeps. Yes, rockets! There was a cream dish!

As for himself? Well, the principal job was to make sure of himself. Of course he had been in numerous combats, and had brought

down five or six enemies; but that success could have been a lucky
fluke. How did he know he would get more Huns—or that they
would not get him? He reviewed his mistakes in combat and found
that most of them were due to overanxiety, impatience over weather,
delays in operations, and the boredom of waiting. He decided to
do away with all that—to stop flying with a heavy foot and use his
head instead. In-an-out would be his operational procedure, and
only when the odds were in his favor. From now on, long running
fights were *verboten* unless sure victory was in sight.

With respect to the Germans and their reputed skill in the air,
well, Eddie was showman enough to know the psychological impact
of that kind of propaganda. He had employed it himself in publi-
cizing the Maxwell racing team—an All-Star Cast of Speedway
Kings!

Eddie caught his breath: An all-star cast!

Why not a Squadron of Shooting Stars—a hard-hitting, high-
flying outfit of American pursuit pilots that would rival and top the
widely advertised Richthofen Circus? What could be better than the
Hat-in-the-Ring 94th to do that job? Who was a better man than
Eddie Rickenbacker to lead it? He knew men, he knew motors; he
was used to teamwork, to leadership.

Having reached this conclusion, he leaned back on his hospital
pillow while Eddie the Strategist took over the job of building a
workable plan. It did not have to come that day or the next. He
would be biding his time.

The following day, just as Eddie was about to leave the hospital
to attend the Fourth of July celebration in Paris, great and good
news arrived: Captain Hall was alive, well, and a prisoner in Germany. His plane had not been shot down but had made a rough
landing with a crumpled wing.

After the Independence Day parade, Eddie played a hunch.
Instead of returning to Touquin directly, he went to the American
Experimental Airdrome at Orly. He wanted to learn how soon the
Spads promised by General Foulois would reach the First Pursuit
Group. At the supply depot, he discovered that the 94th stood first
on the Spad list, and that three of the new planes had already been
cleared for delivery. One, it was understood, was actually flyable.

Eddie's heart stepped up a beat or two as he asked: "If one is ready, how about my taking it now?"

"Certainly. Why not?"

Half an hour later, Eddie was soaring into the French sky in a Spad that might have been well controlled lightning. This was the famous Number One in which he flew to combat stardom as America's foremost ace. But after the joy of possession wore off on that flight he wondered what punishment he might face for this unauthorized moonlight acquisition: he was now both out of uniform on the ground and out of step aloft, for the Nieuport, until further orders, was the one and only plane officially assigned to the 94th. But he got away with it. Where wrath might have destroyed another man, admiration of his audacity won Eddie permission to keep the Spad as his official combat steed. And did he lord it over the humble Nieuport pilots!

When Lieutenant Rickenbacker returned to his base, the German retreat from Château-Thierry had begun. As the foe rolled back, the First Pursuit Group had to use so much fuel in reaching the front that little was left for actual patrols. The outfit moved closer to the lines, but Eddie had little interest in that. On July 10, he suffered a severe mastoid attack, with the formation of an abscess. He was rushed to a hospital in Paris for an operation on his right ear.

He was still in the hospital when the break-through to Paris, on which Germany had staked everything, failed. While this battle raged, he fretted and fumed in bed. Then the doctors implied that he might never fly again—the damage done to his ear might have affected his sense of balance. So! This was serious. Sneaking to a telephone, he called Colonel Mitchell, told him the circumstances, and asked to be ordered back to duty at once. Mitchell issued the order, and Eddie vanished from the hospital and Paris before there could be any change of mind about him. To his great delight, he discovered that he could handle his Spad as well as ever. By now, all pilots in the squadron were getting Spads.

Those days at the end of July, 1918, and the start of August were bitter ones for the Hat-in-the-Ring pilots. Their losses were great, and their victories were comparatively few. Winslow was downed—not killed, but captured.

But the worst hour of the entire fall came to Eddie on the morning of August 18. He had been ordered to stay in bed because of recurring earaches when an orderly came into the room and said: "I've bad news for you, lieutenant!"

"Yes, I know. It is that Smyth and Bruce are dead!"

"How do you know?" The orderly turned slightly green.

"I just dreamed it. Tell me, is it true?"

It was. Smyth and Bruce died in a mid-air collision over the Hun lines at about the time when Eddie dreamed that he saw Smyth shot down in flames, and Bruce following in his fiery trail.

Whenever Eddie began to believe that the life of a pilot was just about the most trying in the whole war, he would jump into a car, drive up to an active part of the front and make friends with the infantry in the muddy, filthy, vermin-infested trenches. He usually remained overnight. Memories of the comfortable barracks, the happy gathering in the clean messroom, the warmth of the fire in the quarters at the airdrome, would come to his mind as he sat in the mud and ate "goldfish" rations out of battered tin cans, with sad-pronged forks. In these surroundings came realization that, while an airman's life might be a short one, it had its compensating points.

Repeated ear trouble took Eddie back to Paris in August for further hospitalization. Following recovery from an operation, he was eager to return to combat. One day just before he left the hospital, Colonel Mitchell telephoned to him from Army headquarters at Chaumont: He had a brand-new Mercedes in a garage in Paris. Would Eddie drive it out for him? Eddie was delighted. He knew the car by reputation, for it had won first place in the hotly contested Grand Prix auto race in 1914. It was a large, powerful car with a double-chain drive. Mitchell had had it changed from a racer into a sport car with four deep leather-lined bucket seats. Like the colonel, it was very swanky indeed; and it was the apple of his eye.

To Eddie, whose love for automobiles had never abated, and who still dreamed of building the Great American Car, driving this Mercedes was an indescribable joy. He was speeding along one of the smooth military highways at about sixty miles an hour when the car went out of control and almost turned turtle into the ditch.

At that very moment a group of French mechanics came along in a truck, and helped him put the car in shape. The trouble was that a chain guard had got out of place.

Eddie reached Chaumont about two hours late but with the car in running order. He explained what had happened, showed the damage that had been done. Mitchell gave him a black look but said nothing.

They had returned to Colonel Mitchell's office when a French general entered. Suddenly, the colonel turned on Rickenbacker and gave him a merciless tongue lashing. All that Mitchell had learned in many years of soldiering from Cuba to the Philippines, from Alaska to Army posts all over the land, went into that verbal dressing down of Lieutenant Rickenbacker before the amused eyes of the French general.

If Mitchell wanted to display temper before this French general, no matter how unfairly, Eddie had to take it silently. But every sharp phrase cut into his heart. When at last the colonel's ire subsided and he was excused, he returned to his squadron boiling with suppressed rage. As the months passed and he rose to combat stardom, his outward attitude toward Colonel Mitchell was always correct; but deep underneath he decided that some day, somewhere, he would call the colonel to task and make him swallow his insults.

In Eddie's absence the Hat-in-the-Ring Squadron was moved up to Erize-la-Petite, some fifteen miles south of Verdun. When he reached his unit on September 11, the whole organization was in a blue funk, and with fairly good reason! The fine start made in April and May, with fourteen enemy planes brought down, had petered out. June, July, and August had netted only six victories, and not one crash had yet been scored in September. Of the four squadrons in the First Pursuit Group, all clustering around the same field, the 94th stood a poor third—the oldest outfit in terms of service over the front. Meanwhile Bill Taylor, Ted Curtis, Harold Buddy, and others in the 95th were shooting their way to fame. And in the 27th, now commanded by Jimmy Meissner, a blustering Arizona cowhand named Frank Luke was using his shooting irons with telling effect.

The very day after Eddie's return, the great Saint-Mihiel offensive was begun, but the everlasting rains prevented combat flying.

The gang grumbled over their bad luck. On the 14th, however, the weather improved, and Eddie had a chance to match guns and wits with a Fokker pilot, who went down: six for Eddie. This tied him with the then leading American flying ace, Lieutenant Tobin of the Third Pursuit Group. Just after dawn on the following day, Eddie had a set-to with another Fokker pilot whom he sent to glory: seven for Rick. Among Americans, Lieutenant Rickenbacker was now the ace of aces. He was stepping high, but in dead men's shoes. Lufbery, with eighteen victories, was dead. Frank Bayliss, with thirteen, was dead. David Putnam, with twelve, was dead. How long would he wear their boots? And would he die with them on—dead men's shoes? Or would some other pilot surpass his score? Eddie did not have to wonder long. In a few days, Frank Luke's roaring guns blasted down a long line of planes and balloons. In six days, alone, Luke downed thirteen balloons as if they had been sitting-duck targets in a shooting gallery.

Eddie's dream of squadron command came true on the afternoon of September 24, when Major Marr was ordered back to the United States and he was promoted to the rank of captain and squadron commander. At that time the 27th, thanks largely to Luke's daring and marksmanship, had a six-victory lead. When Eddie assumed command of the 94th, his driving impulse for mastery took immediate control: not in a ranting and roaring fashion, but according to a plan that Eddie the Strategist had all figured out and ready for action.

Eddie's new orders arrived just before dinner time. Less than five minutes after he had read them, two bulletins were posted. One called for a meeting of all pilots at eight o'clock. The other summoned all mechanics to gather at nine o'clock.

As the pilots and other officer personnel of the squadron grouped themselves in the mess hall, Eddie looked them over. They were young, eager, and new. Of the old gang that had constituted the 94th in March, only two familiar faces looked back at him— Thorn Taylor and Reed Chambers. All the others had gone—some dead, others prisoners, still others invalided out, and a few transferred to different units.

For one solid hour, the captain spoke to his officers. He explained what he wanted: victories! He told them that he was more interested in their mechanical knowledge than in military decorum. He spoke to them, as he did to the mechanics afterward, in the tough short-worded way he had used with his drivers and pit men before races. And he wanted, from the airways, the same results he had sought on the speedways: first place! top position! He told them that he respected the uniform, but that saluting and other military formalities were to be reserved for officers visiting the post —then snap to attention; otherwise, they were all teammates laboring to the same end. He ordered his pilots to work on their planes— learn about engines. He pointed out that his knowledge of engines enabled him to fly his own Hisso about one hundred hours between top overhauls, while the average for the rest of the squadron was little over twelve hours per engine before it went to pieces.

"Save your engines," he pleaded. "Baby them along until you sail in—then open up your guns and your engine too. But don't be overcautious. It is just as dangerous to stop short of your limitations as to go beyond them."

The pilots and mechanics caught the spirit and the letter of their commander's message. From that moment, the squadron's climb to leadership began with a rush that nothing could brake or supersede. Eddie started the ball rolling the very next day, when he sighted two German photographic planes protected by a five-plane formation of swift Fokker pursuit craft. Before any one of the seven pilots had a chance to see him, the captain climbed into the sun and swung astern of the enemy formation until he was well above it. Now was the time! The odds were seven to one against him—but what did that matter?

Eddie nosed down and made a beeline for the nearest Fokker. It tried to pull away, but his bullets were already ripping through its fuselage. The pilot must have been killed instantly, for the machine fell wildly away and crashed. Eddie had planned to zoom upward and protect himself against counterattack; but the four remaining Fokkers were so dumfounded that one fell into a vrille and the other three viraged to right and left in the effort to save their own skins, leaving a space through which Eddie instantly plunged to attack the photographic planes. They had already nosed down to escape, and, as Eddie came on, they drew apart. Both observers were firing at him, although the range was still too long. He dived more steeply and zoomed quickly up at one of the planes from below. But victory was not to be easy. The pilot kicked his tail around, giving the gunner a clear aim, while Eddie had to delay shooting until he had more time for his own aiming. In the meantime, the other Hun stole up behind him. Seeing tracer bullets whiz past, he zoomed out of range, made a reverse turn, and came directly back at his first target.

As this went on, the four Fokkers were still wrangling among themselves about their formation. And all the time the milling planes were getting farther into Germany. Eddie decided upon one bold attack. If it failed, he would head home before it was too late. He suddenly found an opening between the two photographic planes. They were flying parallel and not fifty yards apart.

He made a sideslip until he had one machine between himself and the other. Then he straightened out, leveled his Spad, and shot at the nearest Boche, who passed directly through his line of fire. As flames burst from the plane and it started a blazing path to earth, with the Fokker escort tearing up to the rescue, he stepped on the gas and dashed for home.

September 26 was to be an important day for the whole American Army. It was "D" day, and at the zero hour forty thousand doughboys, following an artillery barrage, would go over the top from the Meuse to the Argonne. Eddie examined the dark but clear sky at four o'clock, wondering how many of his boys Death would claim before this day's work was done! The 94th had an important part in the program. Headquarters had ordered attacks on all Hun balloons along that entire front until the infantry's operations were completed. It was the first balloon strafing party the 94th had been ordered to stage since Eddie was made its commander, and he wanted to make a good showing.

With Lieutenants Cook, Chambers, Taylor, Coolidge, and Palmer, he sat down to an early breakfast at which they went over all the details of their prearranged plan. Two balloons had been assigned to the squadron, and three pilots were delegated to each balloon. The gas bags hung along the Meuse between Brabant and

Dun. Every man had noted the exact location of his target the evening before. It would be difficult, perhaps, to find the balloons before daylight if they were still in their nests, but the pilots were to hang about the vicinity until they found them, if it took all day.

It was still dark when the planes left the ground, but as soon as he got upstairs Eddie saw the most marvelous sight human eyes could behold. A terrific artillery barrage was going on ahead. Beyond the darkness, the whole western horizon was illumined with one mass of shooting flashes. The big guns were belching out their shells so fast that it seemed as if there were millions of them. Looking back, he saw the same scene. It was like a gigantic switchboard which flashed thousands of electric dots and dashes as invisible fingers handled the plugs. These extraordinary fireworks fascinated him so that he was startled when he discovered Verdun below. Noting the dim outline of the Meuse River, he turned to follow that stream, which was as familiar to him as the Indianapolis Speedway's track. He knew exactly the point where he would leave the river and turn left to strike the spot where the balloon had been last night. He did not know what course the other pilots had taken.

Suddenly the long snaky flashes of enemy tracer bullets from the ground pierced the sky. They came from the site of the balloon and either Cook or Chambers was already attacking. But even as the flaming bullets streamed upward Eddie saw a gigantic flame burst out in their midst! One of the boys had destroyed the gas bag! As the glare of the fire died down, he saw the second balloon go up in flames. Undoubtedly the enemy would send other balloons up in their places, but that would take a little time. He decided to fly to Damvillers where there was another balloon. Eddie was near the spot when another gush of flame announced the doom of the very balloon he had decided to attack.

Rick was chortling over the extraordinary good luck of the team's balloon hunt when he was startled to discover a German Fokker flying wing to wing with him barely a hundred yards away. The next instant, the Fokker came tearing at him, and both pilots began firing at the same time.

It was still so dark that the four streams of flaming bullets cut brilliant lines of fire through the air. To Eddie it looked as though the machines were tied together with ropes of fire. All his ammunition was incendiary, and the Hun's ammunition was part tracer and part incendiary. As the planes drew closer, Eddie wondered if this was to be a collision or if the other would get out of his way. The German settled the question by starting a dive. Eddie instantly made a reverse turn which put him close behind the Fokker. He pulled both triggers with one long burst, and the Fokker fell.

Eddie's joy over his victory was dissipated by a sudden violent vibration of his engine. It was out of whack and getting worse. He had to get home, and fast. Throttling down to reduce the pounding, he just managed to keep flying speed. Motor failure now would mean certain doom: he was less than a thousand feet above Hun territory, and could glide only a few hundred yards without power. But the plane cleared the lines and landed without damage. Hastily climbing out to find the cause of the trouble, Eddie discovered that one blade of the propeller had been shot in half.

All the news was good that morning. The First Pursuit Group had shot down ten German balloons. Eddie's victory over the Fokker made eleven victories in one hour, and not a single pilot was lost.

At about this time, the cometlike career of Frank Luke came to an end; and with Luke's deeply mourned departure from the skies Eddie again became the American ace of aces. September brought six victories to his credit, including one balloon, raising his official total to twelve.

Thus the month which began so poorly closed on a triumphant note. But the triumph was mixed with secret tears for Luke and other brave and brilliant American airmen who went west.

Chapter XVI

The guns of Captain Rickenbacker's Number One Spad drummed out the tattoo of death for eleven enemy planes and three balloons during the furious fighting of October. His dominant sweep of the skies that month began on the first day of the month, when he downed a balloon, and ended on the 30th, when he scored a double-header against another balloon and a Fokker. Double-headers came in a wild rush for Eddie in October. On the 2nd, two fighters; on the 3rd, two photographic planes; on the 10th, two Fokkers; and, on the 27th, two more of the same deadly breed. In between, on odd days, he sent other Hun planes crashing and other balloons down in flames.

Captain Rickenbacker's most brilliant victory—his most daring coup in turning almost certain defeat into glorious victory—was on a bright afternoon of mid-October. He had gone out alone on a balloon hunt, but rapidly gathering haze obscured his target. As he roamed the skies for game, the captain saw a German plane shoot down a French balloon near Exermont. Deciding that the lone raider would be an easy victim on his way back across the lines, he set himself for swift attack. He had actually chalked this victory up in his mind when a swarm of leaden fireflies bored through his fuselage and wings. Sensing rather than seeing what was taking place, Captain Eddie knew that one or more Heinies were taking pot shots at him from above. He had been so intent on catching one Hun that he had failed to check the sky against the possibility of a protective formation high above the lone balloon strafer. The whole group had been stalking Rick for many minutes without his knowing it.

Quick as a flash the captain did a climbing chandelle to escape the droning bullets. He did not even stop to look at the position of his assailants. Knowing they were above, he concluded that they expected him to dive away from them, and that a dive would be the thing to avoid. He guessed correctly. As he shot upward, two red-nosed Fokkers, veterans of the Richthofen circus, swept by him. But before he had time to congratulate himself he discovered that only half of the enemies had passed him. Two more Fokkers had remained above, on the chance that the Yank might decline to do the obvious.

The skillful contortions of the two top-side Fokkers made Eddie realize that he was in for the fight of his life. He lost all interest in the balloon strafer, and his one dearest desire was to escape. The masterly way in which the Fokkers met and even anticipated his every movement showed him that he had four crafty fighters against him. He zigzagged and sideslipped in vain. He knew that if he did not keep cool he would soon fall prey to these extremely skillful Huns. The two planes that had first attacked him remained below in a position that invited his attack while preventing his escape in a dive. He decided to take the offensive before it was too late.

Even though it might mean death, the captain decided that action would be better than waiting around for the red-noses to close in for a gang-up kill. Noting a chance for an attack on the nearest man below, he quickly tipped over, went hurtling down with wide-open motor and firing with both guns. The German ran straight through his line of fire, and that left only three Huns to one Rickenbacker. Fair enough! Joyous over this success, Eddie refused to use the open door to escape. Instead he did a sudden loop and reverse turn, believing that his two enemies above would be on his tail and preparing to shoot. Again he guessed correctly. Not only were they in just the position he expected to find them, but they were startled by his sudden and unexpected assault upon their comrade. With the tables turned and the American in the role of top dog, the three Boches dove for home with Rick's faster and heavier Spad gaining on them every second. His blood was up. He forgot all his rules against a hot head and a heavy foot. Here he was three miles behind the lines, where other enemy planes might very easily be lurking. He had just escaped miraculously from the worst trap he had ever fallen into. Yet, he could not resist the mad impulse to destroy the three Huns at any risk.

The fleeing Huns had a slight start, and Eddie did not overtake them immediately. Presently one of them fell behind the others. The ground was getting close and it was growing dark. At about one thousand feet, the captain decided the straggling Fokker was within range. He opened fire, following the Hun's desperate gyrations. Presently the plane dropped, out of control, and he ceased firing. The dead German's two companions were now well out of sight in the shadows, and Eddie awoke to the fact that he was being fired at by hundreds of guns from the ground. All the way back to the lines he was followed by machine-gun bullets and some Archie, but—untouched—he continued to his field, where he put in claims for two enemy Fokkers, his twenty-first and twenty-second victories!

When Captain Rickenbacker was not hammering away at the Boches in the air, he was drilling his pilots and mechanics into greater efficiency. He harped, particularly, on the condition of the machine guns. The forward sweep in the squadron's string of victories was, in a large measure, due to increased plane performance caused by better handling of the engines in flight and the cutting down of gun jams by ceaseless honing of the gun parts. About half the gun jams were cut out when Abie Karp developed a new, quick, and certain way of eliminating off-size and out-of-shape bullets. He made a mock-up breech mechanism that served as a sure-fire test. This brought Abie the highest rank Eddie could bestow on any member of the squadron, that of a Good Gimper.

The *esprit de corps* in the 94th was as high as it was unusual. In line with the captain's orders, there was no distinction of rank. Everybody worked with the will to win. To an out-and-out military person this was naturally a rather strange arrangement, as Majors Carl Spaatz and Maxwell Kirby found out when they joined the 94th on temporary duty, to get some first-hand combat experience.

The very moment the two majors arrived on the field, after proper and punctilious salutes, Captain Rickenbacker took them into his office and told them, cold turkey, what his policies were, and why.

"You came in here as majors, but you know nothing about aerial combat," he concluded. "You have to learn it. The easy way to command respect from these kid combat pilots and from the mechanics, all of them enlisted men, is to take those blasted leaves off your shoulders, and keep them off while you're here. Then no one will have to jump every time you turn around. And whether you like it or not, I won't accept the responsibility of having you here unless you do that."

Majors Spaatz and Kirby laughed as they removed the insignia of their rank. Incidentally, they learned a lot about combat. In fact, the last Hun plane shot down by an American pilot in the war was bagged by Major Kirby on November 10, the day before the Armistice.

On October 30, Captain Rickenbacker landed after downing a Fokker and a balloon, within five minutes, shortly before sunset. These turned out to be his last victories in the war. When the Armistice was signed on November 11, the 94th had a total of sixty-nine Huns to its credit, twenty-nine more than the famous Lafayette Escadrille had downed in some three years of fighting. Captain Rickenbacker's score was twenty-six victories in seven months. His tunic bore such brave ribbons as the Cross of the Legion of Honor, the Distinguished Service Cross with nine Oak Leaves, the Croix de Guerre with four Palms. A decade later, he was awarded the Congressional Medal of Honor.

It was typical of the man that even as he flew on the first combat patrol of the 94th, so the only Hat-in-the-Ring plane that soared aloft in the hour of Armistice was Eddie's bullet-worn Number One Spad. The weather on that eventful day was cloudy and mean. All planes had been grounded. But Captain Rickenbacker craved one more moment in the front row of the theater of war. All morning, he worked on the engine of his plane. About 10:45 he announced that he was going up on a test flight. He did not say where or for how long. The ceiling was under five hundred feet, but the horizontal visibility was not bad as he hedge-hopped toward the front. First he came to Verdun; then he went from Verdun down along the front. Exploding around him in black puffs was the ever frustrated Archie. From the ground came rifle and machine-gun fire. Bullets sang all around him. Some lead even drilled through his wings. Below there was the usual scene of desolation and gray silence of no man's land, broken by the orange stabs of gunfire on both sides.

Then, suddenly, as if some one had pulled a switch or banged a gavel, the firing ended. Eddie looked at his wrist watch. The hands pointed to eleven o'clock. Pushing his nose up, Rick pulled the triggers of his guns and sent a spray of tracer bullets high into the sky. Then, with empty guns, he dipped his wing and sideslipped down over no man's land, which was desolate no longer. He saw helmets being hurled high and rifles thrown into the air as two waves of men moved toward each other—one of them German, the other American. Now the men shook hands and pounded backs. Soldiers who five minutes earlier would have shot to kill, now danced with each other in clumsy gyrations or swapped cigarettes.

The war was over!

The war to end wars had run its course!

Suddenly, as he flew homeward, Eddie realized that he had just seen the closing of the death factory that had been his job.

Peace!

What now?

He was not sure, but as his wheels almost grazed tree tops and roofs on his low-level homeward journey, he made up his mind that, whatever happened, he would never go back to automobile racing. Some day soon, he would build the Great American Car.

About a week after Armistice Day, the 94th was ordered to proceed to Koblenz, Germany, with the Army of Occupation. At the same time, Captain Rickenbacker was ordered to return to the United States to help in the Victory Loan Drive. This order created such a furore in the 94th that all hands, from pilots to grease monkeys, signed a petition to General Pershing asking that it be revoked so that he might lead his own outfit in the great victory invasion of Germany. With the strong support of Billy Mitchell, who had been made a brigadier general in October, Captain Rickenbacker was allowed to proceed with the Army of Occupation. For a few weeks, the squadron was stationed at Koblenz; then it was moved up to Trier, the original Zeppelin Experimental Station. Just before dinner one evening, Lieutenant Alden Sherry of the 94th came into his commander's room.

"Eddie," he said, "I just ran into a German flight lieutenant who wants to meet you."

"Yes, and you know the rules against fraternizing with the enemy!"

"Oh, but this is all right. His parents run a small shoe store up the street. They live right over the shop—the name is Strummer—all you have to do is to go in and look at a pair of shoes."

Captain Rickenbacker decided to have a try at it. A day or two later, he went into the store, was taken upstairs to a small living room where he met Oberleutnant Strummer, a short, stocky, slow-spoken fellow who said that most of his flying had been in photographic work.

That reminded Eddie of his numerous unsuccessful tries at Rumpler 16. As he told the story, Strummer grinned more and more broadly and, presently, he was telling the story too, for he had been the pilot of that plane. He produced some pictures, and one of them showed Eddie's own Number One firing tracers at the cameraman's plane.

Early in January, Captain Rickenbacker turned down an invitation to drive in the 1919 Indianapolis five-hundred-miler. At that time, he and Reed Chambers were interested in reports that American Navy fliers and English pilots were planning to fly the Atlantic from America to England that spring. They felt that the Army Air Service should develop a similar project and beat the Navy and the British to the draw, but they met with little encouragement from high Army aviation officers in France. About this time, Captain Rickenbacker was ordered to return to the United States. He went by way of London, where he found time to visit the Sunbeam factory and pick up the papers and drawings he had been forced to leave with Coatalen in the winter of 1917. At the same time, Captain Rickenbacker wanted to find out what he could about English transatlantic flying schemes. He met Harry Hawker, who planned to fly nonstop in May from St. John's, Newfoundland, to Ireland, and learned about a similar project by John Alcock and Arthur Brown. Rumors had previously reached him about the United States Navy's projected NC–4 seaplane flight to Portugal. He felt keenly that the Army was missing a bet in not having a transatlantic entry. As soon as he got home, he proposed to go straight to Washington and do something about it.

Going to Liverpool to board the *Adriatic*—sister ship of the *Baltic,* on which he had sailed to war with General Pershing and his staff—Eddie recalled his old nemesis, the police sergeant. After searching quite a bit, he found him.

"Remember me?" asked Eddie with a grin.

"Aha," snorted the policeman. "So you're back again, eh?"

"Yeah, and what are you going to do about it?"

The police sergeant clicked the heels of his thick-soled shoes clumsily together as he brought his right hand up in a ragged salute.

"I'm going to salute you, sir," he said, seriously and slowly. "That's what I'm going to do about it. And the port of Liverpool is yours, Captain Rickenbacker, as long as I'm on the job."

During World War Two, several United States military pilots topped Rick's bag of enemy planes. In view of the higher fire-power of more accurate guns, larger numbers of planes in the air and longer duration of fighting, this is not surprising. By the end of the war, his total bag was twenty-two planes and four hard-to-get observation balloons. When it is remembered that, of these victories, he shot down eleven planes and three balloons between September 14th and October 30th, his feats as a flying fighter become so much more remarkable.

Book Five

Commerce

WHEELS, WINGS, AND WAR
1919-1942

Chapter XVII

~~~~~~

As the once famous *Adriatic* followed its methodical course to New York, Eddie took inventory of his assets and evaluated his future. In assets, he had only his skill as a driver, pilot, and mechanic. Financially he had scraped the bottom of the till. The savings of his racing-days had been used up in caring for his mother and eking out his rather meager Army pay. To put it briefly, he was broke. He could always make money as a racing driver; but he had decided that racing, for him, was a closed chapter. In fact, he rejected a very handsome offer from the Sunbeam people in England. No more racing for Eddie. This decision was not because his love for automobiles had been supplanted by a yearning to fly.

Being an absolute realist and a straight thinker, Eddie knew that aviation, as a business that paid off in income, was not even in its swaddling-clothes stage. After mulling things over, he decided that he wanted to get into business for himself, making the Great American Car. To do it he had to borrow money, maybe start on a shoestring and live on the lean side for a while. Well, that was all right so long as he had enough to provide for his mother. His decision was made by the time the *Adriatic* docked at its Hoboken pier.

Scores of reporters and photographers boarded the ship, expecting to get a lot of blood-and-thunder copy from a daredevil racing driver who had turned into a spectacular aerial shooting star. They met with a heavy disappointment. The tall, straight, serious-faced, and serious-minded young captain did not talk about his exploits in downing Germans but said his first mission was to get in touch with the families of men in his outfit who had died overseas. This serious note set the reporters rocking on their heels. Here was a new kind of returning hero.

"What about flying the Atlantic?" some one asked. "Do you think any one can do it, or is it a pipe dream?"

"If the United States Army wants a man to fly across the Atlantic, and will provide the necessary support, I am willing to do the job."

When asked to express his views on the war and the future, Eddie said:

"It makes a fellow think to see so many men die. It makes him think about the meaning of life. Like many others who have gone through battle, I feel that from now on I shall take a greater interest in this country—especially in the young people. It's the young who count. I am going to take the duties of citizenship much more seriously than I used to, and I will take more interest than ever before in helping elect the right kind of men to run America."

The interview was broken up by a sergeant with the brassard of the military police, who elbowed his way politely but firmly through the ring of reporters and said he had orders to escort the captain to the pier office at once.

"What's up?" Rick wanted to know.

"No idea, captain," replied the sergeant. Then, recalling the troubles he had with British counterintelligence on his arrivals in Liverpool, Eddie laughingly observed: "Maybe they think I'm a German spy?"

The sergeant maintained a silence that, to Eddie, seemed ominous. They walked down the gangplank, picked their way through a pier shed cluttered with cargo and people, until they came to the pier office. The sergeant pointed to an empty chair, asked the captain to wait, and knocked respectfully at an inner door. Receiving a brisk but muffled "Come in," he disappeared. A second later a two-star general opened the door and barked, "Rickenbacker—come here!"

More in a tailspin than ever, Eddie snapped to his feet at attention, walked stiff-legged across the floor and past the general into the adjoining room. And there, next to an over-age wood-burning stove, stood his mother—the person whom he loved most in this world. She looked a little older than the last time Eddie saw her before he went overseas. There was a gentle smile on her face as she held out her arms. Then her lips trembled as tears formed in the corners of her bird-bright eyes.

Eddie shook a finger at her and said with a smile: "Don't forget, Mother, I promised I'd never make you cry again." Both remembered the night after Father Rickenbacker's burial. Then Eddie swept her into his arms and, like any woman, Mother Rickenbacker had a good cry.

The stern two-star general, now all smiles over the success of the home-coming surprise, turned out to be Major General Charles T. Menoher who was soon to become Chief of the Army Air Service.

That evening Eddie was the guest of honor, at a mammoth banquet in the Waldorf-Astoria ballroom, of the Contest Board of the Automobile Association of America, the very board which, a few years earlier, had ruled him off the track. Every one in motordom was there, and so were many of the great and near-great in politics, finance, and commerce. Also present were several friends from the speedway world.

Seated on the dais next to Secretary of War Newton D. Baker, Eddie took the chance to boost his idea for an Army transatlantic flight. Secretary Baker had a lot to say on the subject, but it all boiled down to an unqualified *No!* Then and there, Rick buried any hope he had of flying the Atlantic. He knew the Army; knew the Stone Age attitude that prevailed among War Department leaders of that era toward aviation had not changed with the ending of the war, and decided that he might as well drop a hopeless cause.

At the long speakers' table that night was Dr. Henry van Dyke, outstanding clergyman and educator. Having overheard the conversation, he suggested that, since Captain Rickenbacker's plan for a transatlantic flight had evidently gone into the discard, he might like to serve the cause of France by touring the country on behalf of the Fund for French Wounded. Eddie answered that he was not much of a public speaker. However, Dr. van Dyke, who was one of the greatest verbal spellbinders of his day, made him promise that he would give the proposal serious consideration.

As the banquet ran its course and Congressman Clifford Ireland, the toastmaster, introduced speaker after speaker, Eddie became more and more convinced that the silken garments of postwar complacency had already replaced the rough robes of war here at home. Their words suggested that the Dove of Peace had not come to America with a mere olive branch—it had scattered cargoes of olive seeds of peace from coast to coast. Nearly all the speakers talked as if Mars were dead.

Throughout it all, Eddie suffered as only those can whose duty it is to sit and suffer and smile as orators pour out platitudes about themselves. The climax came when the Secretary of War, in the course of his remarks, said of Captain Rickenbacker:

"In his old age, it will gladden his heart as it will ours, to see men walking on Earth unafraid, enjoying liberty and justice, and to feel that in his youth he ventured death to bring that about . . ."

Words! Words! Words that had neither reality nor meaning. In that long speech, not a word about preparedness—not a word about the enemy rising again to strike as he had struck before.

Some one had to deliver that warning—some one had to let America know that the end of the war was not, in itself, the end of danger. Thinking rapidly, Eddie decided that he, for one, would deliver that warning whenever he could. He realized that Dr. van Dyke's invitation to tour the country on behalf of the French Fund would give him the greatest chance to speak his mind to the largest number of people.

Just as he had made up his mind to accept, there was a slight commotion in the central box in the gallery that ran along the wall of the old Waldorf-Astoria's ballroom. He looked up and saw his mother enter the box, with his sister Emma. Taking her seat, Mother Rickenbacker removed her silver-rimmed glasses and started to wipe them as calmly as if in the living room of her home in Columbus. Completely taken by surprise for the second time that day, Eddie stared across the room; then he rose to his feet, waved his napkin, and, unmindful of the thousands of eyes and ears that followed his every move and word, shouted at the top of his voice:

"Hello, Mother! Gosh, but I'm glad to see you!"

The crowd in the room went wild. Automobile tycoons and

racing drivers, the politically and financially great and near-great, leaped to their feet and cheered. Some jumped on their chairs and cheered. Others even climbed up on the tables and cheered. Napkins swished up and down like a Hollywood blizzard. Tears of pride and joy streaked down Eddie's lean cheeks. But the little old lady from Columbus, who never believed everything she read in the papers, and who had known her aviator son would be safe in France because there were no fences in the air and because he flew low and slow, that little old lady simply put her clean glasses back on her high-bridged nose and had neither eye nor ear nor thought for any one or anything in that room but Eddie— her little boy, Eddie! To her he looked so handsome there in his well-fitting uniform, with wings and ribbons on his chest. Still, those were things that did not matter. The big thing was that he had come back! That was all that really counted. For a brief moment her lips trembled and her eyes dewed up; but Eddie, seeing it, shook a warning forefinger.

Only Dr. van Dyke and a few others knew it at the time, but Mother Rickenbacker's entrance had been carefully timed to fit in with the next event on the program, the presentation to Eddie by Dr. van Dyke of a pair of Air Service wings made of platinum and studded with diamonds and sapphires, a gift to America's foremost Ace, by his own "gang"—the automotive industry of America. After the soul-stirring speech of presentation, Eddie was completely wordless. He stood with the beautiful wings in his hands, silent and motionless for fully thirty seconds; then he lifted them toward his mother and said: "I give them to you, Mother!" Again the crowd went mad. It was a great evening for the Rickenbackers— a great evening for Mother Rickenbacker, at any rate. It had some disturbing elements for Eddie, foremost of which was the seeming prevalence at home of the idea that the time had come to turn the swords of victory into stock shares. Choked up as he was with a deep conviction, and being prevented by his uniform from speaking his mind in public, Eddie made a rather halting and poorly articulated response when his time came to talk at the end of the banquet. However, before the dinner broke up he had an opportunity to tell the Secretary of War his belief that America should plan on an Air Service of tens of thousands of pilots and planes, and that this air strength should dominate both the Army and the Navy for "the simple reason that air dominates both land and sea."

The Secretary of War, in a jovial mood, told Eddie that, while airplanes had shown ability to fight in wars, it was open to doubt whether they would ever *win* wars. And, since in all likelihood there would be no more wars, what was the use of stirring up a lot of argument over nothing? This viewpoint called to Eddie's mind a talk he had with General Mitchell in Germany. The General had told him that the biggest fight to maintain peace would be to insure a strong air policy in the Army and Navy.

From the banquet Eddie went with his mother and sister to the hotel which, for several weeks, was to be his headquarters.

Eddie soon discovered that a man did not have to make a mousetrap in order for the world to make a path to his door. There was an endless stream of visitors, telegrams, telephone calls, and letters from people with axes to grind and fish to fry; hostesses who wanted the aerial lion to roar at their dinners; businessmen who knew people he "ought to meet." Delegations from "home towns," where he had driven to fame in racing cars, wanted to give him big home-coming parties. Honors a plenty, but Eddie was fed up on honors. He was rich in honors but low in funds.

Money! Ah, that was easy. Why, all the gold in the world could be his. All he had to do was to sign contracts allowing the use of his name on various kinds of goods from shaving cream to cigarettes—on shirts, hats, shoes, and underwear. Thousands of dollars could have been his for the use of his name; but rich or poor, broke or flush, his name was not for sale.

Publishers, editors, syndicate agents, and ghost writers came with tempting offers, as did vaudeville managers, circus owners, stage producers, and movie fly-by-nights. Every one was ready to hand Eddie a fat check if he would only sign a contract without looking too closely at the small print. Airplane manufacturers offered to back him to the limit in forming barnstorming flying teams. No, thanks! Automobile makers wanted him to drive their racing cars. "Write your own terms, Eddie!" No, thanks!

Carl Laemmle, head of mighty Universal Pictures, put young

Irving Thalberg on a "death watch" with a check for $100,000 as part payment for Eddie's services in making a motion picture. Again and again Eddie said: "No, thanks." Finally, in desperation, he sent Laemmle a wire saying: "One hundred thousand times: *No!*"

Eddie at that point of his life was so low in funds that he had to borrow money. He did not borrow it from friends, but from a bank on a business basis. He did not want a dollar with a single string attached to it. One night, jokingly, he told his mother that they might have to borrow money on the diamond-studded wings . . . the wings she wore with an equal mixture of fear and pride.

"We will not!" she replied firmly. "I am saving those wings for the girl!"

"What girl?"

"The girl you are going to marry when you get set. And you'd better hurry up, Eddie," she added with a twinkle. "You're getting pretty old."

But there was not a girl in his life. Ever since his early boyhood the fight for mere security, to keep his mother's humble little home going, had been so strenuous that he had determined not to fall in love, to marry, until he could offer the thing which, in his opinion, mattered most—security. To obtain that, Rick would have to get into a steady, established business. His own business. And every time he thought about the future, he thought about an automobile —the Rickenbacker Car. Some day, somehow, he would make that car, and it would sweep the roads of America. It would be a car no other car could beat. It would be his pride. It would make him both happy and rich. Then, and only then, would he find *the* girl; then he would get married and have a home. Children perhaps. Ah, it was good to dream about—but many things had to happen before that dream could come true.

Meanwhile, during those early months of 1919, Eddie said No to all comers and all offers except one: Dr. Henry van Dyke's invitation to make a country-wide tour on behalf of the French Fund. Hardly had he accepted, before he wished that he had declined. Being a precisionist in lectures as well as automobiles and airplanes, he discovered that he was a dud as a public speaker. True, he had talked himself hoarse over and over again in bull sessions with his drivers, pilots, and mechanics. But there was a great difference between speaking your mind to your "gang" and delivering a prepared address to an audience. To begin with, he did not even know how to write what he wanted to say. Needing help, he thought of Damon Runyon, a war correspondent on the western front to whom he had taken a great liking. The dour-faced reporter helped him put his talk together, and arranged for vocal lessons under Madame Amanda, who coached the foreign-born stars of the Metropolitan Opera. Day after day, when opera rehearsal and matinee schedules permitted, Eddie would stand on the great Metropolitan stage and make his speech to an audience of one—that one being Madame Amanda, perched in the last row of the top gallery of the dark and cavernlike theater. He would wrestle with his speech on the stage where Romeo courted Juliet and Othello slew Desdemona. Every so often, Madame Amanda would sing out from her Jovian height, "Throw your right arm out here!" or "Throw your left hand up here!" At times, he felt like throwing the whole thing out then and there. His trouble was not merely that he spoke badly, but that he could not remember what to say. So he not only studied such guides to oratory as "Master-Speeches of the Ages" and "Modern Eloquence," but subscribed to the Roth Memory Course and learned all about the famous but evanescent person known far and wide as Mr. Addison Sims of Seattle. Remember him?

Having found a writer to write his speech, a teacher to show him how to deliver it, and a memory course to enable him to remember it, Eddie might be thought to be fairly well set when he launched out on his lecture tour through New England in March, 1919, to "try it on the dog," before he had his big opening at the Metropolitan Opera House in New York in April. But, alas, such was not the case. He was greeted in Worcester, Massachusetts, by a huge crowd. His hands, feet, and forehead were cold and wet, but his throat and lips were hot and dry. After the introduction by a leading local attorney, he stood before the expectant audience and finally declared:

"This is my wirst speech in Fuster!" It not only brought the house down, but almost brought Eddie down.

One night, he spoke in Symphony Hall, Boston. He was scared

almost to death because Major General Edwards' presided and
Governor Calvin Coolidge introduced him. Feeling very small, he
started looking for a friendly mousehole, but he perked up as
Governor Coolidge began to hem and haw his introductory remarks in a small, high-pitched, and rather whining voice.

"That's the Governor of Massachusetts speaking," said Eddie
to himself. "Listen to him, boy, and get hep to yourself. If he
can get away with what he's grinding off, you can knock 'em dead."

And knock 'em dead, he did. He threw his prepared speech to
the blizzard that howled outside and dived into that Boston crowd
with both guns blazing. He gave them a raking over about war and
peace and preparedness that echoed around Beacon Hill for weeks.

That night, Eddie lost his fear of speaking before crowds; and
he had no further trouble assembling the points he wanted to discuss, remembering them, or presenting them in terse, dramatic
language. And he owed it all to Calvin Coolidge. Some years later,
he spent an evening with Mr. Coolidge in the White House, pleading the cause of General Mitchell, who was then about to be
dropped from the Army because of his emphatic views on air
defense. When Eddie told him about that night in Boston the
President showed no change of expression; but Eddie's keen eyes
noticed a slight seismographic disturbance along the rim of the
Coolidge granite jaw.

It was a good thing that Eddie found his stage presence before
his Metropolitan Opera meeting in New York, because in the
middle of that program there was an accident that would have
made almost any performer blow up : the projection apparatus that
threw pictures on a screen to illustrate the lecture went out of
order, and suddenly the stage was drenched in a glaring white light.
There stood Eddie speechless with a ten-foot fishing pole he used
as a pointer. The silence became painful as the audience squirmed
in its seats and the speaker was rooted to the stage. Then some one
yelled :

"Hey, Rick, why don't you go fishing?"

Quick as could be, the speaker came back :

"I would if I had some bait."

That broke the ice. The densely packed house howled, and the next day Eddie's press notices left nothing to be desired. He was a success on the Big Time!

From New York, he made a tour that took him into nearly every state of the Union. Whatever small capacity he might have had at the outset for accepting the acclaim of the crowd soon died out. Before long, he took off his uniform with its wings and ribbons so that he might travel in peace from town to town. He came to dread the big public receptions that were part of the routine; but he dreaded even more looking up the wives and mothers of men in his outfit who had died in the war. Those meetings took the heart out of him, but they reinforced his determination forever and always to do what he could to see to it that the dead did not die in vain. The small children or the younger brothers and sisters of the men who died made Eddie a crusader for youth in the course of the years.

Captain Rickenbacker's tour ended in Seattle, just in time. Another week of lecturing and he would have had to cancel out. The steady strain of playing a public role he hated had taken a heavy toll. He had lost appetite and weight. He could not rest. Nightmares haunted him. After his last lecture, he took to walking in his sleep. He made a quick trip to Columbus, where he arranged funds for his mother, borrowed enough cash for himself to go to Tucson, Arizona, and buy a fourth-hand Model-T Ford, which he filled with the staple provender of a desert rat. Then he pulled out for the hills, to sit in the sun and think and to lie under the stars and sleep. For two months he roamed the mountains and the desert, and in this solitude he found not only peace but purpose. The time had come, he decided, to make or break his dream of the Great American Car. He spent hours planning it, part by part, as he loafed in the Arizona sun. To be sure, now and then—when he saw fat, white clouds float against the sky—he would get terribly homesick for the blue expanse above him; but he would brush those thoughts aside, knowing that for all their limitless horizons, the lanes of the air, just then, did not lead to his most important goal: security.

In making plans for the Rickenbacker car, Eddie had selected three men who might want to help him make it. They were Harry Cunningham, a veteran who had driven Henry Ford's "999" and helped build the Winton car; "Barney" Everett and Walter E. Flanders, also pioneer car builders. These three, Rick's friends from his earliest Mason and Duesenberg days, might want to put up the money for the experimental models of the Rickenbacker car. He met them in Detroit, and they listened with interest and approval to his idea of building a speedy, durable, and smart automobile incorporating features of performance and reliability that he had tested out in the laboratory of the race track. After some discussion, they agreed to put up $200,000 so that the initial model could be built, tested, and produced. It was to have a six-cylinder engine and sell around $1,500. (Eddie insisted that the experimental model should be built at once—in great secrecy—but that the car should not be placed on sale until January, 1922. Candidly, his associates thought that there was no need to take two full years to develop the car. Still, Eddie stubbornly maintained that he wanted "a car worthy of its name." And that, by the way, became its selling slogan even as the Hat-in-the-Ring was the proud insigne on its radiator-shield.

"But," his partners remonstrated, "look at the market we are losing by waiting two years! They're buying cars in our class at the rate of half a million a year!"

"Give me a chance," pleaded Flanders, who created the assembly line for Ford, "and I'll turn Rickenbacker cars out by the thousands before next spring."

"Nothing doing," insisted Eddie. "Everybody nowadays tries to build *more* cars instead of *better* cars. They're putting on fancy gadgets instead of adding real engineering progress. I'll show them up!"

He insisted that he did not want to head the organization as president.

"But it's your car! Your name's on it," spluttered Cunningham. "People will expect you to be the head man of the company."

"That's where you are 100 per cent wrong," answered Eddie. "To most people I am either a happy-go-lucky racing driver or a daredevil wartime flyer. They'll accept me as such, but not as a manufacturing executive. Make me sales manager. That's where I fit in best—demonstrating cars and mixing with people. That's my meat."

And that was the way it was left. Rickenbacker, aided by

Cunningham and a small but select staff of engineers and mechanics, assembled the first Rickenbacker car step by step and with
greatest stealth. The first car "worthy of its name" was, oddly
enough, a car without a name. To the casual observer, it looked like
any popular 1919 make of car; but it had no name tag. This
was part of the plan to keep its real identity a secret. Under the
hood and beneath the chassis of this car were engine and construction changes that had been born on the speedway—such as four-
wheel brakes, reduced engine vibration, greater safety due to a
low center of gravity, a double flywheel, and greater economy in oil
and gas consumption. As soon as the car was ready, Eddie took
it on cross-country road tests that lasted many months and covered
almost 150,000 miles. He drove it through the heat of the desert;
he pushed it to the heights of the Sierras; he fought it through
the gumbo roads of Iowa, the mud roads of Texas and the dirt
roads of New England. That first Rickenbacker car was called
upon to meet every climate and every road condition in America.
In the course of these exhaustive tests, flaws crept out of hiding.
They were corrected. It is estimated that that original Rickenbacker
car used up enough replacement parts to build three new ones. However, by the time Eddie drove it back to Detroit, the veteran car
was a sturdy traveler that had proved itself worthy of its name.

"It's O.K.," said Eddie as he turned it over to his engineering
partners for production. "It has what it takes—and it can take
anything that any skillful driver can hand it."

The partners were jubilant. They knew that Eddie never compromised with perfection. If he said the car was good, it was
good!

"But wait a minute," he continued. "I said that the car is
O.K. in the hands of a *skillful* driver. But how many skillful drivers
are there?"

"Darn few," the partners admitted.

"In that case," ventured Eddie, "our next step is to make this
car so sturdy and reliable that not even the most careless driver
can hurt it."

That was a pretty large order, thought Cunningham, Flanders,
and Everett as they shifted uneasily in their seats. This was a

brand-new Rickenbacker: a man who wanted automobile perfection at a time when horses by the thousand still worked up sweat by hauling stalled cars off streets and highways.

"Got an idea!" exploded Eddie before anyone had a chance to speak. "We'll find two or three boys who know nothing about driving, and will let them drive our first cars any way they want to. Then we'll see how the cars stand up. They ought to get plenty of abuse."

This program was carried out, and it proved most productive. Meanwhile, during his testing run, Eddie had given considerable thought to the sales end of the business—his end. He realized that he had much to learn in every branch of sales management. And, again, Eddie the Strategist set himself to overcoming this deficiency. Finally he had the solution:

A new car, a four-cylinder job that sold around $1,500, had just been placed on the market. It had no sales organization, no dealers, no reputation—all handicaps. It was called the Sheridan, and it had nothing ahead of it but solid and intrenched competition. A four-cylinder car in a six-cylinder market. Eddie thought that here was a tough nut to cut his teeth on. He promptly went after the job of West Coast sales distributor and got it.

Eddie did not know what "sales resistance" meant until he began to try to sell the Sheridan. First, he had to find zone distributors—and they were hard to get. Then he had to help the zone distributors get local dealers—and they were even harder to find. On top of that he had to help the local dealers find purchasers—and that was an uphill job in low gear. But despite all handicaps he reached the crest of that defiant hill. By late fall in 1920, Eddie had a complete wholesale-retail-and-service system and some thirty dealers who, all told, had sold a thousand Sheridan cars. Despite the 1921 depression, his sales organization did rather well; but in midsummer, 1921, he quit the job to return to Detroit, where the Rickenbacker car was ready to go into production. The 1921 depression had been a lucky break for the partners. They had been able to buy plants, machinery, and materials at bottom prices.

Things were moving so smoothly at the factory, and business prospects for 1922 were so good as the end of the slump came in

sight, that Eddie and his partners decided to go to New York
to see the Huggins boys in the American League and the McGraw
men in the National League slug it out for the World Series pennant
of 1921. They and a lot of other members of Detroit's motordom
"gang" took a floor at the Biltmore Hotel and got set for a high
old time. On the night of his arrival in New York the thought
struck Eddie that he had not seen his old friend Billy Mitchell
for several weeks. In fact, the two had had very frequent and
long meetings since General Mitchell's return from Europe after
the war. On the spur of the moment, he sent a telegram to the
general, who was then the storm center in the battle waged between
stone-age-minded military leaders and those who recognized that
the horseless carriage and the flying machine had come to stay,
even in the Army. Mitchell, although he was shoulder-high in a
life-and-death controversy, decided to take time out to fly up to
New York for the ball game. He arrived the next day in full military
regalia: stiff-collared blouse with Sam Browne belt; his cap set at
the typical Mitchell angle; his chest covered with several rows of
well earned ribbons; a swagger stick in his well gloved hands, and
boots on his feet so highly polished that they could have served
as shaving mirrors.

After the ball game, Eddie and his party returned to the Biltmore, had dinner, and made plans for the evening. It was proposed
to visit the "21" and other leading speakeasies of the fabulous Pro-
hibition era. Mitchell, who loved a good time, was all for it; but
his friend voted against his going.

"You look hotter than a firecracker in that get-up, Billy, and
I'm not going to be seen with any billboard like you. Get into civvies,
and you can go with us!"

"But, Eddie," protested General Mitchell, good-naturedly, "I
have no other clothes with me."

"We'll fix you up, feller."

With a shirt borrowed here, trousers borrowed there, shoes, tie,
coat and hat picked up from rooms here and there along the floor,
Billy Mitchell was soon dressed for the "speaks."

Now, ever since the verbal licking Mitchell had given him
before the cynical French officer for damaging his car, Eddie Rick-

enbacker had carried a grudge against him. Eddie loved and respected the general too deeply not to forgive him; but the incident had rankled, and tonight he decided to get rid of his bitter feeling by bringing it into the open. As the party was breaking up, he suggested to the general that they drop into Jim Moriarity's for a nightcap of "real" Canadian ale. That sounded good to Mitchell. They were comfortably seated in Jim's cozy place, and Eddie was just about to launch his offensive when Mitchell said:

"Look here, Eddie, there's something I have always been sorry about. I owe you an apology for the time when I bawled you out about my car—or maybe you've forgotten?"

"Forgotten? Say, I've been lying awake nights wondering how I could make you pay for it. But now"—Eddie laughed—"you spoil it all, Billy, by saying you're sorry."

"And I really am."

"O.K. then." Eddie reached his right hand across the table. "Forget it, and shake on it!" And shake they did.

The sun was fairly high on the sky line of Manhattan before the two parted company: Mitchell to fly back to Washington; Eddie to get some sleep. During the still hours of that night, Billy Mitchell and Eddie Rickenbacker had decided that they had a common goal—the goal of making America air-defense-minded to such an extent that public opinion would demand a military air establishment strong in men, machines, and performance. The ties of that night between Mitchell and Rickenbacker grew stronger with the years. And the role Eddie was to play, visibly on stage and invisibly back-stage, in the great drama of aerial preparedness was written during those hours. Small wonder then that Eddie's head was crowded with many thoughts as he returned to Detroit a few days later to work out his sales campaign for the Rickenbacker car and at the same time shape his course as an apostle of aerial preparedness in America.

By this time everybody knew that Eddie had gone into automobile manufacturing. The Rickenbacker Car Company was publicly organized in August, 1921, with a capital of $5,000,000. Now, $5,000,000 may be a lot of money in some kinds of business; but it is small potatoes in making and financing automobiles. During the latter part of 1921, the Rickenbacker plant worked overtime to roll the new, shining cars off the assembly lines. Every one was kept carefully under wraps because the Rickenbacker car was to be the big surprise of the January, 1922, automobile show in New York City. The Rickenbacker "line" consisted of a touring car, a coupé, and a sedan, six-cylinder cars that sold respectively at $1,485, $1,885 and $1,985. Eddie personally supervised the setting-up of the Hat-in-the-Ring exhibit, preliminary to the opening of the auto show. Like the boy who had dusted off the C.B.C. car in the Chicago show more than a dozen years back, he rubbed the lacquer and polished the metal on these sparkling new cars with his own hands.

Among those who helped him put the finishing touch on arranging the flowers and palms that flooded the exhibit, was a tall and slender woman with prematurely gray hair, clear and vividly blue eyes, a gracious manner, and a ready smile. Her name was Adelaide Frost, and she had only recently come to New York from Paris where she had gone after obtaining a divorce from Clifford Durant. Eddie, who had been so reluctant all these years to speed down the roaring road of romance to the finish line at the altar, suddenly saw Cupid wave the starter's flag, and he was off in the typical Rickenbacker headlong rush. It was not a case of love at first sight, however, because he had known Adelaide for many years.

None of Eddie's or Adelaide's friends ever quite learned how they became engaged, because it all happened with lightning speed. When Eddie came to New York in December, to prepare for the automobile show, he was heart-whole and fancy-free; but when the show closed in January he was engaged to be married in the fall. However, it all tied in with Eddie's over-all plan of life: that where there was no security there could be no absolute stability of happiness. But during those January weeks, his fears of the future vanished.

The Rickenbacker car was the hit of the show. It was selling like coal among Eskimos. Newspapers all over the country—all over the world, for that matter—gave it reams of publicity. Offers to handle the new car came from dealers in the East, North, West, and South. The Rickenbacker was a sure winner, and Eddie was heading for the big money. Big money! He did not want millions—just enough to have a home and wife and kids. It seemed wonderful, as he thought about Adelaide. No more barren and lonely hotel rooms for him; no more meals alone; no more having to solve all his problems by himself. He would have a real partner to share the load; and such a partner—he knew, without hesitation or doubt—was Adelaide.

As Eddie begins the third great phase of his career—his years as a motor maker—it is worth while to stop and look him over. At the age of thirty-two, he is still the tall, slim-waisted, and broad-shouldered athletic type. He holds his head high, and his carriage is young; but the deep lines near his mouth and eyes make him look somewhat older than he is. His eyes are deep-set under bushy brows, alert and questioning but rather friendly, and his smile, always one of his most engaging features, is still on tap. His lips have lost their boyish fullness; his mouth is hard, and his chin has a truculent bulge. His once thick hair is getting thinner and rides higher on his forehead. This gives a misleading intellectual look to a man who still is a rough-and-ready, two-fisted realist with little time for theory. He is neat, almost precise in his personal habits, but no tailor's dummy. His clothes have the inconspicuous look that good and expensive garments always have. His neckties are on the quiet side, and his lapel buttonhole is conspicuously free from any emblem or decoration. Everything about him is neat except his hat. Once he buys a hat, he hangs on to it with grim determination. The older, the more shapeless it is, the better he likes it, and he will not buy a new one until the old one falls apart. It is always a gray fedora, and it never stays new very long.

Despite his busy life, Eddie finds time to read a lot about the world he lives in. His lifelong habit has been to retire early, and since he does not need much sleep he usually rises about five o'clock. Most of his reading, and virtually all of his work on speeches and magazine articles, is done before breakfast. He has no need of a ghost writer.

There, briefly, is the Rickenbacker of 1922, and, for that matter, the Rickenbacker of today.

Twenty-odd years ago, Eddie may sometimes have longed for the freedom and feeling of power that come to men who fly, but he never revealed the longing. He was interested in transportation, and automobiles provided this. Some day the airplane might reach the stature of a transportation medium. On that day he would be ready for it. The plane's role in national defense was a different story. Here aviation was a known factor, and he campaigned late and early for a separate air force. His was the thunder that accompanied Billy Mitchell's lightning.

In the course of the spring and summer of 1922, the Rickenbacker sales organization spread all over America, and the makers of the Hat-in-the-Ring car had to bend all their resources to keep up with the demand. But the automobile business was still seasonal, and when fall brought a breathing spell, Eddie and Adelaide were married. Immediately after the ceremony, on September 16, the couple boarded a steamer for a honeymoon tour of Europe, in the course of which Eddie planned to study the new European cars, and the trend toward a small-cylinder, high-combustion engine delivering a high ratio of power to the gasoline consumed.

Eddie returned to Detroit with a stronger belief than ever in the small-cylinder engine. His partners still were doubtful of it. This widened a rift that had opened when they vetoed the use of four-wheel brakes on the 1922 model, as too experimental. He yielded, but only temporarily. The Rickenbacker car, during its brief existence, pioneered in many engineering features that afterward became standard for all cars. Among these Rickenbacker "firsts" were the small, gasoline-saving, smooth-pulling, high-speed motor; the double flywheel to take the whip out of the crankshaft; balloon tires; the gasoline-eliminating crankcase oil filter; and cradle spring suspension to insure better balance by lowering the center of gravity. It is not implied that Eddie Rickenbacker and his engineers invented all these improvements. He simply applied to cars for general use improvements that racing automobiles had tested, incorporating them in the Rickenbacker car not all at once but from time to time, usually against protests of the company's directors. Some of his partners feared these improvements would incur the wrath of competitors. Adding to the production cost of the car, they would force competitors to change their cars drastically, reducing profits or lifting prices. Either that, or the other manufacturers would have to fight Rickenbacker.

The die was cast when the Rickenbacker car came out with four-wheel brakes. Today all cars have four-wheel brakes, but twenty years ago only the rear wheels had brakes. There was nothing new in the four-wheel-brake idea even then: the Peugeot car Eddie had driven in 1915 races had brakes on every wheel, and many European cars had four-wheel brakes. In the United States there was nothing wrong with them except that they added to production problems and production costs. That, plus the fact that, if the Rickenbacker four-wheel-brake automobile won public approval, it would revolutionize the industry. The entire American trade—from manufacturers to dealers, from parts makers to car owners—had hundreds of millions of dollars tied up in two-wheel-brake automobiles. American owners (so the argument ran) took a peculiar pride in driving high-grade, up-to-date cars, and if the four-wheel-brake idea caught on millions of automobile owners would be dissatisfied. The four-wheel-brake Rickenbacker was greeted by the trade with brickbats and slander. Competitors ran full-page advertisements in the nation's press charging that four-wheel brakes were not only unnecessary but dangerous because— it was claimed—they made cars stop too suddenly. Whispering campaigns told of people who had snapped their necks, cracked their spines, broken their bones, and died in agony from using four-wheel brakes. One company spent almost $200,000 on a single full-page blast against the Rickenbacker four-brake car, saying that experiments had shown that four-wheel brakes caused cars to turn over and wore tires out faster.

All over the country, other dealers ganged up on Rickenbacker dealers. Potential buyers were scared away from the salesrooms by the tens of thousands. Thus it came about that the company's pioneering in four-wheel brakes—one of the greatest improvements of all time in automobile construction and driving safety—brought it to a gradual financial stop from which it never recovered. One factor in this was the 1925 slump, which made money tight for borrowers and strangled the business of hundreds of Rickenbacker

dealers who did not enjoy the credit or the resources which agents
for longer established cars had. Another great blow was the death
of Walter Flanders, who was killed in a crash. Directors and stockholders now got to bickering, and one day Eddie decided that he
had had enough. He scribbled a few lines on a piece of paper, got
up from his chair, shrugged into a topcoat, jammed his old gray
hat on his head and started for the door.

"Goodbye, boys," he said. "Here's where I get off. I can't go
along any further because I don't want to be a party to having any
one lose any more money. The Rickenbacker Company is in the
ditch and out of the race, and the best way I can let people know
that we're out of the running is to walk away from the wreck.
You'll find my resignation on the table!"

He stiff-armed the door open, walked out, and kicked it shut
behind him.

Thus, Eddie's lifelong dream of the Great American Car came
to an end. As he headed almost blindly toward home, he thought
about how hard he had hoped, how hard he had worked, how
hard he had fought to make the Rickenbacker car worthy of its
name. Now, just because of that very determination—just because
he would never compromise with the best—his car had been
crowded into the junkyard of failure. Without taking exact inventory he knew that he was broke, and owed about a quarter of a
million dollars which he could not pay.

Assets? He had none. Oh, yes, he had three: Adelaide and the
two boys—David and Bill.

Suddenly he grinned. Then he broke into howls of laughter.
People on the street looked at him with curious eyes. They could
not know that this man laughed because he suddenly remembered
his lifelong fetish: security. For years he had refrained from marry-
ing because he wanted to build his home on absolute security. Now
here he was, with a mother, a wife, and two baby boys, in the
worst financial mess ever.

Adelaide took it like a soldier. That very week the Rickenbackers gave up their swank duplex apartment, sold a lot of expensive furniture, and moved into a cottage.

Naturally, Eddie's many friends flocked to him. They offered him money, jobs and advice—particularly advice. Some of them urged him to go into bankruptcy and thus get rid of his quarter-million-dollar debt. But he stood firmly by his obligations and informed his creditors that he would pay every single dollar he owed them.

"I want to be able to look at myself in the morning when I shave," was his only answer when bankruptcy was suggested as an easier and cheaper way.

Eddie lived up to his promise. It took work and sacrifice and time, but he paid up.

Chapter XVIII

~~~~~~

When Eddie and his associates in the Rickenbacker Car Company came to a parting of the ways, he received many offers of employment. Some of these were fairly attractive, but he preferred to go into business for himself. Frank Blair of Detroit, head of one of the leading banks in Detroit, encouraged him: "If you can find anything that is worth while, anything you think is good, we will help you finance it. Bring it to us!"

This encouragement meant more to Eddie than mere working capital. It stimulated his morale. If Blair, a hardheaded, flinty-eyed banker, had confidence in him, he certainly had reason to have confidence in himself.

A friend told Eddie that the Allison Engineering Company in Indianapolis might be in the market, as the owner was getting old and wanted to retire. Jim Allison, who had been one of Carl Fisher's partners in building the Indianapolis Speedway, advised Eddie against buying his company on a shoestring, but told him that certain real estate interests were dickering for the Indianapolis Speedway. Having a deep loyalty to the Speedway as a great American institution for automotive progress, Eddie decided that he would try to save it from being cut into suburban building lots. Before he left Detroit, he had a thirty-day option to buy it; but bankers refused to lend money on it as a race track. The option almost expired, but by pulling every rope he could reach he obtained a thirty-day extension. Again he rang the doorbells and called the telephone numbers of financiers, businessmen, and bankers; but nowhere could he raise the $700,000 he needed. His real estate competitors were ready to close the deal against him, and were crowing one hour before the end of the extension—they had forgotten about the Eddie who took the high curve on the home stretch to hit the finish line ahead of the rest. Half an hour before the end, some hitherto reluctant backers promised to underwrite the deal, and, with five minutes to spare, he handed in the check that made the Speedway his.

It was only a moral victory, because the Indianapolis Speedway was in the class of white elephants. In the center of the Speedway oval Eddie built a beautiful $100,000 golf course, the fees from which helped to pull the track out of the red. Today he owns all the stock of the Speedway and expects it to pay off in postwar automobile improvements through the test of racing as it did for many years before and after the First World War. Eddie's firm conviction that in saving the Speedway he has contributed to continuous automotive development perhaps eases the pain he has always felt as a racing driver at his failure to reach his greatest goal: victory in the Indianapolis five-hundred-mile race.

Meanwhile Eddie, ready as ever to start at the bottom and work his way up from it, had taken a sales job with Cadillac Motors. By hard labor and successful salesmanship he soon became division manager for the LaSalle car, a Cadillac product within the over-all framework of General Motors.

At the same time he kept an eye on the airplanes which, in small but increasing numbers, had begun to open up regular transport schedules. In 1924, Reed Chambers (second-in-command in the 94th Pursuit Squadron) came to him with a plan for an air line from Atlanta to Miami. Eddie, who was in the money then, bought stock in the aviation company, together with some of his Detroit friends. Chambers bought five single-engined Fords and, operating under the name of Florida Airways, got the first real air-mail contract in this country—three dollars per pound of mail from Jacksonville to Miami by way of Tampa. Despite the contract, Florida Airways went broke.

During those pioneer days commercial air lines lacked both government and public support. In fact, most of them were only objects of speculation in Wall Street, and there was less high flying by air-line planes than there was by air-line stocks on the Exchange, Board, on the Curb, and on the cuff. The stocks would take off on the ticker in the morning and land back on the tape at closing

time several points higher with no production, no operations, no
real activity or progress in the air to justify the rise. The men in
aviation who tried to make the plane a full partner in the American
transportation system labored against terrific odds. Time and again
they were utterly frustrated by irresponsible market speculators
or financial highbinders. Florida Airways was one of the victims.

Taking the loss in his stride, Eddie made up his mind to get
into aviation despite lack of public support, despite the government's stupidly antagonistic policy toward aviation and despite
the stock speculators. The opportunity came in 1929, when General
Motors bought the Fokker Aircraft Corporation. Eddie was then
well on the way to the presidency of Cadillac. His friends urged
him to keep clear of that will-o'-the-wisp aviation; but Eddie
the Strategist, looking through the fog of finance and indifference
that blocked commercial air progress, could see the day when the
airplane would obtain transportation leadership. When that day
came, he wanted to be aboard. So he turned his back on automobiles for all time and climbed into the airplane, then a limp and
lifeless orphan of the storm. He remained with the Fokker Corporation until 1932, and during those three years he learned everything
he could learn about the construction of heavy aircraft. Under
his leadership Fokker built its famous thirty-two-passenger commercial plane, which was almost a decade ahead of its competitors
in speed, comfort, and stability.

In 1932, Eddie left Fokker to join the Aviation Corporation
of America, which owned American Airlines. He did his best
to knit this tangled skein into a system. He felt that, if Aviation
Corporation would absorb North American Aviation, he might
have a chance to use the air lanes of the latter to tie the routes
of the former into a solid and continuous pattern. There were many
useless odds and ends in North American, he knew; but worth-
while possessions were a big interest in Pan American, a controlling
interest in TWA and—last but far from least—Eastern Air Lines.
In the last, Eddie saw not only terminal links in Chicago and New
York for American Airlines but also feeder lines to Florida and
Texas which some day would lead to Central and South America.
At that time the financial wellsprings of Aviation Corporation were

Brown-Harriman and Lehman Brothers. Whenever he had a chance, he hounded Averell Harriman and Robert Lehman to buy North American or, at least, Eastern Air Lines. He was making headway and might have arranged a deal if E. L. Cord, who had made millions in the automobile business, had not decided just then to play with air-line kites on the stock ticker. Starting with the mid-western Century Airlines, Cord branched out into air lines in other parts of the country. Soon Aviation Corporation bought him out; but, instead of staying out, Cord began to buy blocks upon blocks of Aviation Corporation stock. The battle for control began in the fall of 1932 and lasted well into the spring of 1933, when he had enough stock and proxies to slide into the driver's seat. He won, but the fight had been bitter and dirty, undermining public faith in air-line operations.

Repeatedly, Eddie had warned both sides to stop fighting and come to an understanding. No use. He had no confidence in Cord as an air-line operator, and fought the cash Colossus tooth and nail regardless of the outcome. After Cord had been voted into power Eddie was cleaning out his desk preparatory to leaving when the magnate walked in.

"Well, E. L., when do you want it?"

"When do I want what?"

"My resignation," replied Eddie.

"Why?" Cord lit a cigarette.

"Because, you can't afford to keep me on. Everybody in the organization knows I was against you. I got licked. The people I was with got licked. I don't mind a bloody nose. It will cure itself. I will go about my business—you go about yours."

Cord puffed at his cigarette, looked at the tip for a moment, then grinned broadly at Eddie. "Well, I wish you'd stay and finish up what you are doing. Let's talk about it again, Eddie!"

"All right, I will stay with that understanding."

In April, 1933, Cord decided to move the headquarters of the company from New York to Chicago; and at the same time Eddie had an opportunity to return to General Motors Corporation as vice president of North American, which it had just bought. He announced that he would not move to Chicago.

With General Motors' ownership of TWA and North American's Eastern Air Lines, Eddie thought in terms of a double-utility system. TWA, running over northern territory, was mainly a summer route; while Eastern, operating chiefly in the South, was principally a winter line. The set-up, Eddie thought, was made to order for economical operation through the shifting of planes and pilots from one system to the other with the changing seasons. But Eastern proved to be a much better air line on paper in 1933 than in the air: it had poor equipment, was understaffed, and had almost no income. In spite of this Eastern remained, to Eddie, the dream-princess of all air lines: a Cinderella of run-down airplanes who, on the morrow, would become a dazzling Queen of airways. Throughout 1934, he concentrated on Eastern. He aroused among its employees a devotion to its future as keen as his own. In 1935 Eastern's great promise for the future began to be realized. Its staff —flyers, mechanics, office force—as well as the people in localities it served, came to regard the system as part of their very existence. Eastern became a source of civic pride in scores of localities as "our line." This was not accomplished by either magic or mirrors. It was slow work, hard work on the part of Eddie Rickenbacker. Even then, in those early days of 1933–34, Eastern was really and fundamentally a one-man line—the Rickenbacker Line.

The future looked bright; hard work was beginning to pay off in real progress—when a thunderbolt came from a clear sky: on February 16, 1934, the White House announced the cancellation of all air-mail contracts, instantly and without discussion. The mail, it was officially stated, would be flown by the Army Air Corps until new contracting methods were established. Not trained to fly over regular routes day and night, in all sorts of weather, the Army Air Corps flew the mail at a heavy cost. From February 16 to the end of June, when commercial air transport operators and pilots returned to the air routes, the cost included the lives of a dozen Army pilots killed in sixty-nine accidents that wrecked some four million dollars' worth of Army Air Corps equipment. These operations, which Eddie Rickenbacker attacked as "legalized murder," made a rift between him and President Roosevelt that nothing could bridge. He could have taken—and did take—the cancellation of air-mail

EDDIE AND ADELAIDE RICKENBACKER AND THEIR TWO SONS, BILL AND DAVID, IN NORWAY, 1935.

COLONEL HANS C. ADAMSON

CAPTAIN WILLIAM T. CHERRY, JR.

LIEUTENANT JOHN J. DE ANGELIS

LIEUTENANT JAMES C. WHITTAKER

contracts in his stride. Like many others who were interested in air-line operation, he felt that the whole contract system was wrong, wasteful, and monopolistic. He agreed that the operation of air lines should be divorced from the aircraft industry, with manufacturers forbidden to control air-transport companies. He was also opposed to the costly by-products of interlocking directorates. But the arbitrary manner in which air-line reform was brought about, the arrogance with which tens of thousands of innocent workers were deprived of employment, and the wanton sacrifice of young pilots inexperienced in cross-country flying, Eddie Rickenbacker could never forgive; and he placed the responsibility loudly, repeatedly, and emphatically on the White House doorstep.

When the transport lines went back into business on the enactment of the 1934 air-mail law, Eastern, like most of the other operators, flew its planes over the old routes but with brand-new highs in operating deficits. Eastern alone lost more than $1,500,000 in the air-mail war.

Shouldering his losses, Eddie went to work on putting Eastern more on the airways map than ever. Eastern was still a subsidiary of North American Aviation, which was still owned by General Motors despite the 1934 law because North American was engaged in the making of military aircraft only. General Motors had sold its TWA interest to the banking house of Lehman Brothers, in which John Hertz was interested. This was the same Hertz who had piled up a mountain of millions as owner of Yellow Cab, which he had sold to General Motors for some $40,000,000 back in 1925.

As time went on, Eddie devoted all of his attention to Eastern. In 1935 he became general manager in full charge of all its operations. Never a desk executive, he was forever on the road; holding meetings in the daytime and flying the air line at night, sleeping in a cramped and narrow seat, getting out at stops to talk and observe. His annual mileage easily ran to 75,000, and he came to know personally every employee on his line, on the ground or in the air; governors, aldermen, and community leaders in a dozen states and scores of communities. In 1935 Eastern made a little money; in 1936 it made a little more. The network extended with successful air-mail contract bids.

A unique, and most illuminating, index to the high importance of the human element in Captain Rickenbacker's way of doing business is the following partial transcript of a straight-from-the-shoulder talk he made to the air and ground crews of Eastern Air Lines shortly after he took charge. He pulled no punches when he said:

"The first move was to see where the pilots stood. The pilots were in a quandary. They didn't know whether they were coming or going. We had and we have the finest bunch of pilots in any line in any place in the world. Their record proves it. But they had to be taken care of. A man can't carry the burden of financial worry and pilot one of these big ships loaded with passengers between here and some place else safely in bad weather. Their minds couldn't be on the job.

"I made a secret investigation of their troubles and problems, found many of them worried by debts. They were not supposed to be businessmen. I cured most of their financial ills, not by giving them anything but by showing them the way out and getting some one else to worry for them, clean up their problems and get the mental hazard out of their minds. Many of them had domestic troubles. You can't have a fight with the wife and fly with a free mind. Those things were cured in many cases, without the men's knowledge, by talking to their womenfolk.

"We had some men who drank a little too heavily. You can't burn the candle all night and go on the job the next day—air liners and hangovers don't mix. Quietly we were able to stop excessive drinking. That doesn't mean our pilots are all total abstainers, because they are not. I don't intend them to be. But they know when to drink and when not to drink. Then there were physical problems. A man can't be in the air doing a good job and doing it safely and thinking: 'My God, I am only going to last another year or two, because that bad ear of mine will catch up with me, or this eye of mine will catch up with me, or this stomach will catch up with me.' That is an awful worry. So I went out and got the finest doctor in the United States for the job of chief medical examiner—Dr. Ralph Greene. None can equal him. We set up the Eastern Air Lines Aeromedical Laboratory in Miami, and I don't know of anything that can touch it. Maybe Kelly Field could do a better job. I think they could, because they have spent more money.

"When the laboratory was first announced, many of the men thought I was trying to find their weak spots, so I could railroad them out of the job later if they didn't toe the mark. I tried to tell them that I was not thinking in terms of railroading anybody. My job was to see that they lasted longer at the job that they were working at; and they couldn't do it without having a good body: no flying man can have an alert mind without the help of a good body. My job was to increase the length of their period of usefulness. It took months to convince them. The only way I could convince them was through action and deed. Today I don't think there is a man in the outfit who doesn't realize that his period of usefulness has been increased from five to ten years. We might have had some very serious accidents if it hadn't been for Dr. Greene and that medical department, because there were some things that were pretty bad.

"One of our biggest problems was the copilots. Their wage was not my making. It was made by them, them alone—and the legislators. There has always been too big a jump between the wages copilots were paid and first pilots. I don't begrudge the money the captains are getting. I think they are entitled to it. They are doing a very fine job, and they have a heavy responsibility, an awful lot on their shoulders. They have got to discipline themselves and cheat themselves out of a lot of pleasure in life that ordinary human beings are entitled to. They do it for their job's sake, so that they will not kill anybody. Checking on the copilots' living conditions, I found many of them using up their savings trying to live up to the job. Many of them were being supported or helped by their parents or outsiders. Many of them had families, two and three youngsters. Many of them were working at jobs outside the line of duty. As soon as I could, I raised their pay scale. It is the highest in the business today. I didn't ballyhoo it. I didn't even announce it to them until they got their first month's check. Then I wrote them a little note, telling them what I had done and the reasons for it. Up to that time, copilots had been quitting in droves. What could we do to keep them from doing that?

"I made a hurried check-up, did it by long-distance telephone when one of these boys who is today one of your captains was in my office, and I said: 'What is to prevent forcing every captain to go on a two weeks' vacation immediately, so that the copilots can get a chance to be first pilots, get some experience, and also the earning power that they are entitled to, to help level off their obligations? It was done. The result is that every summer we develop a new set of captains. Every copilot who was on the job when I came on is now a captain.

"We haven't made a lot of money. We have made $140,000 this year so far. I have spent $6,000,000 on Eastern Air Lines since I have been in the company. Today it is the cleanest system in the business. Your working conditions have been improved all along the line, made easier. Why? I will tell you why: because I am interested in you fellows; because it is my job; because the only kick I get out of being in business is seeing that all of us go ahead as a unit. Do you realize that there has been over 100 per cent increase in the personnel in Eastern Air Lines since 1933, three years ago? We had then less than 500 employees, and we have close to a thousand today. We have twice the pilots we had then. We are running twice the mileage. We had fourteen stops, and today we have thirty-four. I have spent money to buy new lines, to open up schedules.

"That is my worry and job, fellows. If you think it is an easy one, by George, try it some day! At two o'clock this morning I was awakened out of my sound sleep, the first time I had been in bed since Sunday night; I had been on the rattler, on the plane, every night in the interests of the outfit, working all day and trying to catch a nap in the ship en route, and at the same time see what was going on at the stations on the field, come to long enough to understand and look around. Do you suppose that I would do that for my own profit or benefit? What can I get out of it? I haven't had a raise in three years. I haven't asked for it. If they offered it to me I wouldn't take it, because it can be used in other places better, bring better results.

"I can go outside, fellows, and get a job any hour of any day I want one, for twice the money I am making with this outfit, and I will put in half the time, and I won't have one-tenth of the worries, and I will have sleepful nights instead of sleepless nights. Some of you know, I have called up here at all hours of the night because I have come to, wondering where So-and-so was, whether he was down or whether the line was going all right; called the traffic office to find out how their business was. Do you suppose I would do that because I am going to get something out of it? Certainly not. I am beyond that point. The only thing I can get out of it is seeing this outfit continue to go as it has gone ahead for three solid years, steady and straight as an arrow, and seeing a happy bunch of fellows, everybody pulling for everybody else.

"It is everybody's business. It can't get along without any one department. It just won't work without any one department. And, as I have said time and again, the greatest safety device in this business is a happy frame of mind, a healthy, happy frame of mind. Give me that, and you can have all the instruments you have on the dashboard—I don't care what they are. I will do a better job with men in that frame of mind than men will do with those instruments if they haven't got it."

There was one blank space on Eddie's air map he was not able to fill with an Eastern Air Lines symbol—the space leading to Brownsville via Houston. In those days, Brownsville had just shown signs of the importance as an airways terminal that he always believed it would have. He was dead set on extending his line to that point so that passengers from New York and Chicago for Latin America could "go Eastern" all the way to the Pan American terminals at Miami and Brownsville. Eastern already had Miami; but Brownsville, alas, was in the territory of Braniff Airways, which had no intention of surrendering that juicy plum on the border of Mexico. It was, for both lines, a case of watchful waiting.

Toward the close of 1937 lightning struck at Eastern Air Lines. It came this time from the astute financial operator we have already mentioned—John Hertz, who was now heavily interested in TWA as a partner in Lehman Brothers. In addition Hertz owned cab companies, bus and truck lines, and was one of the biggest customers on the books of General Motors. Like Eddie, Hertz believed Eastern and TWA would form a fine combination and would be blessed with rich dividends. General Motors owned about 30 per cent of North American Aviation, the parent company of Eastern; and Hertz, with strong friends in General Motors, began secret negotiations for the purchase of North American.

Early in February, 1938, the disastrous news came to Eddie, almost bowling him over. He made a bee line for Alfred P. Sloan, Jr., and William S. Knudsen, the big two of General Motors. Yes, they admitted, Hertz had offered $3,250,000 for Eastern, of which $1,000,000 was to be in cash. The deal had not been closed. After some talk back and forth, Eddie received thirty days to make a counter offer and raise the cash—if he could. Three million dollars —and a quarter! No, he'd have to top it. Three and a half, then!

"I'll get it—I'll get it!" he shouted as he left the meeting.

At that time Eddie did not have a dollar in the bank above the day-to-day needs of his family. True, he had always earned good money; but, on the other hand, he kept himself poor by paying up every cent of the $250,000 debt from the Rickenbacker Car days. He owned the Indianapolis Speedway, but barely broke even on it. All he had was his reputation as a straight-shooter who paid his debts, kept his word, used his head, and knew how to run an air line from the red into the blue. On that record he was able to borrow the $3,500,000 he needed, in cold, hard cash, from Smith, Barney & Co. and Kuhn, Loeb & Co. When the sale of Eastern was announced, Eddie said, "I've saved it for the gang that made it."

Hertz, accepting his defeat like a good sportsman, wished Eddie and Eastern well.

Now that he controlled Eastern, Eddie doubled his efforts to make the Cinderella a queen of air transportation. For her crown he needed that Houston-Brownsville route. Again Eddie the Strategist went into long executive session—and he came out with an idea. When the route was advertised for bids, the Braniff people offered to fly the mail for an infinitesimal fraction of a cent— $0.00001907378, to be exact. They had figured pretty fine, they thought. Then the Eastern bid was opened. Its offer was to carry the mail for exactly nothing. There were loud and long yells from the Braniffs but the Post Office Department ruled that if Eastern wanted to carry the mail for nothing, in return for the privilege of operating an air line over the route, that was its legal right. It got the award.

Running an air line against stiff competition and hanging on to
it against strong pressure, might be thought to be enough to occupy
all of Eddie's time and mind. Instead, as his air line grew, Eddie's
interests expanded. With the years, he became an outspoken and
sometimes unpopular exponent of Americanism, preparedness, and
air power. On trips to Europe he had opportunities to observe the
German rise toward military might; but his repeated warnings
against the Hitler program reached only ears that were deaf. He was
among the stanch few who stood with General Billy Mitchell from
the time of his court-martialing to his death in 1936. Like Mitchell,
who had an unfortunate facility for saying the right thing the wrong
way, Eddie frequently exposed himself needlessly to criticism by
men who did not share his belief that the American way of life had
to be protected at all costs. Realizing the futility of trying to convince the older generations of the dangers that faced the world,
Eddie turned more and more toward the young, with whom the
preservation of fundamental American principles rested. In placing
his cause before the boys and girls of America, he became one of the
greatest and most influential youth leaders of the nation.

There is not room, within the covers of a single book, to deal
fully with the many facets of the civic, political, and patriotic prism
of Eddie Rickenbacker's make-up; nor to describe and analyze the
numerous controversies he entered into, which, to some, made him
an inspiring prophet and, to others, a loud-mouthed pest. But one
thing his friends and foes agree upon: he is a first-class fighting
man. Also he has the peculiar knack of making even his enemies
like him. This was manifested in 1941, when Rick came about as
close to death as any one can come and still survive.

Late on the afternoon of February 26, Rick boarded the Mexico
Flyer (Eastern Lines Trip 21) at New York. The plane made its
scheduled stop at Washington and then nosed southward to Atlanta.
About Spartansburg, the pilot, Captain Perry, came into the sky
lounge.

"Captain Eddie," he said, "we may have trouble getting into
Atlanta. It's thickening up fast."

"Don't worry about me. I'm in no hurry. If you have to, let's
go back to Charlotte. Got gas enough?"

"Plenty," answered Perry, and left.

But the plane kept on past Stone Mountain and entered into a zone of low scudding clouds and scattered showers. The time came when the plane should have been over the Atlanta airport, nose down the beam for an instrument landing. Suddenly lights stabbed through a thin spot in the foggy murk—automobile headlights on a highway instead of the landing-lights of the airport. But Eddie did not worry. The plane droned on. Peering through the window, his heart with the men in the cockpit, he suddenly felt the left wing scrape against something—it might have been tree tops. Now, in a plane that has to make a bad landing, the safest place depends on what kind of landing it is: if the landing is premeditated the center of the ship is safest; but if it is a crash landing the safest place is in the tail, because you stand a good chance of getting free if the plane breaks in two. Thinking fast, Rick jumped out of his seat, started toward the tail, and shouted to his fellow passengers to follow him. But things happened too fast. A split second later the right wing hit so hard that it broke off. The pilots barely had time to cut the main switch before the plane went on its nose and killed them both; but their last act had saved their passengers from burning in the wreck. After bouncing around for a moment or two like a toy in a wind, the plane came to a stop. The tanks were leaking gasoline. The tail was twisted, cutting off all exit for those who, like Eddie, were caught in the center of the body. He had been thrown into the aisle between two bunks at the very point where the plane's fuselage had been twisted like a cord. His head was caught between a bulkhead and a leaking gas tank that sprayed him with 100 octane gasoline. The gas burned his skin like acid. His skull was crushed. His left arm was broken; so were several ribs; his left eye was dangling down his cheek. His nose was bashed in. His legs were broken. His lungs, cut by jagged stubs of rib, hurt so that he could hardly breathe. Every living moment was agony. For the first time in his life, Eddie was almost willing to die, so great was the pain.

Then he caught the sound of voices outside. To his horror, he heard some one shout:

"I'm cold. Let's start a fire to get warm!"

"Yes, do that," screamed a voice in the plane. "That'll help people to find us, too. I'm caught in here—can't move!"

The voice died into a moan.

"Hey, you! Hey, you!" yelled Eddie over and over until he got an answer. Then: "Are you outside the plane?"

"Yes."

"Then, whatever you do," pleaded Eddie, "don't start a fire. Don't even light a match or start to smoke. The air is full of gas fumes and one spark will be the end of all of us. Not one of you will have a chance. The plane will explode. We'll all die."

Throughout the night Eddie was held in the torturing vise of the wrecked plane. With him in the broken hull were the dead and dying. Outside sat those who had been thrown clear. Some had minor injuries but they were all numb with shock and stiff from the wet and chilly night.

The torture-laden nightmare lasted until about seven o'clock in the morning when a searching party arrived. Although the wreck was only ten miles from Atlanta, the country was so rough that neither trucks nor ambulances could get near the plane. The injured had to be carried on stretchers down a steep canyon and then through a half-mile of underbrush to a narrow country road. By his own orders, Eddie was the last of those trapped in the plane to be moved out. It took a full hour to cut him free, and after that there was another hour's wait at the roadside for an ambulance to come back and pick him up. During that hour, he prayed for strength to live. The pain of his bruised, broken, and gasoline-burned body seemed beyond endurance. On arrival at the Piedmont Hospital, Eddie's stretcher was set down on the ground floor and left: the internes who were handling the arrivals evidently thought him dead. They changed their minds when a booming voice yelled, "Hey, what about some room service here?" Cracked ribs cut into his lungs like knives, and he fell into a dead faint; but from that hour on, Rick got all the medical service he needed under the supervision of Dr. Floyd McRae, who had been an interne in Paris at the hospital where Rick was a patient during the First World War.

At the time of the accident, Adelaide Rickenbacker, David, and Bill were in Charlotte, where the boys attended school while their mother worked in the American Women's Volunteer Service. The boys were impressed by the high-speed escort of motorcycle police that led them from Charlotte to Atlanta at speeds of over eighty miles an hour. By the following Sunday morning, their father was doing so well that it was decided to send Bill and David back to school by bus. A few hours later, Eddie took a turn for the worse. Even in coma, his will to live was so great that he heard himself say: "Whoa! Get out of here—swing away, or you'll go over the fence!"

Meanwhile, word had been telephoned up the line to stop the bus with the Rickenbacker boys and bring them back. Two Georgia state troopers caught up with it near the South Carolina line, put the boys in their car and streaked for Atlanta with the siren howling. About twenty miles from the city, they pulled up before a service station.

"Fill 'er up, Pop," one of the troopers yelled to the aged proprietor over the fading moan of the siren.

"What's your rush, Joe?"

"We're bringing Eddie Rickenbacker's sons back to Atlanta. Their old man's very ill. Stop gassin', and shake a leg!"

"It's no use hurrying now," said Pop slowly as he filled the tank. "Eddie Rickenbacker is dead. Heard it over the radio just a few minutes ago."

"Bet you it ain't so," snarled the trooper. "Rick'll be O.K."

As the car rolled toward Atlanta, the two boys huddled together for mutual comfort. This time they understood the gravity of the situation. Happily, they soon learned that the radio report was not true. Their father kept his wheel on the roaring road of life; he didn't go over the fence.

To Eddie, days and weeks and months in a hospital bed, life became a strange but heart-warming parade of well-wishers. He had never given much thought to himself. His picture of himself was as a plain, hard-working man whose interests in his business, his home and family, and his country and community combined to make him a solid American citizen. And now, suddenly, in a small hospital room he discovered that he, Eddie Rickenbacker, was one of the few Americans who had forgotten Eddie Rickenbacker. The influx of telephone calls from people all over America who knew or did not know Eddie Rickenbacker, from men who had fought with and against Eddie Rickenbacker, swamped the Atlanta telephone exchange so that the company had to add an entire long-distance switchboard. In the hospital, too, extra telephone facilities had to be installed. The telegraph instruments in Atlanta clicked out about eight thousand telegrams to Eddie; the mail carriers delivered almost ten thousand letters from well-wishers of every age and every station in life. Letters and telegrams were still arriving in daily batches when Rick was dicharged from the hospital on the 25th of June, after almost four months.

All summer Eddie was at Candlewood Lake with his wife and sons, recapturing his strength. In the fall, when the boys went back to school, his office drew him irresistibly; and he was fully back in the run of things when Uncle Sam, in preparation for possible war, asked the air lines of America to make ready for the role they would have to play. Then—December 7, and Japan's attack on Pearl Harbor. America mobilized her resources and her sons for battle. Watching the streams of men who flowed into the Army, Navy, Marine Corps, and Coast Guard, Eddie felt soberly that he, at the early age of fifty-one, was forever excluded from putting on the uniform for his country. Permanent impairments resulting from the Atlanta crash made it impossible for him to pass any kind of military medical examination. He kept busy—but not happy —applying his knowledge of air-line operations to the winning of the war. Then, one day early in March, 1942, General H. H. Arnold, commander of the Army Air Forces, telephoned to propose a job if he felt well enough to do it:

"I can't tell you over the phone what it is; but if you are interested, I'll send Hans Adamson of my office down to tell you about it."

"O.K.," answered Eddie. "Send Adamson along. I'll let you know after I talk with him."

The job was a tour by air to every Air Force combat unit undergoing final training in the United States for entry into the theater of war in Europe, Asia, or the Pacific. General Arnold wished to have Eddie Rickenbacker instill into the air crews the will to kill, the urging sense of conquest that is the core of combat psychology.

"Tell Rick I want him to put turpentine under their tails! I want him to get those youngsters fighting-mad. Give them the will to kill!" were his parting words to Adamson. They were delivered verbatim.

After brief consideration, Rick said: "You know, Hans, Adelaide is going to kill me for this. Here Dave and Bill are coming home for Easter. I haven't seen them for months and—oh, shucks! —we've both been looking forward to it. But, as you say, a lot of the crews will be gone in a few weeks. This can't wait. O.K. I'll do it!"

Using the plane assigned to Major General Carl Spaatz, then head of the Air Force Combat Command, Rickenbacker left on his mission accompanied by Colonel Frank O'D. (Monk) Hunter and Adamson, both friends of many years' standing.

The tour lasted thirty-two days and covered more than a hundred units scattered all over the United States. Hardly had this trip been completed when Rickenbacker was asked by the Secretary of War to survey American units in Iceland and the United Kingdom. Again Colonel Adamson went along. In the course of their mission, they learned from members of the Allied High Command about the plans for the fall invasion of Africa and the related diversion of most of the American bomber and fighter units from England to Africa. As they made ready, early in October, to return to the United States, Rickenbacker and Adamson were handed a thick, big and heavily sealed, brown manila envelope. It was addressed to General George Marshall, Chief of Staff, and contained the complete plan for the invasion of Africa. Both men were under strict orders never to leave the package out of their sight or possession. This proved rather trying when the two were held by rain in Scotland for three long, dull days. That package became as big and as heavy as a mountain of lead and about as conspicuous. At long last, the weather cleared, they took off, landed in Washington, and surrendered the secret papers to a major and three heavily armed military police who were waiting at the airport in a jeep.

After reporting on conditions in England to the Secretary of War and learning that no time would be wasted in putting nearly all of his recommendations into effect, Rickenbacker was asked to make a similar tour of the Pacific. He accepted and, with barely enough time to change his linen and pack his bags, made ready for a swift trip to the Southwest Pacific area and General MacArthur's headquarters, accompanied by Adamson.

Chapter XIX

Rickenbacker and Adamson left New York for San Francisco on the evening of October 17 by way of Los Angeles so that Rick might visit his mother, who lived in Beverly Hills with his brother Dewey. They had an early dinner at the St. Francis in the Golden Gate city the following day and then boarded the plane for Honolulu, which made the overnight flight through millpond air on schedule time and landed shortly after sunrise.

The day was spent with Lieutenant General Delos Emmons inspecting the island defenses. They learned from General Emmons that the regular air-ferry service to Australia was slow and none too frequent; and after some discussion he agreed to place a Flying Fortress (B-17) at their disposal for the entire trip. He turned the matter over to Brigadier General William Lynd, who promised to have a good ship and a top-notch crew ready to leave that night at ten-thirty. Ordinarily, the steppingstones from Hawaii to Australia included Johnston or Christmas Island, both relatively close to Honolulu, but Captain Rickenbacker was under such pressure to get into MacArthur's realm that it was decided to head straight for Canton Island and skip the in-between stops. This was nothing novel. The hop, of about eighteen hundred miles, which could be made in some ten hours, was virtually operational procedure for a B-17. The members of the crew were experienced over-water airmen who had made the California-Australia ferry run half a dozen times.

At ten-fifteen General Lynd came in a car and drove Rickenbacker and Adamson to Hickam Field, where they boarded a B-17 that stood with idling engines ready to go. Entering the dark interior, they saw shadowy figures; but there was no opportunity for more than a brief "Hello" as the two passengers went forward from the tail, through the radio compartment and the bomb bay, into the control cabin, where Rick plunked into a seat on the left behind the pilot and Adamson slid into a chair behind the copilot. There was no light in the cabin. Both pilot and copilot were so intent on the job at hand that they barely nodded in reply to the greetings of their passengers.

Suddenly, as the go-ahead was flashed from the control tower, the four engines turned from idling speed to open throttle. Bumping and thumping its tail over the uneven surface, the plane wallowed slowly to the end of a runway to take off. It paused briefly and then plunged forward. The huge craft was moving over the ground at about seventy-five miles an hour and was about to rise into the air when the brake on the starboard landing wheel froze. This caused the craft to swerve out of control. With no brakes to help him, the pilot fought the wildly careening craft with engines, rudder, and stick—and a good job he did. The plane barely missed a man-killing crash into one of the hangars, and it was heading for the harbor waters along the field when the pilot succeeded in throwing it into a ground loop that almost tore off a wing and nearly knocked two engines out of their mountings. It came to a stop with a snap that should have cracked the necks of all aboard. The copilot had cut all the switches at the instant of ground-looping, thus preventing fire.

As the plane stood silent and safe with a heavy pitch to starboard, the pilot and copilot unbuckled their safety belts and turned around. Cars rushing toward the ship threw just enough light through the windows to catch the white splash of teeth in the pilot's smile as he said, in a long, low, and lazy Texas drawl: "That's the longest no-hop crash landing I've ever made. I'm Bill Cherry— Captain Cherry. And this is Lieutenant Whittaker."

"Hope this near-take-off wasn't too rugged for you," grinned Whittaker. "But you know the old saying, 'Any landing you can walk away from is a good one.'" Glancing at Adamson, he saw the eagles on his shoulders and said, "Howdy, colonel," with a faint two-finger Air Force salute. Then he turned toward the man opposite and inquired what his name might be.

"Rickenbacker," he was told. "Eddie Rickenbacker."

Neither Cherry nor Whittaker said a word. They just sank back into their seats.

By this time, ambulances and crash trucks with howling sirens had arrived. The entrance door was torn open. General Lynd climbed into the tail without waiting for a ladder.

"Anybody hurt?" he yelled. "Anybody hurt?"

"Nobody's hurt, Bill!" answered Rick as he and Adamson went toward the exit. "Everything is O.K. All we want to know is how soon Captain Cherry and his crew can get another plane so we can get going."

"Huh?" replied Lynd. "You mean you want to take off now in another plane—right on top of this?"

"Certainly," answered Rick. "The sooner, the better—and with this crew too. It wasn't their fault that a landing wheel went wrong."

The second plane, another B-17, was ready shortly after one o'clock. At one-thirty on the morning of October 21 it took smoothly to the air, climbed speedily to ten thousand feet, and headed for Canton Island. The night was made to order. Clear weather and a ten-mile tail wind had been forecast. A three-quarter moon sailed in and out of fleecy clouds as the plane made miles toward the equator. Beneath was the Pacific, placid and peaceful as its name implied.

Much to their surprise, Captain Rickenbacker and Colonel Adamson learned that neither Captain Cherry nor Lieutenant Whittaker knew anything about their mission—where it was to take them, how long it might last, or even whom they were taking. Their orders had been to fly a "hot, top-drawer" mission to the Southwest Pacific and await further orders. Period.

Never having held to the line of rigid military procedure, Captain Rickenbacker told the boys what he could about his mission and his plans as far as these affected them. He opined that they might be back in January.

When the tall gangling master sergeant who presided over the radio pulled a long face, Rick asked jokingly what was wrong.

"Well, you see, captain, we were all heading for home—the United States, I mean—when we got caught for this job at Hickam. I was going to get married next week, home in Oakland. And

Lieutenant De Angelis, our navigator, was married just before he left on this mission—and—and—" Reynolds drew to a drooping halt. Then he snapped out: "But don't get me wrong, captain—I'm glad to have this chance to see a slice of the war."

"Don't let Jimmy Reynolds get under your skin, Captain Rickenbacker," injected Bill Cherry with a laugh. "There isn't a man aboard who wouldn't fight for this chance. Sure, we had all hoped to get back and catch a glimpse of our families—but the mission comes first."

"And," broke in Whittaker, "this mission is going to be more fun than a barrelful of monkeys."

The little staff meeting in the cabin then broke up. The two passengers withdrew into the tail, where two cots had been installed, and went to sleep while the members of the crew tackled their respective duties and the plane sped toward its unscheduled destiny.

Even at the equator it gets cold at night over the ocean, and when Rickenbacker woke up at six o'clock he was stiff and cramped and chilled to the marrow in spite of wearing all his clothes with a trench coat and a blanket on top of them. The sun was just coming up; but the sky was gray, and the sea looked bleak and leaden.

As he shook the wrinkles out of himself Staff Sergeant Alexander Kaczmaczky from Torrington, Connecticut, a chief of ground-crew mechanics, came into the tail from the radio compartment. Sergeant Alex was aboard as an extra crew member, on his way to his outfit in Australia after having been hospitalized in Hawaii for jaundice followed by an appendix operation. He was about twenty years old, sandy, short, and stocky. He was rather shy and short on speech; but his blue eyes were alert, and he had a ready grin. Noticing that he looked tired, Rick motioned him to the cot. Alex threw himself down and was asleep before his head hit the pillow. Rick took the blanket from the floor and flung it over the boy. (Adamson took this in from his cot between sleepy lids and decided to do some more bunk fatigue.) Then Rick entered the radio compartment, where Sergeant Reynolds was bending sleepily over his instrument board. A receiving set was clamped over his ears, and his right hand rested near the sending key.

"What's new, sergeant?" asked Rick as he stopped at the radio desk.

"Nothing—not a thing all night." Jimmy Reynolds's long thin face cracked into a yawn. "You know, captain, being a radio operator on this Pacific run is a lead-pipe cinch because we've gotta keep radio silence. The Japs may be close. So you send nothing— hear nothing and learn nothing!"

"Still got that girl in Oakland on the beam, though," chid Rick.

"Betcha! And the signal is coming in strong—man, oh, man!"

Slapping the sergeant on the back, Rick continued into the control cabin, where Lieutenant Whittaker held the controls. Captain Cherry had swung around in his seat and was checking with Private Bartek, his flight engineer, on the fuel remaining in the tanks. He was trying to estimate the amount of gas he would need when the plane reached Canton Island, still some three hours away.

This was the first opportunity Rick had had to get a good look at his pilots. Captain Cherry, the plane commander, was of medium height. He had clear, level eyes, brown hair and sported a well tended Vandyke.

"So you're from Texas, eh?" was Rick's opening shot.

"Yeah, but how do you know, Captain Rickenbacker?"

"Oh—that's easy! The give-away is those fancy high-heeled Texas boots of yours—or isn't any one supposed to know?"

"You bet my boots I'm a *Texan*," retorted Cherry with mock belligerence. "I'm from Quail, *Texas*, and I learned to fly at Kelly Field, *Texas*, and I was a copilot on an American Airlines run in *Texas*."

Captain Rickenbacker glanced at Bartek. "Don't tell me that you're from Texas, too. What's your name, soldier?"

"Bartek, Johnny Bartek, sir! No, I'm from Freehold, New Jersey, and that's plenty good enough for me."

Bartek had a thin high voice and was inclined to speak through his nose, which was covered with freckles. So was his forehead, although it was shaded most of the time by an overhang of unruly reddish hair. Although still near the bottom of the twenties, he had that air of competency which almost universally distinguishes air crew men of whatever age or rank. He looked like what he was: a mighty solid citizen—a man any one would be glad to have aboard when the going got tough.

So, for that matter, did Lieutenant Whittaker. He was a chunky man with broad shoulders that spoke of great physical power. His face, heavily lined, was dominated by a pair of keen, deep-set eyes. His close-cropped hair was almost gray. For all his forty-two years, Rick noted with surprise that he had the rank only of second lieutenant.

Evidently Whittaker sensed his thoughts, for he jabbed out: "Don't think too much about my shavetail bars, Mr. Rickenbacker. You came out of the last war as our top dog in the air, but it didn't get you more than a captaincy." There was neither gripe nor offense in Whittaker's tone of voice. He just put his chips on the line.

"Shucks!" replied Rick. "If I had ever judged a soldier by what he has on his shoulders, I'd been a dead turkey before the first Armistice Day."

Still Whittaker could see that he was puzzled about this middle-aged copilot second lieutenant in a war where Air Force brigadier generals were regarded as oldsters at forty-two. So he explained that he had been in the Navy in World War I; had taken up flying in 1927 and had owned and flown his own sports planes since 1930 and up to the war.

"When we got into the stew," ended Whittaker, "I figured that if I could do the job of a copilot on a ferry plane as a second lieutenant—or anything—some shavetail young enough to fight could be released from ferrying to combat duty!"

By now Cherry and Bartek had completed their check. Bartek left the cabin, and Rick asked the two stock sunrise questions of passengers on overnight flights: "When do we land?" and "When do I eat?" The answer to the first was at nine-thirty—three hours from that moment. The answer to the second question was brought by Bartek: a large paper cup filled with steaming black coffee, and some sweet rolls, on which Rick fell to. The sun was well up in a fairly cloud-free sky, and the chill of night fled into space as Rick drained his second cup of coffee and lit a cigarette. Time went by. Adamson came into the "office," had breakfast, and joined the contented silence that seems to hold a plane in its velvet grip when all is well.

About eight-thirty Cherry took the ship from Whittaker and put it into a long, slow glide to a thousand feet above the sea. It was time to look for Canton Island. Every one was on his toes, eager to be the first to sight land. But, after an hour of flying, the tiny sandy specks of the Canton group had not yet been seen.

"That's funny," snapped Cherry, whose devotion to precision departure and arrival was almost a creed. "I think I'll go down and check with De Angelis." He ducked out of his seat and crouched at the hatch that led to the bombardier's compartment in the glass-enclosed nose of the plane. Just as he opened it the man he had named popped out with the speed of a jack-in-the-box.

Lieutenant John De Angelis was a short, black-haired, sharp-faced man of twenty-three or so. He was quick, tense, and had the nervous and impatient energy of a fox terrier. He was the navigator who the day before had hoped to plot a course from Hawaii to his bride in Los Angeles.

"I was just coming up to see you," he explained.

"Yes," said Cherry dryly, "and I was just coming down to see you. Where in jumping Jehoshaphat are we? And where the dickens is Canton Island?"

"Come on down, captain," invited De Angelis, "and I'll show you the dope I got."

The two men went down into the nose. The hatch cover closed above them, and the plane droned along.

"How about taking the ship for a spell, Captain Rickenbacker," invited Whittaker. "I'd like to go back and stretch a leg."

"Glad to," responded Rick. "Say, how's that navigator?"

"They don't come any better than De Angelis. He's made the run down under half a dozen times, and he's always hit every landing right on the nose! I don't know where that Pittsburgh boy got it from, but he's got a homing instinct like a carrier pigeon."

"*Homing* pigeon," corrected Adamson. "*Carrier* pigeons fly down flat-tops."

"Pay no attention to Hans Adamson," laughed Rick. "He's

been tied up with the American Museum of Natural History so long now that he's splitting hairs."

Whittaker went back into the tail, leaving Captain Rickenbacker and Colonel Adamson alone in the control cabin. Not a word was spoken between them. There was no unhappy anticipation, no dread that a major calamity was impending. Any one could be a little off-the-beam.

Presently Whittaker came back and took over. Almost at the very instant, Cherry climbed through the hatch from the bombardier's cubicle. His usually placid expression had given way to a deep frown, and De Angelis, who came after him, looked both worried and unhappy.

"We want to check up on some things," said Cherry briefly as he took his seat from Rick. On the "intercom," he ordered Reynolds to come forward.

To make room in the rather narrow space, Rickenbacker and Adamson went astern, where Johnny Bartek was showing Alex some rather fine photographs he had taken on previous transpacific flights.

"But you've got to have the right kind of a camera," Johnny observed. "Me, I paid 482 bucks for mine. When I quit the Army, I'm going to be a news photographer." He put a sudden brake on his tongue, and a speculative gleam popped into his eyes: "Say! If I got some pictures of you, Captain Rickenbacker—that would make some swell news shots."

"Go ahead," laughed Eddie. "I'm for anyone making an honest dollar."

Bartek readied his camera and began shooting. He had made a fair start when Cherry came in looking as solemn as a judge about to pronounce sentence.

"We are in a bad way," he said. "We should have landed at Canton half an hour ago. Now we can't even find it."

"If you want my opinion," cut in Captain Rickenbacker, "I would say that we have overshot the island."

"How do you make that out?"

"Because if we stuck to last night's early tail-wind estimate of ten miles, we've been off by at least twenty miles an hour for quite a spell. I'd say that right now we have a thirty-mile tail wind. Maybe the best thing to do is to turn around and retrace our steps. Unless you've other ideas!"

"Unfortunately, the situation isn't quite as simple as that," explained Cherry. "To begin with, when I tried to get a bearing on the radio direction finder, I discovered that it won't budge. It is frozen. Whittaker says that it worked last night when we left Hawaii, but now the crank won't turn."

"Well," broke in Adamson, "there's always the compass."

"That's another trouble," replied Cherry with a wry grin. "The compass is off. We just checked it."

"Holy Moses!" exclaimed Rick. "We sure got a lemon when we picked this plane. Let's go forward, Cherry, and work this thing out."

In the control cabin, Rick took the seat behind the pilot and slipped a pair of radio phones over his ears. Cherry took the controls while Whittaker reached up and tried, vainly, to break the jam on the frozen homing device. Now and then a signal could be heard in the ear sets, but too faintly to provide any cue whatever.

"Have you any idea as to where we are?" Rick asked Cherry.

"None whatever, captain."

"But what about the navigator?" insisted Adamson. "He should have some glimmer of thought about it."

"He should, but he hasn't, colonel! Trouble is that the plottings De Angelis made during the night don't mean a thing, because his octant is out of whack—it went out of kilter when we ground-looped last night. It was thrown clear across the bombardier's blister —only De Angelis didn't think it was damaged."

"Can't put the blame on him for that," Rick broke in. "That's something none of us thought about. But, look, that's all behind us. It's what we do from here on in that counts. If I'm right about the tail wind being stronger than estimated, we may be as much as two hundred miles below Canton."

"Sure," interrupted Whittaker. "But how do we know we are south or southeast or southwest of it? When we turn around, how're we going to lay our course with any assurance of hitting Canton?"

That was a question no one could answer.

"How much gas have we?" Adamson inquired.

"Enough to keep us going about four and a half hours."

It was then about ten o'clock.

"That gives us a fairly decent margin," mused Rick.

"Yep, but unless we find Canton or some other island by half past two," said Adamson, "we have to put her down on the sea—and that's something else to think about."

"We'll think about that later, Hans," retorted Rick. "What about breaking radio silence and ask for bearings."

"We can't do that until we are in a real emergency—and we . can't call this a simon-pure emergency yet." This from Cherry.

After some discussion, it was agreed that unless signs or signals of land were seen or heard by eleven o'clock, radio silence would be broken.

During the next sixty minutes, the pilots, Reynolds, and Rickenbacker listened on headsets for radio signals. None came in. Adamson, Bartek, and Alex assisted Whittaker in covering various sectors of the sea for sight of land. None was seen. Once Cherry took the craft down within a few feet of the ocean to get a reading of the wind through a look at the waves. They seemed fairly high. Their crests were sprayed by spume driven by a strong wind from the north. In a plane roaring along at some three miles per minute, it was impossible to gauge wind velocity by the fragile threads of froth, but it seemed as if more than a ten-mile wind was needed to kick up the waves they saw. After a few minutes of this, Cherry made a quick grab for higher air and leveled off at five thousand feet. Then he began to fly the box procedure course, old and often reliable stand-by of airmen who have missed their objectives. (This procedure calls for forty-five minutes' level flight on each leg of the compass—forty-five minutes north, forty-five minutes east, and so forth—and gives the plane an area of visibility of several hundred square miles inside and outside its boxlike course.) To complete the square would take some three hours—that is, if their gasoline held out and if their engines kept on perking. While eyes and ears kept eager watch, no one felt particularly uncertain about the outcome. There simply had to be an island.

"Our trouble will be over," predicted Reynolds, "when we open up the radio, establish contact and set up a lost-plane procedure. Then they can get a cross bearing on us and give us a course."

On the dot of eleven o'clock, Jimmy began to pound his key. He paused and grinned broadly as an answer came in. The plane was in contact with a station. Every one tried to hide his great relief at this good news. But the good news soon turned into bad news when it was learned that the station Jimmy was in touch with was not Canton. He was told that Canton's radio station had not been completed. Well, anyway, he asked the station to set up lost-plane procedure. Then came the real blow. The station could not comply because it did not have the necessary equipment. This was a solar-plexus sock. Jimmy asked the operator to stand by while he reached out for another station. Soon one came in. It could be of no help. Sorry! A third responded. Same answer. No dice! Jimmy sweat it out at the key as, from various directions, the invisible but ready hands of radio reached out to give help, but none had the power to guide the plane to a safe landing. Now the first station broke in with the happy comment that it was sending planes up to look for the lost B-17 and that, based on the strength of the bomber's radio signal, the station thought it could be only some twenty-five miles away. Acting on this good news, Cherry told Whittaker to fly in a steadily expanding circle and keep his altitude at five thousand feet. This was just below the bottom of the clouds. A series of expanding circles, which would have brought the plane in sight of an island only twenty-five miles away, was flown in jig time. No island. Station Number Two now suggested that if the plane would fly for thirty minutes in a wide circle at five thousand feet, while the operator sent out a continuous signal, it would try to get a position reading. For thirty minutes, Jimmy pounded the keyboard. At the end of the half-hour the station submitted a course with a northeast to southwest axis which did not mean a thing since those aboard the plane had no way of knowing if the station was on an island southwest or northeast of the plane.

As the craft thundered over the empty sea and the hearts of those aboard got a little heavier, Rick searched the hindmost crannies of his brain for ideas that might help to bring this situation to a happy ending.

Suddenly, in a flash of memory, he recalled how, in World War I, he and his fellow pilots had frequently followed the course of German planes behind our lines by watching the cloudlike explosions of antiaircraft shells bursting along the path of the Hun pilots. There was an idea! Eddie the Strategist took quick steps to put it to use. He asked Cherry to go upstairs above the clouds. In a few minutes, the plane reached eight thousand feet, and at this altitude there was nothing about and above it but sunshine and blue sky.

"O.K.," nodded Rick. "Ask the island if they've any antiaircraft artillery on hand!"

The message brought the quick answer, "Yes."

"Good! Tell 'em to set the shell fuses at ten thousand feet and send up a slow but continuous barrage—meanwhile, we'll keep watch from all positions."

This order was executed, and for the next hour every one aboard, except Reynolds at his instrument board, stared into the sky for the mushrooming cloud puffs of AA shells. None were observed.

The station sent word that the island was doing "the best it could with what it had" to locate the wandering bomber. Shells were bursting overhead. Planes were roaring off runways to join the search. Surface craft had been sent out to sea to aid in the hunt.

Aboard the plane this information was accepted with calm hope. But Rick looked at the problem with grim realism. Time had continued its steady march during this trying period. It was now about one o'clock. The sand was running low in the hourglass of Time and Chance.

"We may get a lucky break, Rick," Adamson said; "but, unless some kind of a miracle shoves an island under us, I think we're going to get very, very wet."

While Adamson continued at his job gazing through the roof blister for signs of rescue AA shell fire or planes, Rickenbacker went forward and learned from Cherry that the gas was holding out as estimated—all would be gone by half past two.

"That doesn't leave us a lot of time to take our pick between the devil and the deep blue sea," said Rick with a tight smile. "I think the best we can do is to keep looking and keep hoping, but be ready for a water landing. What do you think our chances are, Bill, of getting away with it? I mean, putting this plane down on the water—"

"And walking away from it?" cut in Whittaker from the copilot's roost. "Not much, captain. So far as I know, no one ever put one of these babies down on a high-wave ocean and lived long enough to talk about it."

"Yeah," echoed Cherry. "In a sea like this, chances are that our ship would float as long as an eight ball!"

De Angelis came bounding out of his hatch with the speed of a rabbit: "Say, how about some chow?"

The four older men looked at one another. They reached a silent understanding in an instant.

"There'll be no chow now or until we know how we stand, Jack," said Rick slowly. "We better save what we've got in case we have to abandon ship and take to the rafts."

Jack De Angelis nodded. He saw the point.

From this moment—which really was the hour of decision—Rick took charge without obviously doing so and without the formal consent of those aboard. To the great credit of Captain Cherry and Lieutenant Whittaker, they took his leadership eagerly and without resentment. Rickenbacker radiated confidence to all aboard through his words and acts and bearing. And it was not blind hero worship for a World War ace that dictated their acceptance. Every crew man aboard that plane had the self-sufficiency that comes to men who know their stuff and who are experts in their specialized fields —which these men were. Perhaps it was that very fact that made the crew recognize in Captain Rickenbacker a fellow craftsman who knew what to do when an aircraft was in distress. There was no surrender of command by the pilot and copilot. They merely took Eddie into partnership and made him the senior member. It was a wise step. For the man who had directed successful air operations of fighter pilots against human enemies in war, and had supervised equally successful operations of air-line pilots against weather enemies in peace, had resources to draw upon in fighting his way out of this situation which few men were able to muster.

The first decision to be made was how to release the rafts—three of them, two fairly large and one small—and get aboard them. Two courses were open. One was to land the plane on the water, release the rafts, and beat Old Man Gravity to the draw by getting out of the bomber before it sank. The other was to release the rafts from aloft and then parachute down to the sea and climb aboard. The vote was strongly in favor of the first course. It was then left to Cherry and Whittaker to figure out how to land the bomber on the ocean with the best chance of survival.

"Don't forget," encouraged Rick, "that we have the element of time in our favor."

"Time," grinned Adamson as he glanced quickly from the top blister to his wrist watch, "one hour and a half—ninety minutes."

"We'll wait and watch thirty minutes more," continued Rickenbacker. "Then, if nothing has improved the situation, we'll make ready to lighten ship and stand by for a water landing."

"Or more likely a crash landing," suggested Cherry calmly.

"Well," answered Eddie with a wave of his hand, "you two figure out how to do it. I will go back and tell the rest of the boys what the score is."

In the radio compartment, Jimmy Reynolds was still at the key. Somehow, he had lost the stations he had been talking to. No one answered his calls. Having nothing to do at the moment but watch and wait, Johnny Bartek and Sergeant Alex were at their respective lookout stations at the gun ports in the tail compartment, sweeping their sky sectors with vigilant eyes. Neither had much to say when Captain Rickenbacker told them what they were up against. To those steady and courageous boys it was all part of a day's work.

"I know a guy who sat on a raft in the Atlantic for three days," commented Bartek. "He said he felt like a frozen haddock when they picked him up. Boy, that Atlantic must be cold up around Iceland."

"Sure, but this Pacific is a cinch," remarked Alex. "It's like the water in your bathtub on Saturday night."

"So what?" responded Bartek as he expelled a lungful of smoke. "This ain't Saturday."

"You boys keep your eyes open," warned Rick as he went forward again.

Adamson, alone under the blister, stopped him. "Listen, Rick," he whispered. "Have you thought what might happen if Japs found us after we got into the rafts?"

"They'd probably fill us full of lead and send us to the bottom."

"Maybe and maybe not. Suppose they picked us up instead and took us prisoners and began to question us—about Europe. Get me?"

"I get you, Hans."

Cherry and Whittaker were too close for them to discuss the secret they shared—namely, the air program for the coming invasion of Africa by American and British forces. The invasion was one of the most important Allied secrets of the war. A leak, even the merest hint, coming to the Huns from the Japs might upset the carefully conceived plan and endanger the success of the African invasion program.

"We can't run any chance whatever of being taken prisoner," said Adamson with slow emphasis.

Captain Rickenbacker nodded slowly.

"If the Japs find us on the rafts, you and I have only one way to go, and that's *down*."

Rick scratched his head.

"I must tell you this now, Rick. Part of my intelligence briefing was that the Japs have a German-made narcotic that puts you in a talkative mood after you get a shot or two of it in the arm. Those who get it talk their heads off. So it is not a case of standing up under torture if they capture us, but simply a question of telling all we know of our own free will without knowing what we're doing. There it is, Rick! The other boys can afford to be picked up and taken prisoners so long as they don't know anything about this— but we can't."

"Yes," agreed Captain Rickenbacker, "you're right, and that's something to be prepared for *if* we get on the rafts—and *if* a Jap plane finds us. We may be in Jap-controlled waters now for all we know."

"Right! And you and I had better be in the same raft. What's the plan? Will we all drift our separate ways, or tie up together?"

"I'm for stringing the rafts together—I think it will work out better that way."

"So do I," said Adamson. "In that case, let's get Bartek aboard our raft—he told me this morning that he had spent a lot of time as an antiaircraft warning observer in Hawaii. That means he can identify every known type of Japanese or American plane."

"Good idea," agreed Rick. "That's how we'll do it—and if we see a plane and Johnny says it's a Nip and it comes down to pick us up, you and I will take a walk."

Meanwhile, the pilots had steered the plane down close above the sea to study the waves. They found no abatement of the wind since morning. On the contrary, the waves seemed higher and wilder. They also discovered that the swell ran contrary to the direction of the wind. On this basis, Cherry and Whittaker proposed the following procedure:

To use up nearly all the gasoline, so that the empty fuel tanks would help keep the plane afloat; but to come down for the landing while there was still enough for a power glide in case something went wrong with the approach which would be flat from almost surface level.

So far, so good!

The next measure, and the most difficult, was to put the plane down between two swells in such a way that it would not break through the surface, making a nonstop dive for the bottom, or land on the crest of a wave—to be pushed under, or to break in two. The escape hatches over the radio room and the control cabin would be opened to facilitate swift exit from the plane into the rafts.

Cherry came back and said to Reynolds: "Send this message: 'One hour of gas left!' Got it?"

Reynolds nodded.

"O.K.," continued the skipper. "After that, continue to send S O S until we hit the deck!"

It was now half past one. The hours had changed into minutes and it was time to do the final chores. Rick and Bartek opened the bottom hatch in the tail and threw out every loose article they could lay hands on—baggage, parachutes, and mailbags. Adamson and Alex broke out the Mae West life-saving jackets and piled up a supply of canned fruit juice, chocolate bars, sandwiches, and other food, two thermos jugs of water and coffee, together with a large box of emergency rations, close to the escape hatch in the radio room. They also rolled the small three-man raft into place. Several of the men went through their baggage before it was thrown into the sea to take out something that they needed or cherished. Rick stuffed three or four handkerchiefs into his pockets and, as he did so, pointed with pride to the embroidered initials:

"My wife did that," he said.

Adamson took out a leather folder in which he placed a map of the Pacific area. The folder already contained a photograph of his wife. He stuck it under his shirt and buttoned his flying jacket over it. He came upon a handful of *Reader's Digests* and some news magazines he had brought along as gifts for men who served down under. The thought struck him that some reading matter might be welcome on the raft. So he stuck a copy of *Reader's Digest* into his right hip pocket. It broke poor Johnny Bartek's heart to let his camera go; but he allowed that it was too bulky.

"There goes 482 bucks," he wailed to Alex as it disappeared. Next he picked up a pigskin case that contained an expensive pen and pencil set. "What good would that be?" he said, and down it went.

"What did you pay for that?" asked Alex.

"Twenty-two berries." Picking up a pocket Bible in a waterproof cover, Bartek said, "That one, I'm going to keep."

"What did you pay for it?" joshed Alex.

"Nothing—I got it for free," Johnny answered, and put the Bible into the breast pocket of his dungarees. "It was sent to me as a gift from the First Baptist Church, home in Freehold, while I was stationed at Roosevelt Field."

It was now ten minutes past two. Twenty minutes more—and all the gasoline would be gone and Old Man Gravity would take charge. Twenty minutes left to live, perhaps, for the eight men aboard that bomber.

Five of those men were very young. And yet they had faced the grim Hour of Decision and what might lie beyond with utmost coolness throughout that morning—long, suspense-laden hours when they knew they were flying against time. There were no glum faces; no moaning self-pity. Every man did his job like a veteran.

One would never have known, from the behavior of Bill Cherry, Jim Whittaker, and their men, that this plane was not about to make a routine landing. Trying as the hours, days, and weeks afloat on rafts were to be, there was at least a fairly uniform hope that rescuers would arrive by sea or air. Aboard the lost bomber on that 21st of October, however, there was no great expectancy of survival in the crash landing just ahead. Every one had faith in the steady nerves and able hands of Cherry and Whittaker; but every one realized, too, that unless God had both of his arms around them there was little hope that the impact of a twenty-five-ton bomber on a tossing sea would permit any one to escape unhurt and alive.

At a quarter past two every one put on a bright yellow rubber Mae West jacket and got into crash position. The pilots strapped themselves in after Cherry sent out his last message: "We are almost out of gas. Making water landing in fifteen minutes."

He also told Reynolds to keep sending S O S to the last, in the belief that somewhere planes and surface ships were picking up the signal and rushing to the rescue.

In the radio compartment, Reynolds sat strapped into his chair; Rick was seated opposite him, also strapped in. Adamson, Alex, and Jack De Angelis were on the floor, huddled together in the belief that their combined weights would save them from bouncing around too much when the bomber hit the water. Bartek, whose job as flight engineer was to release the rafts stored under the outside skin of the plane, was up forward behind the pilots. The emergency hatches in the roof were open to provide an exit if the fuselage should buckle up in the impact of the landing. Cherry had announced that he would keep the plane at five thousand feet until two-thirty when Cherry would start the landing glide, the end of which, to them, was Judgment Day. There was some conversation in the crowded radio room as the five men awaited the verdict. But it was pointless and brief. There was nothing more they could do. Their fate was in the hands of the pilots and of God. If any one of them said prayers, they were spoken in silence. All the ear could catch was the steady *zzzzt-zzzzt-zzzzt-zzzzt* of the radio and the roar of the four engines. Suddenly there was a change in the tempo of sound. The radio seemed to rise in volume, while the engine noises sank to a murmur. Cherry had cut the two inboard engines. The plane was nosing down in a long slow glide. Rick was the only one in the radio room who could see what was going on. By stretching forward, he could get a glimpse through a porthole of a small slice of wing and sky and water.

"How we doing, Rick?" asked Adamson from the floor.

"Yeah, give us the score, captain," chimed in De Angelis.

"I'd say we are now at five hundred feet," said Rick in a calm conversational voice. After a brief pause: "Four hundred—three hundred."

The long slow hours that had changed into nerve-racking minutes were now running through the hourglass as swiftly speeding seconds.

"About a hundred feet to go!" called Rick in the impersonal tone of a surveyor. "Now fifty feet." Then, his voice rising to a shout: "Hang on to your hats, beebees—*here she comes!*"

And come it did. A crash that seemed like the opening gun of doomsday shook the craft as it hit the water, tail first, and smacked down on its belly. Then a second crash—a third—and the plane rested on the pitching sea.

Each man, to himself, probably expressed wonder that he was alive, and that the plane hung together. It did not seem that anything made by the hand of man could absorb the pounding this B-17 had taken without disintegrating.

The miracle had been performed; the seemingly impossible had been done. The plane was afloat; every man aboard was alive, and no one, it seemed, had been seriously hurt. No limbs were broken; no bones were fractured. True, Adamson—bottom man in the human heap on the floor—had hurt his back; but he was able to do something toward helping himself. Hardly had the plane lost momentum on the water before every one started to scramble out. There was not much time to lose. The tail blister had broken wide open on the first impact, and the ocean was coming in fast.

"Take it easy," advised Rick, as he unstrapped his belt. "Get the small raft out first. Then scramble—but don't pull the triggers on your Mae West air cylinders until you're out on the hull."

Quickly, much faster than it can be told, the men wriggled out.

De Angelis and Alex, who had been assigned to the small raft, got out on the left side of the plane. Then Rickenbacker, giving Adamson a lift, since the pain in his back grew more paralyzing by the second. On the right side of the plane, they found Bartek pushing one of the bigger rafts into the sea behind the wing. By now Adamson had almost lost all mobility, so that Rickenbacker and Bartek had to work with nervous haste to keep the raft close enough to the wing to dump Adamson into it. Bartek cut his hands badly on the sharp trailing edge of the wing. Finally, the three got into the raft; but there was no knife to cut the strong cord that held the inflated rubber craft to the plane. Now, the bomber might sink any second. It had already been afloat longer than any one aboard had dared to hope. Johnny worked furiously to saw the cord in two on the wing's sharp edge. Eddie was fighting like mad to keep the raft from being toppled over in banging against the tail. No one paid any attention to the high-rolling seas that pitched the plane and the raft up and down, but soon Eddie noticed that the raft was almost half full of water. He snatched off his hat and began to bail with good results. Meanwhile, Adamson had been sitting in a half-coma. He did not realize what was going on until he saw Bartek sawing away with the cord on the wing with bleeding hands.

"Hey," he called, "you need a knife?"

Did Bartek want a knife!

Adamson tried to haul his key chain out of his pocket, but could not move his arms. "Fish in my pocket, Johnny," he said. "There's a small penknife on the key ring, I think."

A moment later, the cord was cut, and the raft floated free from the bomber.

Meanwhile there was plenty of action on the left side of the plane. The small manual raft not only opened upside-down but turned over and spilled Jack De Angelis and Alex into the sea. Alex could not swim, and would have drowned but for the strength and swimming skill of Jack, who, after much effort, got him aboard the raft. But he was almost unconscious, and terribly ill from having swallowed too much sea water. Poor Alex was to die thirteen days later, and there is little doubt that, had his companions been able to give him proper first-aid treatment on that first day, he would have

STAFF SGT. ALEX KACZMARCZYK

STAFF SGT. JAMES W. REYNOLDS

PRIVATE JOHN F. BARTEK

EDDIE RICKENBACKER SHORTLY AFTER HIS RESCUE FROM TWENTY-THREE
DAYS ON RUBBER RAFTS ON HIS NEAR-FATAL PACIFIC MISSION.

lived. He never had a chance to get over that almost fatal immersion.

Whittaker and Reynolds got the second big raft ready while Cherry, fulfilling the traditional function of captain, made a final tour of the plane to make sure every one was out. As he climbed through the radio escape hatch, Cherry held four oranges. He tossed two into the Rickenbacker raft and threw the others into his own.

"Well, Rick," he called out in a steady voice, "any landing you can walk away from is a good one!"

"You bet, Bill," retorted Rick, "and this one, take it from me—this one was a beaut!"

Cherry grinned, waved his hand, and slid out of sight on the other side of the plane.

Drifting on the waves or pushed by the wind, the three rafts pulled away from the plane. The folding aluminum oars that were part of the raft equipment were put to use so as to pull them together.

"Anybody hurt on your side, Bill?" Rickenbacker wanted to know.

"Nope," Whittaker answered for his captain. "No casualties here except for Jimmy Reynolds—he cut his nose, but nothing is broken."

"How's it with you?" yelled Cherry.

"Johnny cut his hands and Adamson hurt his back; otherwise, we are O.K."

"Who has the food and water?"

No one had any food or water. It had been left aboard the bomber, covered by the sea that came in through the broken tail. Before this disappointing news had a chance to register too blackly on the minds of the men, Rick called out:

"I'll give a hundred dollars to the man who first hears an airplane."

The plan worked: food and water became, temporarily at least, unimportant as against the thought of early rescue. Not one of them doubted, at that time, that rescue planes or rescue ships would come rushing out of the clouds or over the horizon in an hour or two or, at the very latest, the next morning. Off and on, Reynolds had been in contact with many stations for many hours. They had faded out toward the end, but he had sent out a steady signal almost without pause since eleven o'clock. Surely help was on the way. If not that day, then the next—and what was a night on a raft?

"We'd better save those oranges for breakfast," shouted Cherry.

"Good idea!" agreed Rick.

Although the sea was running rather high, the rafts rode easily on the roller coaster of the sea. The waves were so high that the men caught only occasional glimpses of the plane, which remained afloat, surprisingly enough, more than five minutes after the landing.

Chapters could be written about the manly and skillful job the pilots and their crew had performed in putting the huge bomber down in such a way that every man aboard got out, but, even so, words would fall short of depicting all the things that entered into it.

An ancient Chinese proverb says that one picture is worth ten thousand words—or is it twenty thousand? Well, anyway, Uncle Sam's Navy has a four-word combination that beats a whole picture gallery when it comes to heaping praise on heroic men—and since it fits this air crew with precision, it is proper to use those four words here:

"Well done, all hands!"

Chapter XX

Whether they were too stunned by what had happened to them, or too relieved to be alive, or too confident that rescue was just around the corner, no steps were taken that first night to organize the survivors into shifts with regular duties or to plan for the immediate future. Every one was on watch for the first glimpse or sound of ships or planes. When the sun went down and the moon popped up, the sea seemed to smooth out. The stars shone brightly, and around the horizon, like a frieze along a wall, stood a wonderful collection of cloud pictures ranging from animal outlines to profiles of men and women. This "picture section," incidentally, appeared on all clear nights, just after sunset. Rick never tired of watching it. The long dormant artist in him was intrigued by the figures cut by the wind out of cloud formations.

Throughout that first night, there were many false alarms. Stars swinging low on the horizon were mistaken for blinker signals from ships. Toward morning, the wind died down and a heavy mist crept over the sea. It was at this time Rickenbacker came to the conclusion that he and his companions might have to sit longer on the rafts than they had expected to. Thinking the situation out in his careful objective way, he realized that they might be adrift a week or more before they were found, or they might drift even longer before they struck an island. According to the best estimate Jack De Angelis could make, the plane had landed somewhere southwest of Canton; at any rate, with the aid of a cheap little pocket compass Reynolds had brought along, the sunrise, a watch, and some water-soaked navigator's tables, he figured that they were about ten degrees south of the Equator. After studying the directional drift during the night, the navigator thought it was southerly with perhaps a mild slant to the west. Rick and Cherry browsed over Adamson's map. It looked as if the bomber might have hit the water below the Ellice Islands. Then, if all their surmises were correct, the nearest landfall was the Fiji Islands, some four hundred miles away, or eighteen to twenty days as a raft drifts.

Knowing men, Rick knew that his companions needed a counter hope to drive off crushing disappointment if rescuers failed to arrive; without it, some of them might not stand up under the strain. So he began to plant the seeds of confidence that, even if no plane or ship found the rafts, eighteen to twenty-five days would see them through to the Fijis. He put all his persuasive powers to work and sold the idea to his raft mates. This seed of hope was the real life-saver that kept the men going during the next three weeks. As the days went by without rescue, the men felt that each dragging hour at least brought them closer to land. In other words, thanks to Rick's strategy, every added day was felt to bring them so much closer to a palm-fringed lagoon in the Fijis instead of being another day of hopeless and useless waiting. They had something to sweat it out for.

Inventory aboard the rafts that first day revealed four oranges alone as food; two pumps to keep the rafts inflated; two jungle knives; Adamson's map and Reynolds's compass; a Very pistol with eighteen shells, twelve of which proved duds; Adamson's and Cherry's .45 automatics with twenty rounds of ammunition; two rubber bailing buckets; a first-aid kit that contained only salves for gasoline burns and a bottle of iodine; two fishhooks and a short piece of fishing line. Some of the men had soggy cigarettes and wet matches in their pockets that they threw away.

That was all there was aboard those three rafts except stout spirits and Rick's towering and inspiring leadership. He never gave up hope. He never lost confidence. He supplemented the spiritual strength the men drew from prayers with a physical and mental stability that was rocklike in its firmness. He spoke softly and gently when soothing was in order; and he blasted out in thundering wrath when he thought a dose of anger was the best medicine. That the men were sometimes boiling-mad at him did not bother Rick in the least. He fought night and day to keep alive the will-to-live in Alex and the other sick men, and he did it with a rough tongue and tough words that made the men fight back—fight their way out of approaching coma just because they were mad at him. Lord, how they learned to hate that man! There were times when they would gladly have thrown him into the sea, granted the strength. Even Adamson, whose friendship with Captain Rickenbacker extended over almost twenty-five years, came to say that he had "loved Rick for a quarter of a century but hated him for twenty-four days." Rick's sarcasm was bitter and acid, but the pulsing anger kept the sick men from slipping into listless indifference, the first step into the realm beyond.

There was no real restful sleep aboard the rafts—only intermittent stupor caused by sheer fatigue. Stupor brought dreams: frightful nightmares in which the men squirmed and moaned and screamed; pleasant dreams of home and family and friends; vivid pictures of impending rescue. One afternoon Rick came out of a trance with a broad grin: "I just telephoned Adelaide," he told Adamson, "and she's bringing the car right over." Then he realized where he was, and his grin froze.

Frequently, the men would imagine that they had established contact with the outside world. Their dreams were so real as to bring on long and heated quarrels. These factors duly considered, it was no wonder that they did not want to sleep. They dreaded the disappointment that followed pleasant dreams, and the horrors of the nightmares. Also, the first thought of every one on coming to was that, if he had been awake, he might have noticed something on the sea or in the sky his companions had failed to see. Most of the time, however, the men were less alert than they thought they were, even though they counted the days and the hours. Time is a great factor in life, and the habit of wanting to know the time of day was so ingrained in the men on the rafts that they almost constantly looked at their watches until the all-penetrating sea water stilled the hands of the timepieces. Toward the end, Whittaker was the only one whose watch was running. Every so often, some one would yell:

"Hey, Jimmy, what time is it?"

Patient Jimmy would delve into his shirt pocket, take out a wad of oilskin, unwrap his watch, give the time and intone:

"Through the courtesy of Longines-Whittaker watch time!"

And Rick, in a voice rich with disgust, would glare at the inquirer and say:

"There it is! Where are you going, brother?"

Although every one hoped that wind and current would carry the rafts to the Fijis, no attempt was made to navigate the unwieldy rubber boats. They were seaworthy enough, but too clumsy to be steered in any given direction under sail or even rowed by man power. On the second day (October 22), Cherry rigged a small mast with the oars and made a sail of his undershirt. The contraption was placed in the bow of raft number one, where the lookout —usually Cherry or Whittaker—held it in place by leaning his back against it. Sail was hoisted now and then on number two raft when Adamson was well enough to hold his body quietly against an oar serving as mast. No sail was ever hoisted on number three raft.

The two "large" rafts, which were fairly comfortable at first, seemed to grow smaller each day. Their interior dimensions were about those of an average bathtub, only there was no drain for letting the water out. Water sloshed in constantly from the sea by the gallon and had to be bailed out by hand by the pint. It was an endless routine except during doldrums, and even then seepage kept the rafts wet. Nor were the men aboard them ever dry.

As burning sun and glaring sea took their painful toll and constant friction developed sea ulcers on backs and legs, it became more and more difficult for any man to move without hurting his companions; for feet and legs and bodies were so intermingled that, if one man moved, all had to shift around. On raft number two, Bartek used to complain that Adamson had two-thirds of the space, Captain Rickenbacker had one-third and that the rest was his. But if the "large" rafts were cramped quarters for three men the small one was a veritable instrument of torture for two. Jack De Angelis and Alex, being the shortest and lightest members of the party, drew the small raft; and they suffered tortures of stiffness and exposure that defy description. Imagine two men spending day after day on a space no bigger than a shallow washtub. Neither one could ever lie down. They had to sit with their legs folded under them like tailors or else stretch them over each other's shoulders. Either way was painfully uncomfortable.

Hitler overlooked a good thing when he failed to make two-man rafts standard equipment in his torture camps. Still, at sea in a pinch, a small raft is better than none. The outstanding feature of these rubber boats was the stanchness and sturdiness with which they withstood to the end the punishment of wind and wave, tugging ropes and tossing human bodies. In fact, one day Rick said that he was going to write letters of commendation when he got home to the Goodyear rubber people who built the raft, and to Walter Kidde who made the gas cylinders that inflated the raft pontoons so promptly; he added that he would like to give a piece of his mind to the man who designated the "large" rafts as five-man rafts and the small raft as a three-man raft. That drew a laugh—a very bitter laugh.

After the first few days, to give De Angelis a chance to shake the cramps out of his system, Bartek would relieve him for a spell. Alex did not want to be moved. He said he started out on the small raft and wanted to finish up on it.

After Alex died Bartek had the small raft to himself, and it became a bed of roses. He would loll on his back when the weather was good, sleep, read his Bible, or listen to the talk shouted back and forth between the rafts. Now and then Cherry talked Bartek into surrendering the raft to him. De Angelis seemed to have had enough of it. He liked to stay with Whittaker in number one. To make room for him, Jim Reynolds took Bartek's place in number two.

It was about this time that Cherry began to talk about breaking up the string of rafts. He argued that, by spreading out, the party would stand a better chance of rescue. Whittaker agreed with him. Rickenbacker and Adamson held that they stood a better chance of being discovered if they held together, thus providing a larger object. By the second week, the attempt at daily observations had been given up. Winds shifted too much. The current seemed unpredictable. The compass had been ruined by sea water. The sail was of little use. No regular lookout was posted, but that was not necessary because every man was his own lookout, all around the clock. There was no such thing as ordinary restful sleep because of the heat or the waves or the cold or the sharks forever smacking into the rafts.

Of the two fuels that keep the human engine going—water and solid food—absence of the former builds up the greater craving. Hunger will make men suffer, but thirst will drive them to the point of self-destruction. Rickenbacker's greatest battle was to keep the younger members of the party from drinking themselves to death with sea water. Even at night he kept a vigilant eye on the men aboard his own raft as well as those aboard number three lest some one steal a slug of sea water. As both Cherry and Whittaker could be relied on to prevent any salt-water drinking on their raft, only two of the rubber boats came within Eddie's range of worry; but their occupants gave him plenty of concern. The yearning for sea water did not develop for several days. Strangely enough, it did not show itself until the first pangs of hunger had died down. It was only then that thirst rose to heights of madness; and it stayed there many hours after the men were rescued and came under expert care in Navy hospitals.

Hunger and thirst seem to be more or less related, and the best way of presenting this part of the Pacific mission is to describe them together from the beginning.

As pointed out before, the men were so certain that rescue was only a few hours off that they did not mind greatly that all the food and water had gone down with the bomber. Their sole food supply consisted of four rather pulpy oranges and a few bars of chocolate that had been melted by sea water. The chocolate was thrown away. After the first night of drifting, Rick suggested that rescue might be slow in coming:

"We may be sighted by a land plane, and we would have to sit here and wait until some surface craft comes out to pick us up. So why don't we ration our oranges and eat one every second day."

"Hey," yelled Reynolds, "that's pretty hard on me—and Lieutenant De Angelis, too. You fellows had breakfast yesterday, but I didn't have a bite—and De Angelis didn't either!"

"That's too bad," answered Rick. "If we'd known that before we went down, we'd have taken care of you both; but now it's too late."

So Jack DeAngelis and Jimmy Reynolds, thirsty and hungry as they were, had to be satisfied with their share—one-eighth of an orange.

The four oranges lasted as scheduled, until the seventh day. The peeling, cutting, and distributing of this scant food was entrusted to Rick, and he performed the operation with the care of a surgeon. Long before the last orange was divided, harrowing thirst and acute hunger beset the men. The hunger pangs diminished with the passing days; but the rowels of thirst had keen edges and prodding points. The urge among the men for something to drink made Rickenbacker and Cherry experiment with urine as a possibility. They soon abandoned their experiments. For hours on end, the men would sit and drool over daydreams of glasses full of water— fruit juice—vegetable juice—milk—ice cream soda. Oddly enough, not one of them pined for whisky or beer.

For eight solid days, the thirsty hours piled one upon another. When awake, the men would search the sky for clouds that might deliver rain. At the start, when clouds wasted cool, life-giving rain on the ocean only a few miles off, the men would paddle in a wild frenzy to catch up with the rain. They never did. Off and on for eight days, this game went on, Then Rick put his foot down, because these never-won races aroused false hopes and burned up the men's energies. Somehow, the deadly invitation of the sea water became more acceptable to the men after the rain passed them by—near enough for the men to feel the cool air around its thick columns, but no more. It was heartbreaking.

As for food—the sea around the rafts was full of fish. Rafts were not provided then with the equipment for survival that they have had since the report of the Rickenbacker Pacific mission. There was no fishing tackle of any sort—not even a low approach to the efficient kits designed later by famous deep-sea fishermen, including Michael Lerner of the American Museum of Natural History. As luck would have it, Jack De Angelis had found two fishhooks in the jungle kit in his parachute aboard the bomber and put them into his pocket. With them came a length of green line. As for bait— there was none. It was, to put it mildly, almost homicidally maddening for the men to look into the sea from the rafts and watch the fish life all around them: big fish and small ones; white and black fish and fish in technicolor; single fish, groups of fish, and schools of countless fish. The men would dangle the bare hooks before fish standing under the rafts. No fish! They baited the hooks with orange rind. No fish! Whittaker, with a pair of pliers, broke an aluminum oar into a ragged spear. He jabbed at fish with it. No fish! Bartek offered to cut a lobe off his ear in the belief that a "bloody piece of meat" would draw a bite. Adamson vetoed the idea, saying that blood would draw too many sharks. There were plenty around as it was. Rick made a trolling gadget out of Adamson's key chain, the name plate on his key ring, and a hook. It looked promising as Rick lowered it into the water. But the result was the same—*no fish!*

On the third day, when boredom began to set in, Adamson remembered the *Reader's Digest* in his hip pocket. By this time he was paralyzed so that he could only move his hands, feet, and head. Bartek hauled the magazine out of his pocket for him, but sea water had eaten half of it away and the rest of it was stuck together for good. The only page Adamson could read dealt with a balloon flight by Santos-Dumont over Paris at the turn of the century. It described, in fascinating detail, how the Brazilian airman had lunched on chicken, lobster, ice cream, and champagne as he circled over the city. This was more than Adamson could stand. He handed the soggy mass to Rick, who said, "Maybe we can use the paper as bait." He tore off a lump, rolled it into a ball, stuck it on a hook and dropped it into the water before a placid-looking sea bass, whose jaws went up and down as if it were chewing gum.

"Come on, Mister Bass," coaxed Rick. "It'll pay you to take *Reader's Digest*. Millions do!"

No fish!

Toward the end of the days of drifting, the men were aroused one morning by what sounded like the patter of rain. It baffled them because the sky was clear. Then they discovered that the noise was made by the flapping on the surface of the sea by thousands of tiny fish. They were no bigger than tadpoles.

Despite the fact that the sea was full of these fingerlings, the shark-baiters aboard the rafts caught only a score or so with their bare hands. Hans Adamson, when they gave him one of them, did not quite know what to do when he discovered that the tiny creature had a puny sword on its snout. It looked like a baby swordfish. He recalled how Mike and Helen Lerner had journeyed to the ends of the Seven Seas with rod and reel in the hope of solving the mystery of the migration of the marlin. And, here, in his hands—on this nameless spot in the vast Pacific—he held what might be part of the answer to one of Mother Nature's greatest oceanic mysteries.

"Mike and Helen Lerner would give a million marlin to be here right now," he declared, as he told his fellow drifters what went through his mind. He added that if he had a bottle of alcohol he would preserve the fish for the Lerners.

"Boy, oh, boy! If I had a bottle of alcohol," exclaimed Reynolds, "I wouldn't be sucker enough to give it to any fish."

"Go on, eat your fish, Hans," chuckled Rick. "Science begins in the belly!"

"Say!" exclaimed Reynolds, as he swallowed one of the fish. "I feel just like one of them college boys who eat real living goldfish."

"And that gives me an idea," injected Bartek. "Instead of chewing my three fish, I am going to swallow them whole. Then I will know if they wriggle and tickle going down."

With the grace of a sword swallower, Bartek bent back his head, opened his mouth, and dropped a squirming fingerling plump into his gullet. He sat for a moment with the expectant air of one who waits for a time bomb to burst—wondering if it would wriggle and tickle.

With a self-satisfied smirk, Bartek finally nodded his head sagely. "By golly, it does!"

Some of the men wondered how long a human being could last without food and drink. Strangely enough Mohandas Gandhi and his frequent hunger strikes gave them great encouragement. As Reynolds put it:

"If a scrawny little runt like him can sit and fast for a month or two—we ought to be able to do this standing on our heads."

To this view, the men subscribed with well restrained enthusiasm.

After about a week of drifting, God answered their prayers and gave them food and drink within a few hours of each other. Food came first in the form of a bird—brown and smallish, it might have been a gull—which, evidently tired from a long flight, perched on Rickenbacker's gray-green hat. It arrived about midafternoon on a blazing doldrum day. The sea was tired, the wind was tired, the men were tired; and certainly a lonely little bird flying over that hot and lonely sea had the right to be tired too. After circling the rafts in a steadily closing spiral, the bird braked its wings against the air, let down its feet, and made an easy landing. There it sat, unconcerned and motionless. It did not seem to feel the hungry eyes of seven starving men. Rick, under the hat, could not see the bird; but, with killing slowness, he lifted his hand until it was even with the top of his hat. Then a quick grab, and he held the bird by the legs. It pecked at his hand and flapped its wings to get free until Eddie covered it with his other hand. Now that he had the bird, what to do with it? Feeling its scrawny little body—it was no larger than a small pigeon—Rick knew that it would not provide enough nourishment even to blunt the sharp hunger of his companions. Cherry and Adamson saw in the bird a sign from God of deliverance and wanted to set it free. Whittaker, practical soul, sided with Rick, saying that the meat would at least provide some moisture while the inner parts could be used to bait the hooks. And that is how it turned out. Eddie wrung the bird's neck, plucked it and cut small, ragged chunks from the black and leathery meat on the body and the legs. Afterward, the hooks were baited. Rick threw one over the side, Whittaker the other, and within a few minutes they caught two fish that weighed about half a pound apiece. One was divided and eaten immediately; the other was put aside for the next day. Incidentally, authorities on marine bird life say that there are no gulls in the Central Pacific area, and the bird was probably a tern. Tern or gull, it was a messenger of hope.

The few morsels of fish meat tasted surprisingly good and satisfied the craving for moisture; more than that, they lifted the spirits of the men. There were plenty more fish in the sea, and with parts of these fish as bait, there should be no dearth of food from now on. But they were doomed to disappointment. None of the fish around the raft would bite, probably for the simple reason that their normal food was present in such generous supply that there was no reason to deviate from their regular feeding habits.

A few days later two small flying fish jumped into the rafts. On one occasion the men caught a few dozen fingerlings. They caught half a dozen tiny sea lice that fastened themselves to the raft. And that was all they had to eat during their entire stay on the rafts.

One morning Cherry caught a young shark on a baitless hook. He hauled it in, stabbed it with a knife, and cut the tail off. Every one looked forward to a juicy bit of food, but even a young shark tasted like over-age horse glue. Most of the men spat the meat out, and the carcass was thrown over the side. Some of it was tried as bait. The fish not only would not take it, but actually darted away from the hooks.

Fishing with hooks, unproductive as it was, provided a way of killing time and arousing hopes; but even that soon came to an end. One hook was lost somehow. The other was carried off by a shark. Sharks were ever present. The first telltale fins cutting the surface of the ocean were seen soon after the men boarded the rafts. At first, the sharks filled them with apprehension. There were at least two kinds: rather sharp-nosed fellows that seldom measured more than five or six feet; and packs of white-gray round-nosed specimens ten to twelve feet long. They moved along the surface with terrific speed and had the disconcerting habit of barging head-on into the rafts, sometimes almost tilting the rubber dinghies over. Or they would slide under the rafts and start bucking and tail-thrashing in blind fury. The slashing impact of these creatures not only threatened to rip to shreds the thin rubberized canvas bottom of the raft, but was extremely painful to men who sat on buttocks that already throbbed with salt-water ulcers. When a ten-foot shark got to milling under a raft, he could make it dance; but he probably did not enjoy this any more than the men did. The onslaughts were not deliberate attempts to get at the men. The rafts simply interfered with the sharks' way of life. At first, when the men tried to cool off on hot days by dangling their hands and feet in water, they would yank them up when a shark came close. But soon, with the familiarity that breeds contempt, they would dangle them in the water no matter how close the sharks came. De Angelis and Reynolds even went swimming with sharks all around them.

On smooth days, for hours on end, the younger men would lean over the sides of the rafts, their hands dangling in the water, waiting patiently for a fish to swim within reach. Time and again, their fingers would close on a victim, but it always got away. This elusive food stirred up tempers, though not as much as the rains that came so close but never close enough.

On the eighth night, around sunset, black clouds heavy with rain pushed above the eastern horizon and soon hung overhead. Rain fell within a few miles of the raft. Once again hope lifted the men out of their indifference. Once again they laid out their pathetic implements for collecting rain water: handkerchiefs, undershirts and drawers, socks, even bandages, spread out over heads and laps and the sides of the rafts. As soon as they became soaked, they were to be passed on to Rick and Cherry, who would wring the water into the rubber bailing buckets and, later, transfer the water—mouthful by mouthful—from the bailing buckets into the waterproof insides of the life jackets.

The plan was all thought out on the second day adrift; the only trouble was that it never had a chance to be tried. Now, on this eighth night, it seemed as if rain might come within range. With dry eyes the men stared at the swaying curtains of rain that hung between sky and sea. Rain fell all around them, but not on the rafts. Darkness came. There were no stars, no moon.

Suddenly, out of nowhere, came the whisper of a wind. Swiftly it grew in volume. By midnight it was a hurricane. With the wind came crashing seas. The rafts, pulling and tugging at their cords, swung crazily back and forth like a Coney Island amusement device. In furious succession, wave after wave would push the rafts to its crest, toss them forward, and slide out from under. Often the rafts threatened to tilt over, but each time they recovered balance just before the impending spill. If there are varying shades of blackness, one might say that, suddenly, the darkness of the night seemed deeper and closer than it had been before. The wind rose to full-out concert pitch. The sea appeared to rise and fall with greater violence than ever.

Then, out of the blackness of the night, came a blinding flash followed by an ear-bursting crash. More lightning, more thunder, and rain! rain! RAIN! Right on the rafts! It was not a gentle downpour. It came with the extravagant waste of a waterfall. To the men on the dinghies the slashing, torrential downpour seemed like Niagara Falls itself.

For a moment, they sat stunned. Then, yowling with glee, they got down to business. Whittaker and Reynolds handed rain-dripping rags to Cherry, who wrung them dry into his bailing bucket and handed them back. Bartek and Adamson passed their rags to Eddie, who wrung them out. On the small raft, De Angelis and Alex collected rain in their handkerchiefs and squeezed the water into their mouths. On the small raft, unfortunately, they had no means of storing water. The downpour lasted all night with brief intermissions, and when it ended every one slumped in sheer exhaustion.

It had been exhausting work. To begin with, the rafts pitched so wildly and banged into one another so often that they came close to turning over on several occasions. This was especially true on Cherry's raft, where Whittaker hoisted the sail because it was a good way of collecting water. Although the sail was only an undershirt, it furnished enough expanse for the wind to take hold of. Then there was the endless crashing of waves into the rafts. It was not so much the labor of bailing out that bothered the men as the delays in collecting water imposed by the need for bailing, and for rinsing out the rags whenever they got soaked by salt water. It would take as much as five eternal minutes to clear the salt water out of the rags and make them fresh again.

But there were two major calamities. One came when a wave, for all that Rick could do, filled his half-full bailing bucket with sea water. This made all the rain water he already had in it undrinkable.

The other tragedy occurred just before dawn. Shortly after it stopped raining, a mountain of a wave crashed into the rafts. When the spume cleared away, the men on Rick's boat could see that the leading raft had turned over. Yelling like a man possessed, Rick hauled in the cord that held rafts number one and two together. Peering into the gray light, he saw Cherry, Whittaker, and Reynolds clinging to the life lines of the overturned raft. He helped them to shift over to the life line of number two raft, then tackled the righting of number one. How he ever got the strength to do it, how his own raft kept from tumbling over, no one but the Lord will ever know; but, leaning out over the stern of that storm-lashed gadget of cardboard-thin rubber filled with air, he got the other raft right side up and helped the chilled and exhausted men climb into it.

Three lives were saved that morning, but among the things forever lost was a life jacket half full of rain water—water the three men had worked so hard to collect. Bill Cherry had a smaller harvest of water in a Mae West that hung around his neck; its weight did not help him any in his fight against drowning, but the persistent cuss made up his mind that he was going to hang on to that jacket of water, no matter what happened. And he did.

From that night on, it rained more frequently, and the men were never long without water. True, they had to dole out their slender stores so that each man barely had a tablespoonful of water morning and night on flush days. There were days when they had only one gulp of water, and days when they had none. People inclined to doubt that God, in making man in his own image, imparted to him almost godlike qualities of kindliness of spirit could find clear proof of this in what happened aboard those rafts during those terrible days when water was doled out. Before the first rain, the men had nothing to drink for eight solid days. Sea water! Yes, some of them drank it; but of drinkable water there was not a drop.

Bill Cherry was made custodian of all the water collected in the first rain: about a quart and a half. When drinking time came, the rafts would be pulled together in a waving sort of string. Cherry, sitting at the bow of number one raft, would siphon a mouthful of water out of the rubber air tube on the life jacket and spit it into the empty shell of a Very light. Then the shell—a six-inch aluminum cylinder about as big around as a quarter—would be passed on to Reynolds, to Whittaker, to Rickenbacker, to Bartek, to Adamson, to De Angelis, to Alex—for Alex, being very ill and weak, was always the first to drink.

People who need only go into a near-by room to get a matter-of-fact glass of pure, wonderful water will never understand what a tribute it was to the inherent kindliness of man that these men, each clinging to life and striving for survival, had the generosity and guts to give life-sustaining water to two men on whom it might be wasted —Sergeant Alex and Colonel Adamson. But, instead of being deprived of the boon of water, Alex and Adamson were always the first to drink, and their portions were usually a few drops bigger than the rest received.

One amusing feature at water time was the everlasting effort of every one to get an extra drop. As the empty cartridge went from hand to hand back to Cherry to be refilled, every man would put it to his lips, lean his head back and try to garner an extra drop to drink. And each obtained—nothing! Because the man whose turn it was to empty the cartridge always made sure that he got every drop that was coming to him.

There were occasions, after the first, long-awaited rain, when the men went without water for a day or two. But after that first rain there were at least five squalls which contributed anywhere from a pint to a quart of water.

The last rain came to the number two raft on the day after the raft flotilla broke up. Some twenty hours had passed since Cherry had pushed off in the small raft, and Whittaker, Reynolds, and De Angelis had vanished below the horizon in the other. Because of their exhausted condition, Bartek and Adamson could hardly handle the rags during the downpour. But the one who suffered most was Rick. By this time, the skin on his hands had been almost completely burned away leaving infected salt-water ulcers in pits of inflamed, skinless flesh. With those hands, he painfully wrung the water into the bailing bucket. It was unadulterated agony, but he stuck to the task with gritted teeth. He knew that this was the last call for water. That, even if it rained again, neither Adamson nor Bartek would be able to help, and maybe his own hands would have given out. As he poured water into the cartridge case for Adamson and Bartek, Rick's hands shook so that he could hardly do the job. Although Bartek and Adamson were almost famished with thirst, they could hardly hold the cap to their cracked and sun-dried lips. Most of the water ran down Bartek's chin and it flowed drooling out of Adamson's mouth. Both were so played out that nothing made any difference—not even a mouthful of water.

Chapter XXI

Were the days aboard the rafts worse than the nights? The answer is that both were insufferable, but in wholly different ways. During the long furnace-hot days, the men prayed for the cool nights. And, during the interminable marrow-chilling nights, they were cheered by the thought that, with the sunrise, would come rays that would warm their bodies and dry their wave-soaked clothes.

Naturally, they did a great deal of griping; but they did not feel too sorry for themselves. They realized that this break every twelve hours from hot to cold and back to hot was a blessing in disguise. It provided a change in pace; offered different targets for complaint. Toward twilight each day, they would see that hateful sun vanish with great relief; and, at the end of each cold wet night, they would welcome it as bringer of light and warmth. They were poorly equipped to fight the daily attacks of the burning sun and the glaring sea. Waves would wet them down and cool them off a little, except during doldrums. Then they would fill or soak whatever was handy with sea water, and pour or squeeze the water over themselves.

For rather obvious reasons, Captain Rickenbacker and Colonel Adamson never told their companions about the decision they had made to head for the bottom in case the party was discovered and rescued by Japs. However, they did warn them to try to identify any passing plane before it discovered the rafts.

"Johnny Bartek knows every Nip plane by sight," said Cherry.

"Yeah," admitted Bartek, "I can spot 'em miles away!"

"O.K.," snapped Rick. "Keep your eyes open, and if we hear a plane and it's a Jap—we'll all pile into the water, turn the rafts over and hide under them."

"Why do we have to do that?" Reynolds wanted to know.

"Because we don't want to be found by Japs if we can help it. If they see us first, chances are ten to one that they'll drill the rafts full of holes—or they'll take us prisoners. If we turn the rafts over and hide under them, the Japs will have a hard time seeing them. The rafts are sea-blue on the bottom and blend right into the ocean."

"Who gets the hundred bucks for hearing the plane first, if it's a Jap?" asked Bartek with a grin.

"Nobody," laughed Rick. "If he's a Jap, there's no pay-off!"

This escape procedure in case Jap planes should find them was agreed on the first afternoon but never carried out—and a good thing too since Whittaker, Alex, and Adamson could not swim.

By and large, after the first few days, there was little conversation among the men. The crew aboard raft one was more talkative than the others. On raft two, Rick was always grimly silent and motionless unless he had something definite to say—never expending a single fraction of his energy unless there was some reason for it; but when it came to bailing, pumping, and paddling he did nearly all of the work. As for talk, it was remarkable how soon the wells of conversation dried up. Soon there was little left to think about. After the first two weeks, silence hung over all the rafts. Then the sudden shift of an arm or a leg or a body might hurt the next man, and there would come a quick interchange of wrathful profanity. The third man would join in, and every one on the raft would be shrilling hysterically at every one else. Then, as abruptly as if some one had turned a dial: absolute silence again.

Thus things went on for what seemed like an endless eternity during which the men looked vainly to sea and sky for help that was almost too late in coming. That is, human help held off. Spiritual help—the strength of faith, prayer, and hope—came almost at once, and the men were never without them. Bartek's little Bible, which he had got "for free" and kept instead of his expensive camera, became the most precious possession of the group. It passed from hand to hand during daylight hours. Every one read it, and every one found consolation within its pages. It guided men to prayers who had forgotten how to pray and brought a measure of peace into hours of pounding and prodding anxiety. The dramatic coming of food and rain on the very heels of a flow of feverish prayers was enough to shock any man into a strong realization of the nearness of God. Not even Noah could have been more reverently happy when the dove returned to the Ark than these men were when the scrawny little gull came to roost on Rick's hat. Also, the lightning and thunder heralding the first rain after almost nine days of thirst seemed like a message from the Lord. Every morning, noon, and sunset, the rafts were pulled together, and every man would offer a prayer, if that is what it could be called. They were not formal prayers, but rather each in turn talked to God. After every one had had his say, they would sing a hymn or two and then return to the routine of drifting.

The greatest consolation, and yet the greatest source of sorrow and anxiety, among the men aboard the rafts was the recollection of their loved ones. In those long hours of doubtful survival, the one thing that kept their hopes up, next to Faith, was Love. The men kept themselves strong by speaking about and thinking of their womenfolk—mothers, wives, sweethearts. Proof of this may be found in two notes Adamson wrote to his wife and gave to Rickenbacker for safekeeping.

While the Twenty-third Psalm was the most widely read part of Bartek's little sea-worn Bible, the real subject of their spiritual introspections could easily have been taken from John 13:35: "By this shall all men know that ye are my disciples, if ye have love one to another." Aside from Whittaker's diary, the only messages written were Adamson's notes, on paper he borrowed from Whittaker's small notebook. The first was written on Tuesday October 27:

DARLING:

This afternoon we will have been adrift 144 hours. We do not know where we are nor where we are heading. We hope to stick it out until we find rescue, but so far we have seen no sign of anything other than sky and water.

This has not been a pleasant trip, but you know that without my telling you. If the end of this journey is the end of my journey through life itself, the end of "our" journey, I want you to know that your shining eyes and tender smile were with me to the last. And don't grieve over me. Don't forget me, no; but find new happiness with some other man who may be even more able to appreciate your fineness than I have. If this is our final goodbye (my dear, I hate to say it, but believe me I say it as you would want me to), chin up and smile. Elsker dig. ＨＡＮＳ.

On Thursday October 29 he added:

We are still hanging on. Still hoping. Rain yesterday gave us a quart to divide among us, and it should last three days. Alex and I got extra rations. Poor Alex! He is heading out. All he talks about is his girl. But that is what all of us talk about, and think about, just our love. We seem to have no thought of anything but Home and Love. Oh, my dear, I don't know why I write this! You will never see it anyway. What bothers most is that this is not a nice fixed way out but one of uncertainty and worry for you at home as to what really happened to us. I have, I believe, made my peace with God and look forward with frank eyes. Goodbye, Little People.

But, powerful and helpful as the strength from prayer was, Rick never forgot the old maxim: "God helps those who help themselves!" His eternal concern for the welfare of the men would have been amusing if it had not been so earnest. In a way, he felt responsible for the plight they were in, and his sense of responsibility rode him around the clock. His concern over the sick men—Alex and Adamson and later Bartek and Reynolds—found expression in a driving urge to help, an urge that was constantly beaten down by a sense of absolute frustration. For the first time in a life crowded with action, he faced a situation in which there was very little that he could do. Night after night he would hold either Alex or Bartek in his arms, with a tenderness that was almost maternal; for his voice and hands could be very gentle and soothing. When Alex was aboard raft two the second night before he died, Rick held him as he would have held his son David or Bill. Perhaps he was thinking of them back home and wondering—wondering. At any rate, he whispered very softly: "Poor little boys—poor Adelaide!" Then he came back to reality and whispered: "It will be O.K., Alex. It'll be O.K.!"

Alex died of starvation, thirst, and exposure before dawn on the thirteenth day. He spent his last hours on the small raft where he wanted to be. Johnny Bartek had volunteered to spend the night with him. During the early part of the night, Alex talked almost continuously in a mixture of Polish and English. Toward dawn, he suddenly became quiet. The still of the night was cut by a sharp call from Rick:

"Hey, Johnny, what's happened? Is Alex O.K.?"

"No," came Johnny's hesitant reply. "I think he's dead!"

The rafts were pulled together, and Rick felt Alex's pulse and heart. Both had stopped. But he wanted to be sure.

"Can you stick it out to morning, Johnny?" he asked.

"Sure. Sure I can stick it out. Alex and I were pals."

Shortly after sunrise, Cherry and Whittaker made sure that Alex was dead. Then their friend's body was lowered over the side and allowed to float off.

Some of the men who were ill began to wonder how soon they would follow Alex, and Adamson gazed after the body with a deep foreboding. He wondered if he would be the next one, if he would float off like that—

"Cripes, Hans, why don't you answer me!" screamed Rickenbacker.

Adamson turned his eyes. "I didn't hear you say anything!" he snarled. "What is it?"

"Nothing, nothing. Only rub my left leg if you can."

Rickenbacker, reading the sick man's mind, had attained his purpose—drawn his gaze from Alex before his fever-clouded eyes saw what Rick saw—the fins of sharks cutting through the sea toward the body with purposeful speed.

During the long waking hours, Rick, like all his companions, found endless opportunity for self-exploration. He made the journey back through the years from man to youth to boy time and again. He thought about the goals of fame and fortune he had sought to reach and the ideals he had fought so strenuously to preserve. He came to realize how all his efforts through life had been concentrated on security: economic security for his mother, younger sisters and brothers, wife and sons; industrial security for his business, his stockholders, and his employees; security of the American way of life for the youth of the land. All his life, in war and in peace, he had fought for security of one kind or another for himself and for others—but mostly for others.

And now he and his companions sat on the face of the sea with no security except the security of Faith. Never religious or irreligious, Rick had gone through life in matter-of-fact acceptance of the Golden Rule. Now, suddenly, appreciation of the only worth-while security in life came to him: the security of Faith! It came through a firm understanding of the nearness of God. It came with the sharpness of lightning in darkness. And with the same almost terrifying reality.

The only man whose strong and determined grip on life and hope never weakened was Eddie Rickenbacker. Next after him was Jimmy Whittaker, whose stout heart and even temper made him a good crutch for his companions to lean upon in recurrent attacks of despair.

Early in the third week, Rick sensed that the morale of the men was slipping. There was nothing he could put his finger on—a general letdown as they saw Adamson daily sinking and both Reynolds and Bartek became more and more ill. He tried to bolster their courage by predicting that the Fiji Islands would heave within sight any day now. In this Cherry and Whittaker backed him up; but, to the sick, these arguments were not very convincing, and it was a pretty bleak lot of men who drooped aboard the rafts in the afternoon heat of the seventeenth day. Suddenly Cherry got up with a jerk that almost turned his raft over.

"I hear one—I hear an airplane engine!" he yelled.

Every one sat up and listened. There it was, distant and hardly audible but coming closer—the sweet song of an airplane motor. Eager eyes swept the sky.

Bartek saw it first. "It's at three thousand feet, about five miles away," he announced. "About nine o'clock."

Now every one saw it. Rick and Adamson exchanged glances: Was it a Jap?

"What kind of a crate is it?" asked Rick as casually as he could. If it were a Jap . . . Well, then he and Adamson would "take a walk."

"Single-engined—pontoon job. Navy Kingfisher!" Eddie felt a wave of indescribable relief creep through him.

Every one smiled and laughed and yelled, waving whatever was at hand. Here was discovery. Here was rescue. Here was life coming on the wings of a good old United States Navy plane. But the plane never came closer. It remained on a course that quickly took it out of sight. For a few seconds help had seemed to be within reach. Now it had gone. No one spoke, for words could not express the crushing weight of disappointment. After a silence of many minutes, Rick dipped into his well of Hope.

"Listen," he said, shaking an admonitory forefinger. "Snap out of it. Sure that plane missed us, but there'll be other planes—tomorrow or next day—maybe ships. We may be close to an island, or we may have drifted down on the convoy lanes. That plane was a good sign, even if it did not sight us. Wait until tomorrow, and you'll see! Where there's one plane, there's more!"

Rick's talk made sense to the men. They cheered up considerably, and he succeeded in hiding his own disappointment. He had believed firmly that the three bright orange-colored rafts strung out on the sea would be easily visible to any pilot. Now, he knew differently. He did not share Bartek's easy confidence that the plane they had seen was a Navy Kingfisher. The Japs too had single-engined body-pontoon seaplanes. But of one thing he felt sure: where there was one plane, there were more. He was confident that more planes would be seen the next day or the day after, and that discovery was near at hand. His guess was correct on one count. More planes were seen on the eighteenth day, and on the nineteenth; but none of the pilots saw the rafts. On the morning of the twentieth day, no planes were seen, and the men were swept by a dread that they had lost their opportunity, that rescue had passed them by. Captain Cherry, who from time to time had expressed the belief that they would do better in letting the rafts drift their separate ways, now announced that he had decided to cut free. Both Rickenbacker and Adamson protested, but he had made up his mind and nothing could stop him. He had an iron hunch, he said, that three scattered rafts had a better chance of being seen than three strung together. Bitter words were exchanged, but by the time he drifted off in the small raft good feeling had been restored.

Hardly had Cherry drifted beyond the half-mile horizon of the two remaining rafts when Whittaker and De Angelis got itching feet. They, too, wanted to go places. Bartek and Adamson were completely unconscious when this happened, and Rick let number one raft go with a shrug. Soon it too had drifted out of sight, and Rick's world had been narrowed down to one raft and two near-dead men. There was nothing to interrupt his thoughts that long and lonely day except the dry rattle of Adamson's labored breath and the swish of the sea. Bartek lay across the raft as dead. The sun went down, and the darkness brought welcome unconsciousness to Rick.

During the night he had a dream, a dream that he had had many times before. He relived the day of his father's funeral. He was again a small boy in the tiny room above the kitchen in Columbus. He saw the light shoot up the stairs and through the open doorway as his mother lit the kitchen lamp. He went down to the kitchen, saw his mother at the table with tears on her cheeks, and promised her that he would be a good boy and would never make her cry again.

Then a wave swept over the raft, waking him. He thought of his mother as he slowly bailed the water out of the raft. He thought about Adelaide and Bill and David. He thought about the "gang" at Eastern Airlines—the pilots and mechanics and others for whom he had fought financiers and politicians to a standstill. Cold, wet, and bedraggled, he took stock of his chances. They were not too good. It seemed to be only a matter of hours before Adamson and Bartek would die. They had no food and no water. The faithful raft was losing air so badly that it was questionable whether he could pump enough air into it to keep it afloat. He wondered what was happening to the men on the other rafts, particularly Reynolds—he was a sick man. Again he passed into the deep stupor of exhaustion.

In the gray dawn a strong icy downpour shocked Bartek and Adamson as well as Rick to consciousness. Such was the will to survive that the two sick men joined in spreading out rags under the rain, from which Rick squeezed the water into a bailing bucket, later transferring it to his life jacket. When the sun drove the clouds away Adamson and Bartek covered up as best they could, and Rick sat in his end of the raft with his soggy and sea-faded hat pulled down over his eyes and a ragged handkerchief drawn across the lower part of his face. This arrangement, which made him look like a down-at-the-heels bandit, was his usual protection against sunburn and sea glare. Bartek and Adamson slumped in semicomatose huddles. Water was doled out at sunrise and again at noon. The blowtorch in the sky climbed to the zenith with torturing slowness and started its equally slow glide toward the western horizon. Would the good cool evening ever come? The silence of sea and space was suddenly ripped apart by the roar of airplane engines. The sound was from the west, and it came closer. Bartek heard it first. Rick shaded his bleary and bloodshot eyes with a shaking hand and searched the western sky for the plane. Presently, he saw two slim silhouettes. They grew larger as he looked. Two seaplanes plunged straight toward the raft. There was one tense moment when he wondered if the barking of machine guns would be added to the rhythmic explosions of the engines. But no bullets zipped past; instead, the pilots pulled up a few yards above the raft and revealed United States insignia under their wings.

"Wave and shout," Rick yelled to Adamson and Bartek. "Wave your arms—do anything. Only don't lie still, or they'll think we are dead."

According to Lieutenant Commander William F. Eadie, the pilot of the plane that rescued Rick and his companions, the raft was sighted by two Navy Kingfishers about four o'clock in the afternoon of November 13. The planes returned to their station at Funafuti in the Ellice Islands to report. In short order, Eadie, together with Radioman L. H. Boutte, volunteered to fly out to the raft and stand by until a PT boat could pick the three men up. Eadie fueled up, took off, and reached the raft about sundown. He circled overhead until seven-forty-five, when the PT boat hove into sight. Then, satisfied that the surface boat had established contact, Eadie put his plane down upon the sea, taxied over to the raft, killed his engine, climbed down on the pontoon, and shouted:

"Well, Captain Rickenbacker, here we are!"

"And thank God for that. But how did you know you'd find me and my friends?"

"Oh, Captain Cherry told us to look for you."

"Then Cherry is safe!"

"Yes, Boutte, here, and Lieutenant Woodward picked him up yesterday."

"But there's still another raft, three men—"

"They are all accounted for too," answered Eadie cheerfully. "They landed on an island."

"You seem to know all the answers. You wouldn't know where we could get something to drink?"

Eadie shouted to Boutte, who climbed down the wing and handed Rick two canteens. There was soup in one, water in the other, and both tasted like vintage ambrosia.

Suddenly Eadie laughed—a deep, pleasant laugh.

"What's so funny?" asked Rick.

"Oh, I was just thinking," chortled the Navy pilot, "that the Army let you down, Captain, but the Navy picked you up."

"Izzatso?" retorted Rick in mock anger.

Here it was again, even on a raft in mid-Pacific, the old but friendly ribbing rivalry between the Army and the Navy. He found a fast comeback:

"This stuff you're handing us, the soup and the water: it's just like the Navy to dish out cold soup and warm water."

Every one roared. Even Adamson managed a snicker. Then Rick continued:

"As for the Army letting us down and the Navy picking us up— I say, Thank God for you and the Navy! You fellows had the guts to come down and get us; but, believe me, it was the hand of God that set your course for us."

While the castaways drank the soup and water slowly, Eadie told them that they were some forty miles from Funafuti, which had been taken from the Japs only two weeks before.

"What day is it?" Rick asked.

"This is your lucky day, Captain! Friday the 13th of November!"

Placing Rick and Bartek on the wings of his plane and Adamson in the rear cockpit, Eadie taxied toward the PT boat. When he reached it, the two wing passengers were transferred to the surface craft. Adamson was kept aboard the plane because he seemed so close to death that every second counted in getting him to shore and into medical hands. Bartek, on the other hand, burst into a flare of energy and was talkative and happy until he was put in a bunk aboard the boat; then he passed out cold. Rick, the iron man, stayed awake for quite a spell talking with the skipper of the boat and expressed his intention to get another Army plane as quickly as he could and carry on with his mission in the Southwest Pacific for the Secretary of War. Navy doctors, who took the men in charge at Funafuti, had different ideas and prescribed several weeks' rest. With Cherry and other members of his party Rick was flown to Samoa, and placed in a Navy hospital. Adamson also, whose clock had almost run down with lobar pneumonia and diseases caused by starvation and exposure, was flown to Samoa, where full surgical facilities were available for a crucial lung operation. Reynolds and Bartek were kept on Funafuti for treatment.

On December 1, aboard another Army bomber, Rick left for Australia, New Guinea, Guadalcanal, and other 1942 hot spots. Returning to Samoa twelve days later, he learned that Cherry, Bartek, and Whittaker had been sent home, but that Adamson and Reynolds were still in bad shape. Adamson was critically ill and might die, Commanders John Durkin and Fred Robbins said.

"If Hans is going to die," Rick told the Navy doctor, "he would prefer to die at home. If he gets home, chances are he'll get a new lease on life. I'm not a doctor, but I know men! Take a chance. Let me take him home."

The medical people talked it over, and the result was that both Reynolds and Adamson were flown back to the United States aboard the bomber placed at Captain Rickenbacker's disposal by the War Department. Commander Durkin and an Army nurse came along. At Hamilton Field, Whittaker was on hand to look after Reynolds, who was taken to his home in Oakland.

The next day, the big bomber left for Washington; but it stopped first at Burbank Airport, Los Angeles. As its four engines sputtered into silence the door was pushed open, a flight of steps was rolled over, and a little old lady in a black bonnet and a black dress walked firmly up the steps and stood on the threshold.

"Mother!" whispered Eddie Rickenbacker in complete surprise.

"Mother!" he shouted. He had planned to run out and surprise her at home. And here she was springing one on him.

She smiled slowly and tenderly as she held out her arms to her son.

Forgotten, for the moment, were those terrible weeks of waiting, of wondering, of worrying. The days upon days when her hopes of ever seeing Eddie again clung to the thin thread of a telephone wire clear across the country to Adelaide and David and Bill.

Forgotten for the moment, too, was that flash of almost painful happiness when Adelaide telephoned her one early morning: "They've been found—they've been found!" All she thought about, if a human soul thinks when it turns to God, was that there, thanks to the dear Lord, stood the child who had always been her greatest source of worry.

"Oh, my Eddie! My little Eddie!" she whimpered softly as her tall son rushed to her. Her head was held high, but her lips were trembling softly.

He threw his arms around her, squeezed her tightly, then bent and gave her a resounding kiss. Holding her by the shoulders at arms' length he grinned—the grin she knew and loved.

Mother Rickenbacker looked at her son through misting eyes. Tears began to roll down her cheeks. Near tears himself, Eddie pulled a handkerchief from his breast pocket—one of those embroidered by Adelaide which he had used to wring out rain water on the raft. Now he used it to wipe the tears from his mother's eyes— tears that came like a soft and gentle rain.

"Now, now—don't you cry, Mother," he said in a soft voice, shaking a forefinger playfully before her eyes. "Remember—I promised I'd never make you cry again!"

Presently, the pilot came back and suggested it was time to take off. After brief goodbyes, the bomber soared quickly aloft and set its course for Washington. That night Adamson's condition suddenly got worse. Commander Durkin suggested leaving him in a hospital in Dallas, but Eddie would hear nothing of it.

"We've got to get Hans to Washington," he insisted. "The best medicine for him is to get back to his wife. As I told you before, I'm no doctor, but I know what I'm talking about. Adamson wants to go home. I want to go home. We all want to go home. And, hang it all, I'm going to see he gets there!"

At nine o'clock in the morning, the plane made a smooth-as-silk landing at Bolling Field outside Washington. Although nearly all the Pentagon air staff brass hats, from General Arnold down, were on hand to meet Eddie, the target of all this attention had eyes and mind for only three people on the crowded field: Adelaide, David, and Bill. He saw them through the window. Before the plane could stop, he pulled the door open and jumped to the ground. The wind from the churning propellers almost bowled him over, but he recaptured his balance and ran toward his wife and sons, who, hand in hand, were rushing toward him. Without a word, he swept the three into his arms.

Hundreds of people—most of them hard-bitten soldiers or even more hard-bitten reporters—cheered themselves hoarse. News photographers flashed dozens of bulbs. Newsreel men cranked their cameras. Overhead fighter planes snarled in steep power dives and roared in vertical zooms. The Air Force band played a stirring march. It was a heroic welcome for a hero.

For the moment, Eddie neither heard nor saw the clamorous greeting. Holding Adelaide and David and Bill in his arms—close and solid and hard—he knew that here, at long last, he had all that he had prayed for during those hours on the raft when he sought and found the security of Faith.

Suddenly a different thought shot through his head. He looked up and saw Hans Adamson's wife standing a few steps away between General Arnold and Colonel Trubee Davison.

"Hi, Helen!" he shouted as he pointed a thumb over his shoulder toward the plane. "There's an old soldier in there who needs some of your medicine badly."

Even at a moment like that, Eddie found time to think of some one else.

Postscript

The principal handicap in writing the life history of a living person is that it must end at some appropriate milestone along the subject's road of life. In the opinion of the author, the terminal point of this first volume covering the career of Eddie Rickenbacker is his return to America from the Southwest Pacific ready to contribute, at all costs, whatever he could to the winning of the war.

Rickenbacker's vigorous warfare against absentee labor, selfish employers, and sluggish public opinion, and his important but secret missions to world-wide battle fronts, form rich and full material for another book another day.

That day will come when war restrictions—that have held Captain Rickenbacker's military missions in the top-secret class—are lifted, and when the dust of controversy stirred up by his offensives on the home fronts has settled, in the manner of all dust, and left a clearly defined picture of the pros and cons.

CPSIA information can be obtained
at www.ICGtesting.com
Printed in the USA
BVHW042214271120
594405BV00031B/678